THE EARLY MODERN AGE

SECOND EDITION

L. E. SNELLGROVE

LONGMAN

LONGMAN GROUP UK LIMITED,
Longman House, Burnt Mill, Harlow,
Essex CM20 2JE, England
and Associated Companies throughout the world.

Published in the United States of America
by Longman Inc., New York.

First published 1972
Second edition 1989

Set in 11/13 point Plantin (Linotron 202)
Produced by Longman Group (F.E.) Limited
Printed in Hong Kong

ISBN 0 582 31784 3

British Library Cataloguing in Publication Data
Snellgrove, L. E. (Laurence Ernest), *1928–*
   The early modern age. – 2nd ed. (Longman secondary
   histories).
   1. England, 1399–1603
   I. Title
   942.04

Library of Congress Cataloging in Publication Data
Snellgrove, Laurence Ernest.
   The early modern age.

   (Longman secondary histories)
   Includes index.
   Summary: An overview of the historical period during which
explorers conquered "new worlds" and England was governed
by monarchs from Henry VII to William of Orange.
   1. Great Britain – History Tudors, 1485–1603 – Juvenile
literature. 2. Great Britain – History – Stuarts, 1603–1714 –
Juvenile literature. [1. Great Britain – History – Tudors,
1485–1603. 2. Great Britain – History – Stuarts, 1603–1714] I.
Title. II. Series:
Longman secondary histories (Unnumbered)
DA300.S65   1989   942.05   89–8015
ISBN 0-582-31783-5

CONTENTS

PREFACE

This book has been designed chiefly for pupils aged about thirteen or fourteen, that is, those in their third year at secondary school. Great care has been taken to keep the language clear and simple. As an aid to clarity, and in the hope of stimulating genuine interest and understanding, some topics, such as the Renaissance, are given a more generous allocation of space than is customary in a book of this kind. It is felt that most pupils derive little benefit from a brief and superficial coverage of history.

As far as possible social and economic topics, particularly of the Elizabethan period, have been fitted into the chronological framework. In this way the flow of events – their causes and effects – may be better understood. At the same time reference has been made to European events in order to avoid a narrowly based 'British' view of the subject.

This *second edition* takes account of significant changes in the approach to history teaching since the early 1970s. Frequent attempts to relate the narrative to its sources were a feature of the first edition, but now longer passages are quoted in the text, pictorial evidence is made more explicit, and, above all, extensive documentary work sections have been included. The book contains nine collections of documents and questions built around particular topics, and most chapters have shorter 'Sources and questions' sections. The latter contain at least one substantial piece of documentary evidence and usually some 'picture' questions.

The many documents in this new edition have been selected on grounds of interest, relevance to the text, and, not least, accessibility to the young reader. All have been carefully edited and glossed to remove barriers to understanding. Original source material – whether documentary or pictorial – is, of course, not an end in itself. Its function in this book is both to sharpen historical knowledge and understanding and to develop pupils' ability to use and evaluate evidence critically.

I should like to thank Roger Lockyer and Richard Cootes for their advice in the final preparation of this manuscript and Jean Snellgrove for help and hard work beyond the call of wifely duty.

L. E. Snellgrove. 1988.

ACKNOWLEDGEMENTS

We are grateful to the following for permission to reproduce photographs: Alte Pinakothek, Munchen, pages 56–57; Archbishop of Canterbury, copyright reserved to Church Commissioners and Courtauld Institute of Art, page 87 *above right*; Archivo General de Indias, Sevilla, pages 24–25; Armouries Museum, H. M. Tower of London, page 88; Ashmolean Museum, Oxford, pages 216–217, 218; The Bridgeman Art Library, pages 75, 121, 178–179; Bodleian Library, Oxford, page 266; British Library, pages 15, 118, 123, 128–129, 140 *above*, 159, 168, 186, 250; J. Allan Cash, pages 22, 34; The Commodore, HMS Drake, page 120; Department of the Environment, pages 204, 255 *below*; Edinburgh University Library, page 140 *below*; Mary Evans Picture Library, pages 27, 97, 108–109; Fitzwilliam Museum, Cambridge, page 156; R. B. Fleming, page 189; Fotomas Index, London, pages 99, 141, 162, 184, 191, 205, 242 *above*; Glasgow University Library, Hunterian Collection, page 152 *below*; Robert Harding Picture Library, page 26; Dean and Chapter of Hereford, page 10; Reproduced by permission of The Lady Herries, page 90 *below*; Michael Holford, pages 23 (photo: Ianthe Ruthven), 116; Hulton, pages 20–21, 82, 96–97, 11, 155, 173 *below*, 176–177, 210, 213, 216, 233, 238, 255 *above*; A. F. Kersting, pages 64, 85, 240; The King's School in Macclesfield, pages 94–95; Mansell Collection, pages 17, 38 *below*, 40, 41, 48, 52, 55, 58, 62, 103, 108, 114, 117, 124, 135, 136–37, 150–51, 175, 196, 223, 229, 231, 235, 245, 253, 267; Master and Fellows, Magdalene College, Cambridge, pages 90 *above*, 237, 246 *right*; The Methuen Collection, Corsham Court, page 164; Museum of London, pages 236–237, 239, 246 *left*; Musee du Louvre, Paris, page 35 (photo: Edimedia); National Gallery of Art, Washington, page 38, *above*; National Maritime Museum, page 12 *right* (photo: Michael Holford), 228; National Portrait Gallery, London, pages 59, 70 *above*, 79, 81, 95, 98–99, 104, 124–25, 131, 144, 166–167, 173 *above*, 199, 234, 248, 254–255, 263; The National Trust, page 209; Marquess of Northampton, page 182; Marquess of Salisbury, page 112; Photographie Giraudon, Paris, pages 57 *above*, 69 *below*, 72–73, 86–87 *above*; Public Record Office, London, pages 62–63, 130; Royal Commission of Historical Monuments (England), page 93; Marquess of Salisbury, page 112; Scala, Firenze, pages 37, 39, 42, 43, 44–45, 47, 54, 56 *above*, 74 *below*; Science Museum, London, pages 12 *left* (photo: Michael Holford), 18; Battleplan from *Battles in Britain* Vol 1. 1066–1547 by William Seymour, Sidgwick & Jackson; Brian Shuel, page 178; Edwin Smith, page 230; Society of Antiquaries, page 242 *below*; Staatliche Kunstsammlungen, Kassel, page 138; St. Faith's Church, Kings Lynn, page 136; Urbino Gallery Nazionale, Firenze, page 36 (photo: Scala); Walker Art Gallery, Liverpool, page 67; Windsor Castle, Royal Library © 1989 Her Majesty The Queen, page 86 *below* left; Woodmansterne, pages 70–71 *below*, 74 *above*; Reproduced by Gracious Permission of Her Majesty The Queen, pages 78, 86–87 *below* (The Royal Collection), 197 (photo: A. C. Cooper). We are unable to trace copyright holders of the following and would be grateful for receiving any information that would enable us to do so, pages 29, 31, 193, 207.

Cover: Detail of the painting entitled 'Rainbow Portrait' attributed to Isaac Oliver, circa 1600, reproduced by permission of the Marquess of Salisbury.

EXPLORATION AND CONQUEST

CHRISTIANS AND SPICES

World discoveries 1415–98

There is an old map preserved in Hereford Cathedral, England. It was drawn in about 1300 and, because educated people of the time wrote in Latin, it is called *Mappa Mundi*, or World Map. This map shows the earth as a disc with Jerusalem, the Holy City, at its centre. Around Jerusalem are the three parts of the world known to Europeans – Europe, called the region of light, Asia, the region of mystery, and Africa, the region of darkness.

The *Mappa Mundi* is a copy of a Roman map. The original had two circles, one for each hemisphere, or half sphere. The copy shows only the northern hemisphere. It gives the impression that medieval people thought the earth was flat. In fact, most educated persons in the middle ages knew that the earth was a sphere. A scholar living in the thirteenth century wrote, '. . . if there were no obstacles a man could go round the earth as a fly crawls round an apple'.

'Mountains of gold'

In medieval times some foreign places seemed more interesting than others. Europeans were fascinated by Asia. After all, had they not called it the region of mystery? Of course, India and China had been known to the Romans. Later, travellers like Marco Polo brought back amazing tales. Polo had spent many years in Cathay (China) in the thirteenth century. He said it had a gigantic port called Zaitun. Its capital city, Quinsay, was defended by a hundred miles of walls. In his book *Description of the World* Polo wrote:

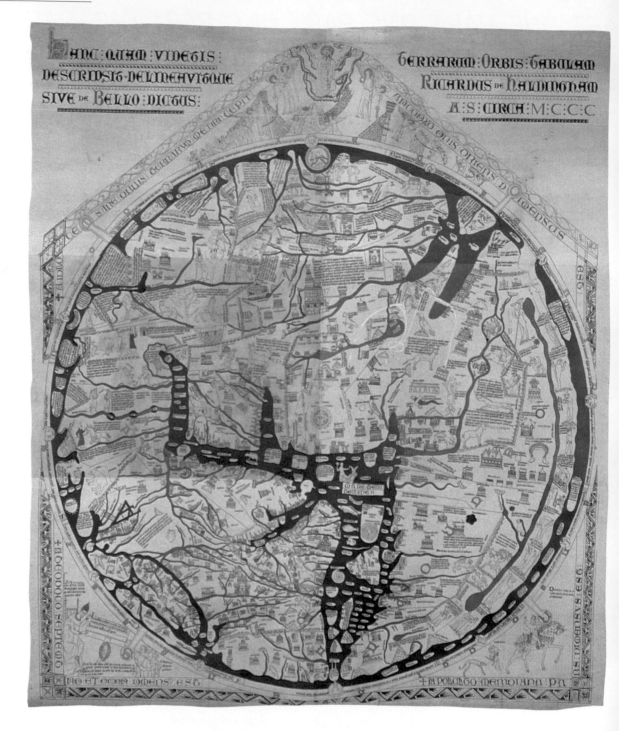

An early view of the world. The Mappa Mundi *in Hereford Cathedral*

Zaitun is the port for all the ships that arrive from India laden with costly wares and precious stones of great price and big pearls of fine quality . . . . I assure you that for one spice ship that goes to Alexandria [*Egypt*] or elsewhere to pick up pepper for exports to Christendom, Zaitun is visited by a hundred.

Other merchants described India as a paradise with sweet-scented bushes, highly coloured birds, and forests whose tallest trees touched the sky. There was said to be a mountain of gold there. Some of its people were thought to be the descendants of a Christian community stranded there long ago.

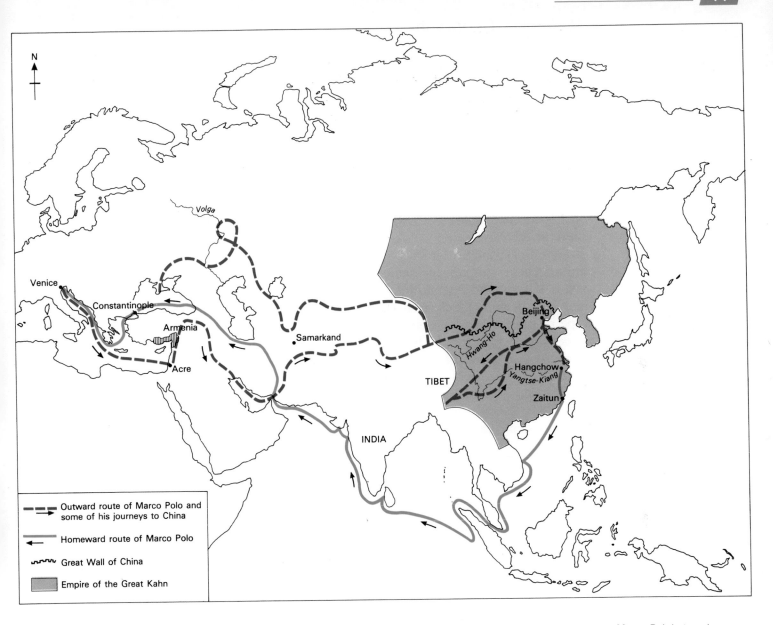

Marco Polo's travels, 1271–1295

Were these only tall stories? On his deathbed, Marco Polo was begged to admit that he had told lies. 'I have not told one half of the truth', he replied. In later years most travellers and merchants came back with similar stories. And although no mountain of gold was found, gems and spices began to arrive regularly from the East. Spices could mean nearly a hundred different things, from pepper, sugar and dyes to perfume and glue. They were in great demand and fetched high prices.

By the fifteenth century a regular trade route had been established between Europe and India. It ran across the Indian Ocean, up the Red Sea and overland to the Mediterranean. From there, goods were brought to Europe in Italian ships, usually those of Genoa or Venice. This Italian monopoly made goods very expensive. Spain and Portugal, of course, were not limited to the Mediterranean. They had Atlantic coastlines. What if they sailed to the East? 'If there were no obstacles . . .' the medieval scholar had written. How many obstacles were out in that grey mist of waters?

Ptolemy's Geography

Among many manuscripts known to fifteenth-century explorers was a book simply called *Geography*. It was written by a Greek, Claudius Ptolemy, who had lived in the second century AD. Ptolemy's book contained useful information about the shipping routes used by sailors in ancient times – from the Canary Islands in the west to Ceylon, India and China in the east. It was not always correct. For example, although Roman seamen used latitude and longitude, Ptolemy's estimate of a degree of latitude was too short. Consequently 'his' world was much smaller than the real one! Nevertheless, his book was very useful in the search for a sea route to the east.

The ships available for such voyages had just undergone a major improvement. Sailing ships have always needed to sail against the wind. If the wind is contrary, the best method is to set the sail along the deck and tack from side to side in a zigzag fashion. This type of sail is called a lateen, as opposed to a square sail which is set *across* the deck. The development of three-masted ships meant that a variety of sails could be carried. These were adjusted quickly if there was a change of wind. So this kind of ship represented a 'new technology' for crossing the oceans.

A fifteenth-century captain navigated with a compass, a lead-line to check depth, and, perhaps, a coastal chart of the area. Far more was needed for long ocean voyages which went out of sight of land. The master had to 'fix' his position on a map as often as possible to avoid getting lost. To find latitude he measured the height of the sun or Pole Star above the horizon with an instrument called a quadrant. The difference in angle since last reckoning represented the degrees of latitude travelled. Finding longitude was far more difficult. A sailor used 'dead reckoning',

A German astrolabe made in 1548 (right) and left, an Italian mariner's compass, 1580

that is, he worked out how far and in what direction he had travelled in twenty-four hours.

A rough and ready way of estimating the ship's speed was to drop a piece of wood, tied to a knotted rope, over the side. The seaman then counted the knots as they ran out. That is why a ship's speed is still measured in knots. Changes in course were marked on a pegged board. Such calculations were only approximate. Different speeds, side drift and compass errors might put a vessel way off target. No captain of those times could count on following the same route twice. The Solomon Islands, for example, were 'found' in the sixteenth century and 'lost' for the next two hundred years!

Henry the Navigator

One possible sea route from Europe to India was west and then south via Africa. It was a forbidding thought to sail into the 'region of darkness' and to see if the African continent ended! Yet from 1415 until 1460 Portuguese expeditions were financed and organised by the King of Portugal's son, Prince Henry. Henry was so interested in exploration that he was nicknamed 'the navigator'. Actually he was a soldier, not a sailor, whose interest in Africa had been aroused by fighting in Morocco as a young man. Henry wanted to spread Christianity as well as to increase trade. So he set up a base at Sagres on the Portuguese coast. Here he collected information from Arab sailors as well as from his own captains.

Henry's first aim was to explore the Guinea Coast of Africa. His men were spurred on by tales of gold. Although not much gold was found, the trips became profitable because of fishing and slave-trading. Hardly a season passed without small fleets of caravels – the name given to these lateen-sail ships – leaving Lisbon, the Portuguese capital. In 1415 the Canary Islands were reached and colonised. Five years later Portugal took possession of Madeira. It was hard, dangerous going. Cape Juby was only rounded after twelve years' effort because of its treacherous currents and the fierce sand-winds which blew off the land.

By 1448 Henry had sent fifty expeditions south. But when he died in 1460 there was still no sign of the turning point to India. In 1475 a captain named de Sintra came to a coast where the thunder of the surf reminded him of lions roaring. He called it 'Sierra Leone' – the mountains of the lioness. Seven years later Diogo Cao entered a river whose fresh water extended 30 kilometres out to sea. As far as we know he was the first European to see the River Congo, or, as it is now called, Zaire.

'Who brought you hither?'

In 1487 Bartholomew Diaz at last rounded the southern tip of Africa. He landed and erected a large cross to thank God. Back home in Portugal he told the king of the 'Cape of Storms' which

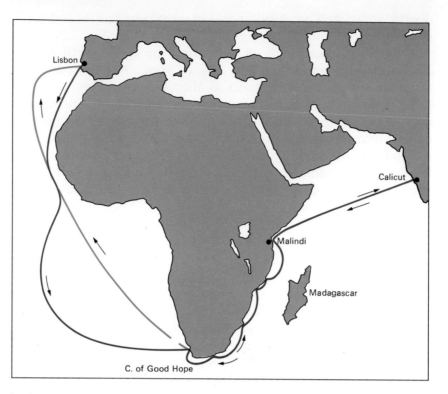

Vasco da Gama's sea route to India, 1497–8

had nearly destroyed his ships. The king was optimistic. He renamed it the 'Cape of Good Hope'. Ten years later another fleet was prepared at Lisbon. When all was ready the sailors walked with their commander, Vasco da Gama, to a solemn service in the cathedral. Afterwards they went to the beach, accompanied by chanting priests and watched by weeping crowds. From this 'beach of tears' they sailed in quest of spices.

Da Gama did not intend to struggle down the African coast as other captains had done. Instead he sailed boldly out into the Atlantic in a great sweep south, covering 6,000 kilometres without sight of land. His daring was rewarded. The ships rounded the Cape after three unsuccessful attempts. On Christmas morning, 1497, da Gama named the coast they were passing 'Natal', meaning 'birth', in honour of Christ's birthday. It is still the name of a province of South Africa.

What the Portuguese needed now was a guide across the Indian Ocean. They managed to recruit Ahmed Ibn Majid, a famous Arab pilot. After a difficult voyage of twenty-five days, their lookouts sighted tall mountains. Here is a description by one of the Portuguese sailors of what happened next:

> That night we anchored two leagues from the city of Calecut . . . after we were at anchor, four boats approached us from the land, who asked what nation we were . . . . We told them, and they then pointed out Calecut to us . . . . On the following day [*21 May 1498*] these same boats came again alongside . . . . The first greeting that he [*da Gama*] received was in these words: 'May the devil take thee! What brought you hither?' They asked what he sought so far away from home, and he told them that we came in search of Christians and spices.

Trade and conquest?

This voyage was a great achievement. Unfortunately, there was another side to the story. When the local people did not want to exchange the goods da Gama had brought he seized some Indians and threatened to kill them if he did not get the spices he wanted. On a later visit he behaved with great cruelty, cutting off the hands, feet and tongues of some fishermen in order to terrorise the ruler of Calecut into doing what he wanted.

The king of Portugal had given da Gama the title, 'Lord of the conquest, navigation and commerce of Ethiopia, Arabia, Persia and India'. The key word was conquest. Da Gama had gone 'in search of Christians and spices'. There were no Christians in India and the spices were to be obtained, if necessary, by conquest.

Vasco da Gama, from a painting on the wall of his palace at Goa, India

THE NEW WORLD

The Portuguese were exploring an eastern route. Others dreamed of another way – west across the Atlantic. It was an old idea, inspired by tales and legends. Far out in those stormy waters, it was said, lay an island called Atlantis. Centuries before, several bishops and their congregations had fled to this spot to escape persecution. Their descendants now lived in happiness and peace. How pleasant it would be to meet these 'lost' Christians! Further-more, their island could prove a useful stepping stone to Cathay and Cipangu (Japan).

One person who believed in such a route was Christopher Colomb, the son of a weaver in Genoa, Italy. We usually know him by the Latin form of his name, Christopher Columbus. As a young man, Columbus had travelled a great deal. In 1478 he married the daughter of one of Prince Henry's captains. From his wife he probably heard stories of the Portuguese voyages down the coast of Africa: there is even a chance he may have sailed on one.

In 1484 Columbus suggested to King John of Portugal such a western voyage to the Indies. This monarch was more interested in the African route. When John said no, Columbus went to Spain which was then ruled by Ferdinand and Isabella. After much discussion with the religious Queen Isabella, Columbus persuaded her to let him go and look for the 'lost' Christians. In April 1492 Isabella ordered Columbus to take three ships and 'discover and acquire islands and mainland in the ocean sea'. The great search was on.

The voyage to the Indies

On 2 August 1492 Columbus sailed from Palos in Spain with three ships, the *Santa Maria*, *Nina* and *Pinta*, and ninety men. The fleet stopped in the Canary Islands to take on fresh stores. Then the ships made good time with favourable winds until they reached the Sargasso Sea, a stretch of water covered with a greenish-yellow seaweed. This strange sight worried the sailors, who feared they might be trapped in it. Actually the ships ploughed through it quite easily since the seaweed merely floats on the surface.

Columbus sets sail. A drawing made during his lifetime

Day after day anxious lookouts scanned the horizon, often mistaking cloud-banks for land. The men grew frightened, complaining loudly that they would never see their homes again. Columbus deceived them with false figures which made it seem that they had not travelled so far. When they still grumbled he declared he would rather be killed than turn back. On 7 October flights of birds were sighted, passing by on their autumn migration from North America. Columbus remembered that the Portuguese had reached the Azores by observing bird-flight. He altered course and tracked the birds south-west. This was a lucky move. Had he not done so he could have been driven north into icy waters where they might all have died from cold or starvation.

After thirty-two days sailing, a cliff appeared in the moonlight. The captain of the *Pinta* lowered his sails and fired a gun as a signal to the *Santa Maria*, rolling and pitching behind. By noon

A model of the Santa Maria

on 12 October 1492 the little fleet was anchored in a large bay, watched by curious natives from a long sandy beach.

Christians or slaves?

Columbus decided to impress the onlookers. He dressed himself in a green velvet suit, purple stockings and a red cloak. He was rowed ashore in a boat displaying the flag of Castile, a Spanish kingdom. When he landed he knelt down, thanked God for their safety and named the island 'San Salvador' which means 'Holy Saviour'. It is now known as Watling Island and is part of the Bahamas group.

This is what Columbus wrote about the natives in a letter to Queen Isabella:

> I am convinced, Illustrious Princes [*Ferdinand and Isabella*], that they would all become Christians had they religious instructors who knew their language, and so set I my hope in the Lord that it will please your Graces to interest yourselves in bringing so numerous a people into the Christian fold and to convert them.

However, in his diary, a few days after the landing, he made this entry.

> These men are totally unversed in the art of arms . . . . A force of fifty men would be sufficient to subdue them with complete ease and compel them to do whatsoever we like with them.

Christians or slaves? What was it to be?

America, not Columbia!

Columbus's expedition went on to visit Cuba and Haiti. The *Santa Maria* was wrecked when it ran aground. Columbus returned to Spain with six Indians, a parrot, some fish and a small amount of gold, probably from Cuba. It was disappointing for a man who the monarchs of Spain had entitled 'Admiral of the Ocean'. On later voyages he reached several more West Indian islands. In 1496 he landed on the mainland of South America near the mouth of the River Orinoco.

As the years passed, Columbus became unhappy at not finding India or China. In Spain the courtiers laughed at this foreigner with his proud ways, who found little gold and no spices. In the Americas he became involved in wars with the natives. Even his own men grew tired of his high-handed ways and mutinied. As a result he was sacked as Governor and even imprisoned for a short time.

Columbus died in 1506, believing himself a failure. Future ages have not agreed with this verdict. As early as 1494 some experts suspected the truth about Columbus's discoveries. One wrote, 'When treating of this country one must speak of a new world'. For Columbus had 'found' a vast continent; he had supplied the *Mappa Mundi* with its missing region.

Whether this great achievement would have pleased him we do not know. What would have annoyed him is that a man named Amerigo Vespucci went to South America and wrote a book about his travels. This became so well known that America was named after Amerigo, not Columbus!

The 'division' of the world

Columbus thought that Japan was 5,000 kilometres from Europe. The real distance is three times that figure. As exploration continued, sailors realised that an even larger ocean than the Atlantic barred their way to the east. In 1513 Vasco de Balboa, a Spaniard, crossed the Isthmus of Panama and became the first European to see the Pacific. He strode into the water, waved his sword and claimed the ocean for Spain.

Spain and Portugal had already quarrelled about who owned the new-found lands. In 1494 they appealed to the Pope. He divided the 'unknown' world between the two (see the map on page 20). Later, another Pope said the Portuguese could have all the lands

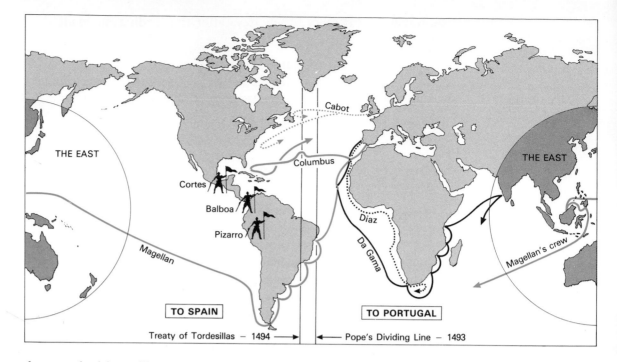

Discovery and exploration

they reached by sailing east. Nobody was sure about these boundaries, so each country sent expeditions to seize territory before the other got there.

In September 1519 Ferdinand Magellan, a Portuguese in the service of Spain, sailed from Seville with five ships and 265 men. His orders were to reach the Molucca Islands and claim them for Spain. Magellan felt certain that he could round the tip of South America and reach the Pacific. So he struck south and west.

'First didst thou sail round me!'

From the Cape Verde Islands Magellan's fleet crossed the Atlantic at its narrowest point and then followed the South American coast as far as the River Plate. Here, in a land they called Patagonia – after the 'patagons', or leather shoes worn by the people who lived there – they found huge men who performed acrobatics and tricks like pushing arrows down their throats. In October 1520 the fleet set off through a narrow channel, cluttered with shallow reefs and small islands. Magellan Strait, as it is now called, is a grim spot, lashed by freezing gales which roar through gaps in the hills. During a desperate voyage lasting thirty-eight days, one ship was sunk and another turned back.

After such an experience the seamen were delighted to see a vast ocean stretching before them. On a lovely sunny day with a calm sea, Magellan named this ocean, 'El Mare Pacifico' – the Pacific, or peaceful ocean. It was not really a suitable name and quite soon his men discovered that the sheer size of this ocean presented particular dangers. One of Magellan's sailors, Antonio Pigafetta, wrote this about the Pacific crossing:

The voyage across this calm ocean lasted three months and

Ferdinand Magellan (1470–1521)

twenty days. During this time we had no fresh food; it was a dreadful time. The biscuits we had to eat were no longer bread but only dust with which worms were mixed . . . . The water we had to drink was yellow, foul and stank to heaven. So as not to starve to death we were forced to eat . . . leather. In our dire distress we frequently consumed sawdust. Even rats . . . were a much-sought delicacy . . . . Nineteen men died . . . .

This is the first known crossing of the Pacific by Europeans. It ended in March 1521 at Sebu in the Philippines. A local chief gave the crew food and supplies and then asked these well-armed strangers to help in a tribal war. Magellan was a brave soldier. He plunged into the thick of the fighting. He was struck several times by poisoned arrows and finally killed with a spear thrust.

The expedition's navigator, Sebastian Cano, took command. His two ships, the *Trinidad* and *Victoria*, sailed round Borneo and at last reached the Moluccas. The *Trinidad* was captured by a Portuguese warship which was prowling around looking for 'invaders'. Captain Cano drove on, crossing the Indian ocean on his way home. Thirteen of the 265 men who first set out landed in Spain on 6 September 1522. Their achievement was a mighty one. They had proved the world was round.

The King of Spain gave Cano a coat-of-arms which featured a globe encircled by the words, 'First didst thou sail round me!'

Sources and questions

1. Here Marco Polo describes the port of Zaiton, called Chuanchou today.

> At the end of the five days' journey lies the splendid city of Zaiton . . . which is the port for all the ships that arrive from India with costly wares and precious stones . . . and big pearls of fine quality. It is also a port for . . . merchants . . . of all the surrounding territory, so that the total amount of traffic [*trade*] in gems and other merchandise entering and leaving this port is a marvel to behold. From this city and its ports are exported goods to the whole province. . . . And I assure you that for one spice ship that goes to Alexandria or elsewhere to pick up pepper for export to Christendom, Zaiton is visited by a hundred.

Source: Travels of Marco Polo, *translated by R. E. Latham, Penguin, 1958*

(a) Marco Polo was sometimes laughed at as a teller of tall stories. What parts of this source suggest that he did exaggerate?

(b) What evidence is there in this source that European travellers visited Egypt?

(c) What does this source tell us about the valuables of Polo's time? What things which he mentions are still regarded as valuable? What commodities are no longer as important, and why?

(d) Polo called his book *Description of the World*. What continents of the world

    i) had he not visited?

    ii) did he not know existed?

2.

(a) This monument stands beside the river Tagus in Lisbon, Portugal. It commemorates a voyage which took place in 1497–8. Why do you think it was built on this particular spot?

(b) It was built in 1960 because this was an important anniversary to the Portuguese. Can you remember what the anniversary was?

(c) Which two historical characters might you think of when looking at this monument?

(d) This monument shows how proud the Portuguese are of their 15th-century explorers. What can be said in favour of these men, and what can be said against them?

3. Make up a short play about Columbus at the court of Queen Isabella.

4. Can you guess which Italian city has a Christopher Columb airport, and which has a Marco Polo airport?

THE CONQUISTADORS

Close on the heels of the explorers came the conquistadors – the Spanish word for 'conqueror'. Some large West Indian islands and the mainland near the Isthmus of Panama had been settled by the Spanish within twenty years of Columbus's first landing. These colonists brought slaves from Africa and settled down to farm with cattle and horses. The more adventurous went to the mainland, attracted to quick riches by tales of gold and silver. Here they found a land far stranger than any lost Atlantis. Deep inland lay ancient civilisations, the Aztecs of Mexico and the Incas of Peru.

The Aztecs were a warlike people who had just conquered their neighbours. They were farmers who had no iron tools, no wheel and no animals for carrying or pulling. They used a form of picture writing. Aztec towns consisted of houses made of baked earth, overshadowed by large temples shaped like pyramids. The

Ruins of ancient Mexico. The Pyramid of the Sun and Street of the Dead at Teotihuacan, built at least a thousand years before the Spanish arrived but typical of what they must have seen

Aztec world was a mixture of beauty and savagery. The capital city, Tenochtitlan, was set on the waters of a lake. Its buildings stood on wooden piles; its 'streets' were canals. Aztec gods had pretty names – Plumed Serpent (Quetzalcoatl) and Humming Bird (Huitzilpochti). However, Aztec priests taught that such gods needed constant human sacrifice. Only a large supply of blood, it was believed, could please Huitzilpochti in particular.

Hernan Cortes

In 1519 a conquistador named Hernan Cortes left Cuba with a small force which landed at Tabasco. Almost at once there was a battle with an Indian people called the Mayas. They were slaughtered by cannon fire and charging horsemen; they had never seen horses and at first thought animal and rider were one creature!

After this victory, Cortes led 400 soldiers, with 15 horses and 10 cannons, out of the steamy jungles of the coastal plain and up to the cold, thin air of the Mexican plateau. By now he knew he had to conquer an empire. The odds against the Spaniards were high but the clever Cortes was optimistic. He knew that the Aztecs had many enemies who could be useful as allies. He had also heard that the Aztecs were expecting their god, Quetzalcoatl, to return to earth that year. Thus it was possible for the Spaniards to pretend to be gods.

Montezuma, the Aztec emperor, was sure that the white-faced strangers were from heaven. Instead of fighting, he sent messengers with gifts of gold who begged the conquistadors to go away. It was no use; the greedy soldiers were not likely to turn back after seeing such riches! They marched into the lake-city of Tenochtitlan, watched by silent, wondering crowds. And when it seemed that they might attack, Cortes daringly took the emperor hostage. At one stroke he had paralysed an empire. No Aztec would move against him whilst their god-king was a prisoner.

After a short stay Cortes had to leave the city. The governor of Cuba had sent an expedition to arrest him for disobeying orders. Cortes defeated his opponents and returned to Tenochtitlan with more men and horses, where he found a dangerous situation. Some of his soldiers had behaved badly, grabbing extra food, melting down gold idols and even murdering Indians during a solemn religious festival. The Aztecs had decided that the gods no longer favoured their emperor. When Montezuma tried to calm them he was hit by a stone and died. His death was the signal for thousands of warriors to attack the Spaniards.

It was night when the fighting started. The Aztecs, wearing animal skins and feather head-dresses, charged to the screech of war-pipes and the steady beating of drums. They fired arrows and hurled stones at Cortes's men who were greatly outnumbered. Only skilled swordsmanship and discipline saved some of them from death. Step by step, they cut their way through the Aztec army, out of the city and along a broken wooden causeway across the lake. The Spaniards managed to lay a temporary bridge across

D. FRA

the gap but it collapsed, drowning many of them. Eventually they crossed using sunken guns and waggons as stepping stones. A tall soldier vaulted one gap, using his lance as a pole!

The end of Tenochtitlan

A number of Spaniards did not escape. Some were stabbed or clubbed to death. Others were taken prisoner, stripped naked, led up the steps of Huitzilpochti's temple and cut to pieces in sight of their horrified comrades. These terrible scenes were lit by fiery sparks streaming into the sky from the nearby volcano, Popacatopetl. By morning about half the conquistadors were safe. The rest were floating dead in the lake or lying in pools of blood on the temple altar.

A grim Cortes swore to be revenged on the Aztecs. Next year he came back with a large army of Indian allies. He broke all the causeways leading to the lake-city and, after a long siege, fought his way in. What was left of the starving population was allowed to leave. The Aztecs had held out for 80 days and suffered at least 250,000 casualties. Cortes had the city totally destroyed.

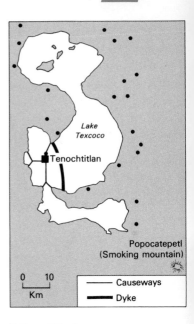

Valley of Mexico

Pizarro of Peru

Francisco Pizarro

Another American Indian people, the Incas of Peru, were conquered by the Spaniards at this time. The Incas ruled an empire which stretched south down the continent and covered areas which are now Ecuador, Bolivia, Peru and northern Chile. The Incas were good at making gold, silver and copper objects and they could weave cotton and wool. They were also fine engineers who had built roads across some of the highest mountain areas in the world. In some place they made rope bridges and long tunnels.

The Incas lived on root crops, particularly potatoes which were at that time unknown in Europe. Their beast of burden was the llama, a woolly-coated animal of the camel family. Inca laws were simple: nobody was to lie or steal and, if they did, they were to be stoned to death or thrown off a high cliff. Sometimes a whole village might be wiped out for breaking a law. The Incas worshipped the sun and rain and thought the moon was the sun's wife.

The Inca capital, Tiahuanaco, was possibly more impressive than Tenochtitlan. Its great stone pyramid-temples were decorated with gold and jewels and set against a backcloth of snow-capped mountains. The Sun Temple at Cuzco, another Inca city, was crowned by a dome which was a huge sheet of gold. Messengers who ran from town to town in relays carried news and government orders. The news had to be remembered because the Inca language does not seem to have been written down.

Such was the empire which was about to suffer a fate more dramatic than the Aztec empire of Mexico at the hands of a man more cruel than Cortes. In 1532 Francisco Pizarro marched into Inca lands.

Ambush at Cajamarca

On 25 November 1532 Pizarro led his men into the deserted town square of Cajamarca. He had arranged to meet Atahualpa, the Inca emperor, who was camped nearby with a large army. The conquistador sent a message saying he would be pleased to meet the emperor 'as a friend and a brother'. Actually, he had hidden his soldiers in back streets around the square.

Atahualpa was a fierce warrior who had just won a civil war against his brother. He was carried into the square on a litter which one eyewitness described as 'a golden castle'. Servants hurried in front, dusting the ground over which their god-king was to pass. A group of singers and dancers followed, ready for the celebrations. When the emperor's cavalcade stopped, a Spanish friar gave Atahualpa a Bible. The Inca held it for a moment before throwing it on the ground. It is doubtful whether he could read any language, least of all Latin. At this, a friar called upon the soldiers to take

The Inca city of Machu Picchu

revenge for the insult to Christianity. The Spanish opened fire, killing many Indians. In the confusion they rushed forward and seized Atahualpa. This action paralysed an empire, just as Cortes's seizure of Montezuma had done in Tenochtitlan. The Incas would not fight whilst their god-king was a prisoner.

More provinces than towns

Atahualpa soon realised that the Spanish were greedy. He offered to fill his cell with gold if they would let him go. Pizarro agreed and Indian servants were allowed to fill the 50 cubic metres of the cell with gold. But once this was done, Pizarro had the emperor strangled. The conquistadors were millionaires, in modern terms. Pizarro even had gold shoes put on his horse.

Pizarro was an efficient but very cruel ruler. In the end he was murdered by his own officers. Spanish people at home did not always admire the conquistadors and their achievements. Possibly they were horrified by the tales of cruelty and greed which reached Spain. Cortes, in particular, felt bitter about the way he was treated. Once, when he claimed the high honour of standing on the step of the Spanish King's coach, Charles V asked who he

To Seville

WEST INDIES

MEXICO
Vera Cruz

hides

NEW SPAIN

CUBA

HISPANIOLA

ATLANTIC OCEAN

Nombre de Dios

Panama

To Philippine Islands (Spanish)

BRAZIL (Portuguese)

• Cajamarca

• Lima
PERU

• Potosi
silver

PACIFIC OCEAN

Spanish colonies

Route of Spanish treasure to Seville

Spanish colonies in the Americas

was. 'I am the man who has given you more provinces than your father had towns!' Cortes replied angrily. It was true. In a few years, conquistadors had given Spain the largest empire since the days of Rome.

DOCUMENTS: AZTEC AND SPANIARD

Document 1

When news reached Montezuma that Cortes and his men had arrived at the coast, he sent spies to watch the strange invaders. These men climbed a tree and watched the Spaniards fishing. They made a report (**a**) and drew a picture (**b**).

(**a**) Until quite late they continued to fish, and then entered a small canoe and reached the two enormous towers and climbed inside; there must have been about fifteen of them, who wore a kind of coloured jackets. . . . Some of their faces had a pinkish hue, and on their heads they had coloured pieces of cloth; these pieces of cloth were scarlet caps, some very large and round like small maize cakes, which must have served a protection against the sun. Their flesh was very white and they all wore long beards and hair to their ears.

Source: Tezezomoc, Hernando Alvarado. Cronic Mexicana, *Editorial Leyenda, Mexico City, 1944*

Questions

1. Why did the messengers stress the whiteness of the Spaniards' skin?
2. What evidence is there in (**a**) of the staple diet of the Aztecs?
3. Why did the Aztecs call the Spanish ships 'enormous towers' and say the Spaniards were fishing from a 'canoe'? What does this tell us about the Aztec's own ships?
4. Imagine you are writing a similar report about the Aztecs. Explain to the Spanish emperor what the Aztecs were like.
5. Pick out the differences between (**a**) and (**b**). Do you think they are important or unimportant?
6. Can you think of a reason why Montezuma needed a *picture* as part of the spies' report?

Document 2

Once the Spaniards had landed, Montezuma sent important officials to see Cortes. This account was written by Bernal Diaz, one of Cortes's officers, who, when an old man, wrote down his experiences in a book called *The Conquest of New Spain*.

> . . . when these people [*the Aztecs*] arrived before Cortes they kissed the earth and perfumed him . . . with incense which they had brought in earthen-ware containers. Cortes received them kindly and seated them beside him. The prince who carried the presents welcomed us to the country and after a long speech ordered the presents to be brought forward. The various objects were placed on mats. . . . The first was a disk in the shape of the sun, as big as a cartwheel and made of very fine gold. It was a marvellous thing engraved with many sorts of figures . . . worth more than ten thousand pesos. . . . There was another larger disk of silver in the shape of the moon. The Aztec lords asked Cortes to accept them with the same kindness as Montezuma had shown in sending them. Then the lords repeated a message from Montezuma. First, that he was pleased such brave men had come to his country. Secondly, that he would send the Spanish emperor a present of precious stones. . . . But as for meeting Cortes, he told us not to think of it . . . and he put forward many objections.

Source: Bernal Diaz, The Conquest of New Spain, *translated by J. M. Cohen, Penguin, 1963*

Questions

1. What parts of this source suggest that Montezuma and the Aztecs thought the Spaniards were gods?
2. Was Montezuma pleased that the Spaniards had come to Mexico, as he said? Use the source to answer this question.
3. What evidence is there in this source that the Aztecs worshipped the sun and moon?
4. Do you think this account betrays the real reason for the Spanish expedition to Mexico? Give reasons for your answer.

Document 3

Here Diaz describes an important incident when Aztec met Spaniard.

> It was the hour of Ave Maria, and at the sound of the camp bell, we all fell on our knees, in front of a cross which we had erected on a sand-hill, to say our prayers. Two Aztec nobles, being intelligent men and seeing us on our knees, asked us why we humbled ourselves before a log cut in that particular fashion. On hearing this question, Cortes made a speech so suitable for the occasion that no clever priest could have done better. . . . Cortes also told them that our great Emperor's purpose in sending us to their land was to abolish human sacrifices and other evil things they did . . . .

Source: Bernal Diaz, op. cit.

Questions

1. Is there any evidence in this source that the Spaniards were Catholics?
2. Cortes is famous as a man of action. What other qualities does he seem to have possessed, to judge from this source?
3. What do you think Cortes explained to the Aztecs when they asked him why they knelt before a wooden cross?
4. Do you think Cortes was being honest when he told the Aztecs why the Spaniards had come to Mexico? Explain your answer.

Document 4

Aztec pictures are now collected in sets called 'Codexes'. These are often copies by Spaniards of the original drawings. This page, from the 'Codex Mendoza', illustrates how Aztec children were educated. The dots show the ages of the children and the round objects are the number of tortillas they are allowed.

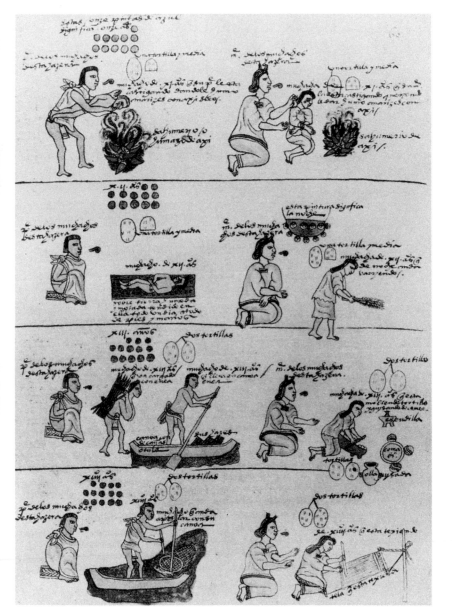

Questions

1. Does the fact that Spaniards were involved in making this source make it more or less reliable?
2. What unusual punishments, by western standards, were given to naughty Aztec children (top row and left, second row)?
3. Using these pictures, describe everyday clothing worn by ordinary Aztecs.
4. The pictures on the right show girls being taught crafts; those on the left the skills learnt by boys. Imagine you are an Aztec boy or girl. Describe your childhood and education.
5. Imagine you are a conquistador. Describe why you went with Cortes, what you thought of the Aztecs, how you felt about the final destruction of Mexico City.
6. Using the sources and the facts in Chapter 3, justify *or* condemn the tactics Montezuma used to deal with the Spanish invasion.

THE RENAISSANCE AND REFORMATION

THE WORLD OF FIFTEENTH-CENTURY ITALY

In 1453 the Turks captured Constantinople. For over a thousand years the city had been the capital of a Christian empire called Byzantium. Over the years much of its power had been whittled away. Turks already ruled most of Asia Minor. Many Byzantine scholars and artists had fled to Europe. Nevertheless, Constantinople's fall shocked the Christian world.

The empire which ended in 1453 was more than a Christian dam holding back the Muslim flood. It was also a vast storehouse of art and literature. The sculptures, paintings and writings of the ancient world were crammed into its palaces and libraries. When the Roman Empire fell in the fifth century many of these treasures were ignored by the west. From Crusading times onwards, however, trade links between Europe and the Middle East increased western knowledge of Greek and Roman art and learning.

The capture of this historic city by people of a different religion and civilisation highlighted a development which had been going on for centuries. Westerners were becoming more curious about the achievements of the ancient world. We call this awakening interest the Renaissance, a word which means 'rebirth'.

The medieval world

Renaissance is a misleading way of describing what happened. It suggests something sudden, as if the curtains were drawn back to let in light after the 'darkness' of the medieval world. The Middle

Ages were not a time of ignorance. Students studied law, Latin literature and the Scriptures. Monks produced beautiful, highly decorated manuscripts. Artists painted lovely religious pictures. Craftsmen built churches and cathedrals whose beauty is still admired today.

Even so, the Church did not encourage medieval scholars to think for themselves or find out more about the world. The Bible, and the teachings of the men who founded the Church (Church Fathers), were believed without question. Greek and Roman writings were also studied, providing they did not directly contradict church beliefs. The opinions of Aristotle, a Greek philosopher, were the last word on most things; to quote his opinion was thought the best way to settle an argument! Where science was concerned, physics, chemistry and medicine were treated as kinds of magic. Doctors, for example, sometimes cast spells over their patients.

So medieval people took too much for granted. During the Renaissance, on the other hand, scholars and artists started to look more closely at Man and Nature. They asked questions. As a result, nothing was ever the same again.

Humanism

The Renaissance began in Italy. There were several good reasons for this. Cities such as Venice, Genoa, Florence, Mantua and

Renaissance Italy

Urbino, Italy

Naples had become rich on the profitable trade with Byzantium. Their ruling families had the money to collect art treasures and books and to employ artists to create new works. In addition, many Italians lived near impressive Roman ruins; in a way it was their 'past' which was being rediscovered.

In the fourteenth century two Italian writers, Petrarch and Boccaccio, started to collect Greek, Latin and Hebrew manuscripts. They were nicknamed 'humanists' because they were interested in 'human' literature of the Greeks instead of the 'divine' works of the Church. Petrarch's searches took him to France and Germany. The work of both men encouraged rich, educated persons to form libraries. Nicholas V (Pope 1447–55) collected over 5,000 manuscripts which now form the basis of the Vatican library in Rome.

It was not only popes who could afford such expensive hobbies. The ruler of the small town of Urbino in Italy, Federigo da Montefeltro, made a fortune selling his services as a soldier. With the profits he built this fine palace which still dominates the town.

Baldesar Castiglione

A writer of the time, Vespasiono da Bisticci, had this to say about this tough warrior's leisure activities:

> We come now to consider in which high esteem the Duke held all Greek and Latin writers, sacred as well as secular. He alone had a mind to do what no one had done for a thousand years or more; that is, to create the finest library since ancient times. He spared neither the cost nor labour, and when he knew of a fine book, whether in Italy or not, he would send for it . . . .

'Renaissance man'

Federigo represented a new fashion. In earlier times a prince's fame depended on how successful he was in war. The painting of Federigo (page 36) illustrates both sides of his character. Because he loved books he is shown reading. But because he was a famous soldier he is reading in full armour!

The ideal for such men was explained by Baldesar Castiglione in a book called *The Courtier*. Castiglione was a scholar who could also wrestle, joust and fence. He served Federigo's son, whom you can see in the painting. He also worked for the Emperor Charles V,

who valued him so highly that he is said to have always had
a copy of the book at his bedside.

The Courtier takes the form of a conversation between high-born
men and women. In this extract, a lady has just been refused a
dance by a gruff soldier:

And when at length the lady asked what his business was, he
answered with a scowl: 'Fighting.'

'Well then,' the lady retorted, 'I should think that since you
aren't at war at the moment and you are not engaged in fighting,

Federigo da Montefeltro

it would be a good thing if you were to have yourself well-greased
and stowed away in a cupboard with all your fighting equipment,
so that you can avoid getting rustier than you are already.

A century before it is unlikely a warrior would have been made fun
of in this way. Later, Castiglione says this of a courtier's training:

I maintain myself that it is more fitting for a warrior to be
educated than for anyone else; and I would have these two
accomplishments, the one helping the other, as is most fitting,
joined together in our courtier.

In other words it was no longer enough just to be a good warrior.
The ideal Renaissance courtier had to be educated as well.

The Medici

Some of the most famous Renaissance princes were members of
the Medici family, who ruled Florence for much of the fifteenth
century. Florence was already rich from the profits of a flourishing
cloth trade. The Medici, although cruel and unpopular, made the
city famous for its arts.

Petrarch, Boccaccio and another Italian poet, Dante, had lived
there. With Medici help the city now produced more beautiful
paintings, sculpture and architecture than any city since ancient
Athens. The first Medici ruler, Cosimo, built a gorgeous palace.

The Medici palace in
Florence

Here he entertained some of the greatest men of the time, including the emperor and several popes. His grandson, Lorenzo, employed fine artists who produced many masterpieces. His taste was so admired that he was nicknamed 'Il Magnifico' – the Magnificent.

Three of the world's greatest artists – Botticelli, Michelangelo and Leonardo da Vinci – worked at one time or another for Lorenzo Medici. Of these three Leonardo was a true 'Renaissance man', a writer, a scientist, and a military engineer. He studied the flight of birds and produced designs for an aeroplane and a helicopter. He painted two of the most famous paintings in the world, the 'Mona

Painted bust of Lorenzo de Medici by Andrea del Verrochio, a famous Renaissance artist

Leonardo's sketch of a flying machine

Leonardo's 'Last Supper'

Lisa' and the 'Last Supper'. His drawings of flowers, plants and the human body show scientific accuracy as well as artistic skill.

Michelangelo is said to have disliked Leonardo. But then his quarrels were as well-known as his paintings.

THE RENAISSANCE

Painters, popes, princes and prophets

Michelangelo was born in Florence in 1475. He was trained as a sculptor and his great skill soon attracted attention. In 1503 Pope Julius II invited him to Rome. Julius was more of a soldier than

Pope Julius II

Michelangelo

a priest. When Michelangelo suggested a statue of him holding a book in his hand, Julius laughed and said, 'What! A book! A sword! I'm not one for book-learning!'

Julius told Michelangelo to make him a grand tomb. The artist set to work enthusiastically, picking assistants and touring the local quarries for suitable stone. Then the pope changed his mind, deciding instead to concentrate on the rebuilding of St Peter's church in Rome. This caused the first quarrel between pope and artist. Here is Michelangelo's version of what happened, written in a letter to a friend:

> As for my departure [*from Rome*] it is indeed true that on the Saturday morning before Easter . . . I heard the pope say as he sat at table . . . he could not spend another farthing for stones, little or big. Nevertheless, before my departure, I asked him for part of what was my due for carrying on the work. His Holiness replied, asking me to call again on the Monday. I did call again on Monday and on Tuesday and on Wednesday and on Thursday, as you well know. At last, on Friday morning, I was sent away, that is to say, thrown out – by a miscreant who said he knew me but was acting under orders . . . .

'Whims of men of talent'

Julius ordered Michelangelo to return. The artist refused. This worried the rulers of Florence, who told Michelangelo that even the French King thought twice before disobeying *this* pope! In fact, Michelangelo was afraid he might be punished if he returned. Julius realised this, and wrote as follows to his ambassador in the city:

> The sculptor Michelangelo, who left without reason, fears to return we hear though on our part we hold no anger against him, well knowing the whims of men of talent . . . we trust in your convincing him . . . that in the event of his return no harm or injury shall come to him . . . .

Michelangelo came back to face a different task. The pope now wanted him to paint the ceiling of the Sistine Chapel in the

God creates Adam. A detail from the ceiling of the Sistine Chapel

Vatican. Michelangelo protested that he was a sculptor, not a painter. Again the pope insisted. So Michelangelo set to work.

Decorating the ceiling was expected to take seven years. Michelangelo finished it in four, perched high on a scaffold, often lying on his back to paint. It was hard work, particularly as these were frescoes, that is, painting on wet plaster. An artist has to work quickly before the plaster dries.

'The Pope is well satisfied'

Michelangelo chose as his subject the story of the creation of the world as told in the Bible. Here you see his idea of the Great Flood and Noah's Ark, and the story of Adam and Eve in the Garden of Eden. The painter was a fast worker. The head of Adam, for example, was painted in a day. But he was not quick

The story of the flood, Sistine Chapel

enough for the old pope. Each day Michelangelo would help him up the ladder to the scaffold. Each day Julius would ask when the work would be finished. Once the quick-tempered Michelangelo snapped angrily, 'When I am able!'

After a year Julius ordered the scaffolding to be taken down so that the decorations could be seen by the public. Michelangelo protested that this would delay the work. There was a furious row which ended when the pope shouted, 'Would you like to be thrown off the scaffold?' The timbers came down and on 1 November 1509 Rome's citizens got their first glimpse of a masterpiece. They were amazed and delighted with what they saw.

In October 1512 Michelangelo wrote to his father, 'I am done with the chapel where I have been painting the decorations. The pope is well satisfied . . . .' The next year Julius died. Today, when few people have heard of him, tourists and art-lovers flock to Rome to see the masterpiece he bullied Michelangelo into painting.

The Borgias

There was another side to this world of artistic achievement and courtly ideals. Medici rulers were brutal and treacherous as well as clever and sensitive. The princes who encouraged Renaissance art were almost continually at war with each other. Cities formed leagues against neighbouring cities, families struggled for control of a town, armies spread devastation far and wide, brother fought against brother, husband murdered wife and wife poisoned husband. Federigo was not the only soldier to make a fortune out of war. It was a time as notorious for bloodshed as it was famous for art.

By the fifteenth century, princes competed to be pope as if it were just another monarchy. We have already heard of one irreligious pope, Julius II. His predecessor and great enemy, Alexander Borgia, was a professional soldier who bribed his way to the papacy. Once he had become Pope Alexander VI, he lived anything but a holy life, having many mistresses and spending fortunes on wild parties which went on for days. As a ruler he was quite efficient but his main concern was to make his family rich and powerful. Since he was getting old, he let his son Cesare command the papal army.

Cesare Borgia was as ruthless as his father. He set about uniting Italy under the pope's rule, using bribery, trickery or sheer terror to get his way. Niccolo Machiavelli, a Florentine civil servant, knew him well. In a book called *The Prince* he says this of Cesare's problems as his father's life drew to a close:

> . . . his chief cause for anxiety was that the next successor to the papacy might prove unfriendly and might endeavour to take back what Alexander had given him. He [*Cesare*] sought to guard against this eventuality in four ways: by destroying all the families of the rulers he had despoiled . . . second by winning

Cesare Borgia

over all the patricians [*nobles*] of Rome . . . in order to hold the pope in check; third, by controlling the College of Cardinals [*who elect popes*] as far as he could; fourth, by acquiring so much power before Alexander died that he could on his own withstand an initial attack.

'Old Nick'

Machiavelli believed that in politics it was success or failure, not right or wrong, that mattered. He also thought that any action which led to the unity of Italy was good. This is why he admired Cesare Borgia, whose eventual failure he excused like this:

> If, when Alexander died, he [Cesare] had been well himself everything would have been easy for him. And he himself said to me, the day Julius II was elected, that he had thought of everything that could happen when his father died, and found a remedy for everything except that he never thought that when he did so he himself would also be at the point of death . . . . So having summed up all that the duke did, I cannot possibly censure him . . . .

Niccolo Machiavelli

The man who Machiavelli 'could not censure' almost certainly murdered his own brother!

Nobody could have been less like a Borgia or a Medici than Machiavelli himself. Yet this hard-working, honest civil servant wrote a classic which has given him a bad name. Today, when people refer to the devil as 'Old Nick', they are speaking of Niccolo Machiavelli. And a treacherous politician is often called 'Machiavellian'.

The print 'explosion'

The spread of the 'new' knowledge was helped by the invention of printing. Hand-written books took a long time to produce. When Cosimo de Medici started his library he employed forty-five scribes who took two years to copy 200 books. And, because books were scarce, only a few rich people could afford them. Thus the spread of knowledge was limited.

Block-printing – the carving of a single page on a wooden block – had been known in Europe for some time. Unfortunately, these blocks took a long time to make and were no use afterwards. The breakthrough came when Johan Gutenberg (1397–1468), a German from Mainz, found a way of making movable type. Knowledge about the technique spread rapidly. In 1477 William Caxton set up his presses at the 'Sign of the Red Pale' in Westminster, London. Presses were set up in other countries at the same time. The first printed books looked like hand-written manuscripts. They were often beautifully illustrated with woodcuts.

Savonarola

Not everybody admired tyrants like Cesare Borgia as much as Machiavelli. The prior of St Mark's monastery in Florence in 1494 was Girolomo Savonarola. In that year a large French army invaded Italy, led by King Charles VIII. Savonarola told the people that this invasion was a punishment for the sins of the rich. It was a sign that God was displeased.

The Florentines were terrified as the French soldiers drew nearer every day. They decided that Savonarola was a prophet of God and forced their Medici rulers to flee. For a time Savonarola was supreme in Florence; he even met the French king and persuaded him not to damage the city. The monk tried hard to make the citizens live better lives. He closed gambling houses and recruited children to spy on their elders and report immoral behaviour. At a huge bonfire in the square an enthusiastic crowd burned perfumes, mirrors, false hair, musical instruments, carnival masks, paintings and books, including one by Petrarch.

It seemed as though Florence had turned its back upon the beauty as well as the wickedness of the Renaissance. But Pope Alexander was furious. He expelled, or excommunicated, Savonarola from the Church. People of the time believed that this meant Savonarola would go to hell when he died. They turned against him. On the very spot where they had burned mirrors and musical instruments, they now burned Savonarola himself, hanging him up in the flames.

The debris was swept into the River Arno. Nineteen years later another monk denounced the wickedness and luxury of the Renaissance papacy. His name was Martin Luther.

Sources and questions

1. This extract from Castiglione's *The Courtier* helps to explain why there was plenty of work for good painters in Renaissance Italy.

> I think our courtier should certainly not neglect . . . drawing and the art of painting. . . . And do not be surprised that I demand this ability, even if nowadays it may appear . . . hardly suited to a gentleman. For I recall having read that in the ancient world, and in Greece especially, children of gentle birth were required to learn painting at school . . . subsequently, a . . . law was passed forbidding it to be taught to slaves. . . . And there were plenty of celebrated painters belonging to illustrious families. In fact, from painting . . . many useful skills can be derived . . . for military purposes . . . to sketch towns, rivers, bridges, citadels, fortresses and similar things.

> *Source: Castiglione*, The Courtier, *Penguin Classics, 1967*

(a) What does Castiglione mean by 'gentle birth' and 'illustrious families'? What was his purpose in writing this? What relationship did he have in mind?

(b) What parts of this source suggest that war was common?

(c) Castiglione gives two reasons for learning to paint. Which reason was more likely to appeal to young noblemen?

(d) What evidence is there in this source that Castiglione

    i) admired the ancient world

    ii) wanted only upper-class people to be taught to paint.

2.

This painting by Raphael tells the story of Christ's miracle of the fishes which will be found in the Bible (St Luke, Chapter 5, verses 6–9). The kneeling figure is Simon Peter, and others include James and John.

(a) Why are some figures shown with haloes?

(b) Why do you think Raphael chose a Biblical subject to paint?

(c) How is the painting of the figures different from that of earlier religious paintings? Why did Renaissance painters use this style?

(d) What evidence is there that this picture was painted in 16th-century Italy, *not* the Holy Land where the incident occurred?

3. Try to find the names of a painting by Leonardo da Vinci or Michelangelo.

4. Turn the story of the painting of the Sistine Chapel into a play.

'ON THIS I TAKE MY STAND'

Martin Luther

Martin Luther was a friar who taught religion at Wittenberg University in Germany. In October 1517 he pinned a long protest in Latin on the door of Wittenberg Castle church. This was not unusual; doors were used then as we use notice boards now. Luther was protesting because another friar, John Tetzel, had arrived in Germany to sell 'indulgences', or pardons. In those days the Church taught that sinners who felt truly sorry could be forgiven if they did a penance. Indulgences were supposed to let the person off. At first they were given to soldiers going on a Crusade in case they were killed. By Luther's time, however, they could be bought by any Christian.

The idea was that a person would repent and then give money. Tetzel knew this but he also told people,

As soon as the gold in the basin rings,
Right then the soul to heaven springs.

Luther claimed that Tetzel was deliberately misleading people. 'Simple folk will not understand that they should feel truly sorry for what they have done. They will think they are buying a pardon from God', he commented.

At first Luther's action attracted little attention. So he wrote his protest out again in German. Immediately there was uproar, as crowds gathered to read it. Germans were sick and tired of paying taxes to a pope they thought of as a foreign prince. Luther's arguments lit the fire of their anger. An enterprising printer got to work and soon Luther's words were spread far and wide.'Within a fortnight it made its way across Germany . . . because everyone was complaining about indulgences', wrote Luther. He felt sure the pope did not know what Tetzel was doing. He hoped to right a wrong. What he never expected to start was a religious revolution.

Promise in a storm

Luther was born at Eisleben in Germany in 1483, the son of a copper-miner. As a young man he was not particularly religious. Then, at the age of twenty-one, a strange experience changed his life. He was walking home from college when he was caught in a violent storm. Dark clouds suddenly blotted out the sun. Heavy rain flooded the fields and lanes. A flash of lightning struck the ground so near him that he fell over.

Luther was afraid. He took the storm to be a sign from God. 'Encircled by . . . terror and fear, I made vows [promises]', he remembered later. In fact recent events had made him take life more seriously – a friend had died, he had visited a plague-struck village and had nearly been killed in an accident. Nevertheless, Luther always claimed that it was his experiences on that stormy afternoon which made him decide to be a monk.

The young man took his new career very seriously. He studied hard, spent hours at prayer and went without food for days on end. 'If ever a monk got to heaven by monkery, I would have got there. . .', he recalled later. As he studied, doubts about some of the Church's teachings entered his mind. Then in 1510 he visited Rome. It was not a good time for a keen Christian to be in the city. Michelangelo was decorating the Sistine Chapel but Julius II was pope (see Chapter 5)! Luther saw the luxurious way Julius lived and wondered, 'If Christ was poor, why is the pope so rich?'

The righteous shall live by faith

Luther was worried by the problem of salvation (eternal life). Could Christians be saved by being baptised and going regularly to Mass? Or should they fast, become pilgrims and worship 'holy relics' like pieces of wood supposed to have been part of Christ's cross? This is what the Church encouraged people to believe, but was it true? Or was there some other route to God's forgiveness?

One day, sitting at his desk in the monastery, Luther read again St Paul's phrase in the Bible: 'The righteous shall live by faith.' For a long time it had puzzled him. Now, in a flash, he was sure what it meant. St Paul was saying that God would pardon all people who believed in Jesus Christ, no matter how many good or bad deeds they did, how many Masses they attended, how many times they went on pilgrimage. Faith in Christ alone would lead to salvation.

This idea became the basis of Luther's teaching in later years. He denied that people needed Church ceremonies to be saved. This was not an opinion which the Church authorities of those days would tolerate. In the past, men and women who 'by-passed' the Church in this way had been burned. Luther had set out on a dangerous path.

'The die is cast'

It would have been better for the Church if the pope had ignored Luther's protest. The German was not the first to grumble about indulgences, Church taxes and bad-living popes. Even Church beliefs had been attacked in the past. But Tetzel was a Dominican

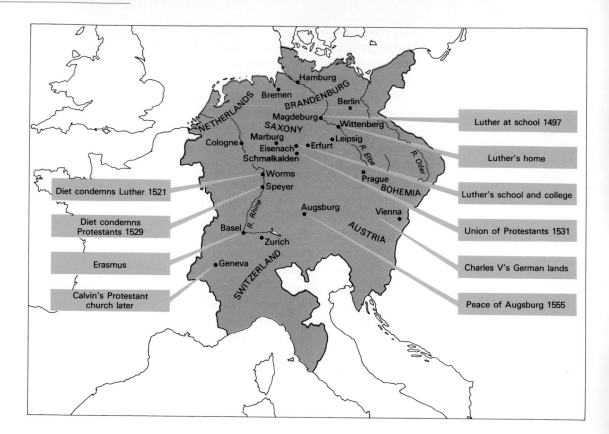

Reformation Europe

friar and Luther was an Augustinian. The rivalry between the two brotherhoods caused Dominican scholars to rush to Tetzel's defence.

The quarrel soon turned into a battle of books. Since books could now be printed, the incident got far more publicity than it would have done in earlier times. As the contest heated up, Luther started to condemn other things besides indulgences. A true Christian, Luther claimed, did not need popes, bishops or priests. In a way every person who believed in Christ was their own priest. This was too much for the easy-going Pope Leo. He gave Luther sixty days to change his mind. After that time he would be expelled from the church (excommunicated) and declared an outlaw.

This news was greeted with anger by Germans. All their hatred of 'foreign' popes surfaced. A spy reported to the pope: 'Nine-tenths of Germany are crying "Luther" and the other tenth are at least crying "Death to the Roman Court"!' A religious quarrel was about to become a political one.

The Diet of Worms

A new figure now entered the story. Charles V had just been elected Holy Roman Emperor, that is, overlord of the different German states. Rarely in history has one person ruled so much territory. Charles was born in Ghent (now in Belgium) in 1500. From his father he inherited the Low Countries (Belgium and

Holland); from his mother the kingdoms of Spain, Naples and Spanish America.

Charles found that there were more problems than pleasures in ruling his far-flung dominions. The pope and the king of France were his sworn enemies. They were jealous of his power and plotted to ruin him. Charles guessed that he would soon be at war with France. He needed German taxes and German soldiers to fight his battles. This was not easy because the Germans looked upon him as a stranger; he could not even speak their language. So when the emperor summoned one of his subjects, Martin Luther, to meet him at the Diet of Worms in 1521 (a 'diet' is a parliament), the rebellious monk seemed a minor irritation. Other leaders felt the same. It was a fatal mistake which was to lead to years of war and persecution.

Charles listened carefully to what Luther had to say. To his surprise the monk defended himself well and refused to change his mind. At one point Luther is supposed to have said: 'On this I take my stand. I can do no other. God help me. Amen'. This made Charles angry and he condemned him as a heretic, ordering all Christians to treat him as an outlaw. However, he gave Luther a safe-conduct out of the town, probably because the monk was guarded by German knights!

Even so, it was only Luther's bodyguard who prevented him from being waylaid and murdered on his way out of Worms. The danger was so great that soon afterwards Frederick of Saxony,

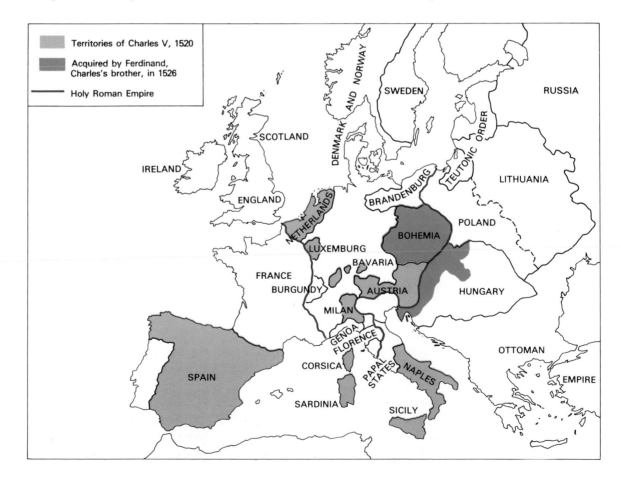

European lands ruled by Charles V. He also ruled Spanish America

Luther at the Diet of Worms. Probably a nineteenth century drawing

lord of the town of Wittenberg, staged a fake ambush. Luther was carried off and hidden in Wartburg Castle, near Weimar in central Germany. It was announced that he had disappeared. From his forest hideout, Luther carried on a war of words against his enemies, writing pamphlets and books. He also began a translation of the Bible into German. The break was now complete. In later years patriotic Germans set up 'Lutheran Churches' independent of Rome. Similar churches were also established in Norway and Sweden.

The Anabaptists

Luther's revolt was religious, not political. Yet his defiance was certain to affect politics. In Germany there were princes prepared to use the religious weapon Luther had given them in their struggle against the Pope. This is why they supported the reformer and why Frederick hid him in a castle. The ordinary people too, were inclined to see the affair, not as a religious quarrel, but as a political battle with an Italian prince.

Among the thousands who now called themselves 'Protestants' were Christians far more extreme than Luther. Wittenberg City Council abolished Mass altogether and allowed mobs to damage churches and attack priests. Fanatics roamed Germany, condemning princes as well as the pope. A group nicknamed Anabaptists, because they practised adult baptism, predicted that

Christ would soon return to earth. A man who sympathised with them, Thomas Muntzer, claimed that Christ would save only poor people. Muntzer placed himself at the head of a peasant army which murdered noblemen and burned their castles.

Charles V formed an alliance of German princes to stamp out this peasant revolt. At the battle of Frankenhausen in 1525 Muntzer's army was beaten and he was beheaded. Ten years later Anabaptists led by John of Leyden defended the town of Munster for nearly a year against an army led by the local bishop. During the siege John went mad, announced he was king of the earth and married a dozen women. When the town fell, nearly all the inhabitants were killed and John was tortured to death with red hot tongs.

Calvin at Geneva

Another important church founded during these years was the brainchild of John Calvin, a French priest and lawyer. Calvin settled in the independent city of Geneva, Switzerland, in 1541. He gathered so many supporters around him that for some years the Geneva authorities let him run the city.

Calvin had described his ideas of a well-organised Church in a book called *Institutes of Christian Religion*. In Geneva he was able to put his theories into practice. Each parish had its own preachers, plus teachers, elders and deacons. These men were responsible for health, welfare and education as well as worship. They were elected democratically. Because the preachers and teachers were called 'presbyters', Calvinists are sometimes known as Presbyterians.

News of Calvin's 'godly city' spread throughout the Protestant world and many refugees from religious persecution joined him. A Scotsman, John Knox, was delighted by what he found. He described Geneva at that time as 'the most perfect school of Christ that was ever on earth since the days of the Apostles'. Knox introduced a similar system to Scotland in 1560.

To modern eyes there was a less pleasant side to this 'most perfect school'. Each year inspectors visited every home to find out if any 'immorality' was going on! Children were encouraged to tell tales on their parents. Wrong-doers were tried by church courts. Punishments varied from fines and whipping to death. A girl who put non-religious words to a hymn was beaten. A boy who struck his parents was beheaded. And when Michael Servetus, a Protestant with different ideas from Calvin, came to Geneva he was put on trial, condemned and burnt.

Very often, however, it was Calvin's followers, not the man himself, who were so severe and gloomy. Calvin's work and teaching was very influential. Scotland, Holland and parts of Germany adopted the Presbyterian system. Most French Protestants were his followers. The 'poor timid scholar', as he called himself, brought spiritual happiness and education to millions. His church also became a well-organised, powerful enemy of Roman Catholicism. If Luther had lit the fire, Calvin showed Protestants one way to control it.

The Counter-Reformation

This is the painted ceiling of St Ignatius Loyola's church in Rome.
In the centre is Christ, rising to heaven with His cross. Below, flying

saints fill the space between heaven and earth. To the right, Catholics are seen triumphing over Protestants. To the left, pagans who have become Christians kneel before Christ. A foreign king bows before a lady who holds a lamp representing 'true religion'.

This painting is propaganda with paint and brush instead of pen and ink. It expresses, in an explosion of writhing figures and blinding light, the essential spirit of the Counter-Reformation. Here was the Catholic Church's response to the Protestant revolt. It proclaims that God can only be reached through the Church and its saints. Heretics must return to the true faith. Lands overseas must hear the Catholic 'Word' so that their inhabitants can join the Church. Everywhere Christ through His Church must conquer.

It is no coincidence that St Ignatius's church contains the tomb of the saint himself. For this Spanish nobleman spearheaded the Catholic counter-attack.

Ignatius Loyola

Loyola's 'Spiritual Exercises'

Loyola started life as a soldier. He fought bravely until in one battle his leg was shattered by a cannon ball. As he lay in bed recovering from his wounds, he found himself reading some lives of the saints and the Bible. This experience gave him a new purpose in life. He decided to become 'a soldier of Christ', converting both Protestants and non-Christians.

To prepare himself for this religious battle, he devised a set of 'spiritual exercises'. This intense 'assault course' occupied four weeks. The first week was spent thinking about the problem of sin. During week two Loyola considered Christ's 'Kingship on Earth'. Week three found him meditating on Christ's trial, execution and ressurection. Week four's topic was Christ's life after he rose from the dead. These exercises became the basis of all training given to Loyola's followers, the priests who formed his 'Society of Jesus', or Jesuits.

In the years which followed the founding of the Society in 1540, Jesuits went to many parts of the world as missionaries of the Catholic faith. It was often a dangerous task. In some Protestant countries they were hanged, drawn and quartered. In foreign parts they were sometimes burnt. In Japan they were even crucified like their Master. But everywhere they were feared and respected. These 'shock-troops' of the Counter-Reformation became a by-word for discipline and devotion.

The Council of Trent

The Society of Jesus was only part of the wind of change which swept the Catholic world after the Reformation. Equally important were several deeply religious popes who tried to undo the damage done in the bad old days of the Renaissance. It was Pope Paul III who gave permission for the Society to be formed. He and his successors took part in a series of meetings held in the

Pope Paul III

Emperor Charles V

Italian town of Trent. The meetings, known as the Council of Trent, were spread over a number of years, from 1545 until 1563.

At the Council of Trent, some of the reforms demanded by Luther and other Protestants were carried out. At the same time Church organisation and teaching was completely overhauled. Many of the decisions made at Trent have lasted to the present day. For example, the Tridentine Mass, or Mass of Trent, remained the standard Latin service for all Catholics until the 1960s.

Trent showed that the Catholic Church had at last woken up to the danger of a permanent split in the Christian world. It was also the last chance to heal the wounds. But the rivalries of the great powers ruined such hopes. Catholic France, for example, refused to send representatives to Trent because the Council took place in territory ruled by France's enemy Charles V. The Catholic authorities rarely invited Protestants to the meetings. So the quarrel grew worse until Christian Europe was divided for good.

Catholics and Protestants will always disagree as to whether the Reformation was a good or a bad thing. But both would agree that the horrors which followed it were bad. When Charles V condemned Luther at Worms, he said: 'His teaching makes for

The Council of Trent in session

rebellion, war, murder, robbery, arson and the collapse of Christendom [the Christian World].' Not everybody would have blamed Luther, but Charles was certainly right in his predictions.

Sources and questions

1. It has contributed greatly to the advantage of the Church that several Popes in succession have been men of good lives; hence all the citizens [*of Rome*] are become better, or at least pretend to be so. Cardinals and priests attend mass punctually; their servants are careful to avoid anything that can give scandal; the whole city has put off its old recklessness and is become much more Christian-like in life and manners than formerly.

Paolo Tiepolo, 1576

(a) The writer speaks of several good popes setting a better example. What sort of behaviour by 'bad' popes had he in mind?

(b) Why do Catholics think it important to attend mass?

(c) Why should Rome, in particular, have been expected to set an example to the Christian world?

(d) Tiepolo wrote in 1576. What events in particular had led to this change of behaviour in Rome?

2.

(a) Why do you think Tetzel is shown riding a horse with a wolf's head?

(b) What is the bird above Tetzel's head meant to represent?

(c) What is the middle figure in the drawing doing? Why did this make Luther angry?

(d) Why is there a bowl on the top of the money-chest?

3. Re-enact the 'Luther story' in three scenes:
   (a) Tetzel's arrival in Wittenberg.
   (b) Luther's protest and quarrel with Tetzel.
   (c) Luther's condemnation by the Emperor at Worms.

4. What countries have Lutheran churches today? How are their services different from Church of England or nonconformist church services in Britain?

TUDOR TRIUMPH

A STRONG MONARCHY: HENRY VII 1485–1509

On 22 August 1485 Henry Tudor defeated and killed King Richard III in a battle fought near Market Bosworth in Leicestershire. He became King Henry VII – the first of the Tudor rulers of England. Bosworth is an important landmark in English history. First, it settled an old quarrel between two branches of the royal family – the Yorkists and the Lancastrians – in favour of the Lancastrians. Second, it established the Tudor dynasty which ruled England until 1603. Finally, it founded a royal line which has lasted until the present day; every later monarch of Britain is descended from the victor of Bosworth Field.

The body of Richard was slung naked over a horse 'as an hog or another vile beast' and carried to Leicester for burial. At the time, few people expected the new king to reign for long. After all, the 'Wars of the Roses' between the white rose of York and the red rose of Lancaster had seen kings rise and fall. Edward IV, the most successful Yorkist king, had won the crown, then been driven out. He had returned to win more battles and become undisputed ruler. Two kings, Richard II and Henry VI, had been murdered. Noblemen of both sides had given their lives as battles were lost or won. By the time of Bosworth, Henry's claim to the throne was the best of any Lancastrian but weaker than several Yorkists.

Perhaps for this reason Henry always claimed that God had given him victory. 'The crown which it pleased God to give us . . .', he wrote in his will.

Henry VII

The princes in the Tower

Henry hoped Bosworth would end the feud between Yorkists and

Lancastrians. Before his victory he had promised to marry Elizabeth, a daughter of Edward IV. In this way the red and white roses would be united. Three months after his coronation Henry kept his promise and married the Yorkist princess. But his troubles were not over. Many Yorkists in England, Ireland and on the continent longed to overthrow him. They were helped in this plan by the mystery of the 'princes in the Tower'.

When Edward IV died in April 1483 he left two young sons – his successor as king, Edward V, and Edward's brother, Richard, Duke of York. The dead king's brother, another Richard, at first protected his nephews. The boy king was lodged in the Tower of London with his younger brother. In July 1483, however, Richard and his Council announced that the princes were illegitimate. Apparently their father had already agreed to marry another woman when he married their mother, Elizabeth Woodville. This meant that neither boy could inherit the crown. Their uncle became King Richard III and the two lads were never seen again. The story that Richard had them suffocated may well be true. They were almost certainly murdered. In 1674 their bones were supposed to have been found under a stairway in the Tower.

What really happened to the princes in the Tower may never be known. In 1485 nobody knew whether they were dead or not. Consequently, 'lost' Yorkist relatives of Edward IV, including the missing princes, appeared to challenge Henry's grip on the throne.

Simnel and Warbeck

In 1487, Irish lords who supported the Yorkists claimed they had found Edward IV's nephew, the Earl of Warwick. In fact, the twelve-year old boy they crowned King of England in Dublin was Lambert Simnel, the son of an Oxford tradesman.

The real Warwick was a prisoner in the Tower. This did not stop some people believing in the impostor. An army of Yorkist supporters and foreign troops landed in England in 1487. It was a serious crisis but Henry managed to win a fierce battle at Stoke in June. Simnel was captured and brought to London. The lad admitted that he was not Warwick. Henry realised that Simnel was just a puppet in the hands of the Yorkist lords. He pardoned the boy and set him to work in the royal kitchens.

Another challenge to Henry's throne came from Perkin Warbeck, the son of a customs' officer in Tournai (now in Belgium). Warbeck was said to look very like Richard, Duke of York. He spent some time in Ireland where the Yorkist lords announced that he was the missing Richard. Edward IV's sister, Margaret, saw him in the Netherlands and declared he was her nephew. Margaret's hatred of all Lancastrians, and of Henry VII in particular, probably helped her to 'recognise' him!

'A low-born foreigner'

Perkin Warbeck became a thorn in Henry's side as he commuted between Ireland and Scotland trying to whip up support. The Scots king, James IV, really believed the young man *was* the Duke of York. He allowed Warbeck to marry his cousin, and helped him when he led an unsuccessful invasion of England in 1496.

That same year a rebellion in Cornwall against Henry's heavy taxes gave Warbeck another opportunity. He slipped into England and joined the rebels. They decided he was the missing prince. The Cornishmen tried to capture Exeter but failed. As Warbeck's army melted away, he took refuge in Beaulieu Abbey in Hampshire. Then he surrendered to the authorities, clothed, we are told, 'in gold', and went to see the king.

Their meeting was described by Raimondo de Soncine, ambassador from Milan:

> The young man was brought into the royal presence, where many nobles of the realm were assembled, some of whom had been companions of Richard, Duke of York. He kneeled down and asked for mercy. The king . . . then spoke as follows: We have heard you call yourself Richard, Son of King Edward. In this place are some who were companions of that lord . . . see if you recognise them. The young man answered that he knew none of them, he was not Richard . . . .

Warbeck was imprisoned for two years. Then, when more Yorkist rebellions broke out, he was put to death, together with the real Earl of Warwick. After these executions, relations between England and Scotland improved. In 1503 James IV married Henry's daughter, Margaret. It was their descendants who ruled England and Scotland as the Stuart kings and queens from 1603.

King, council and commons

An English king of those times had to be obeyed but he was expected to ask the advice of his nobles and gentry (gentlemen) on important matters. Henry governed with the help of councillors, although he rarely summoned all its members to meet together, preferring to consult them individually or in groups. Occasionally, when very important matters were discussed, the king, his council and his lords (including lawyers and clergymen) met as a Great Council.

A parliament of Lords and Commons could only meet if ordered to do so by the king. English monarchs only called a parliament if they needed money for war or wanted new laws passed. We shall see how this worked when we come to the reign of Henry VIII. Henry VII called seven parliaments during his reign. They met for a total of sixty-nine weeks. Henry was proud of this, claiming that so few parliaments had saved his subjects the MPs' travelling and lodging expenses. His people probably agreed with him.

The Commons Assembly consisted of two knights from each county and two representatives from each borough. A borough was a town with a royal charter allowing it to govern itself. Knights from the thirty-seven shires were elected by landowners with property worth forty shillings or more a year in rents.

A Tudor king in Parliament. The king shown is Henry VIII in 1515

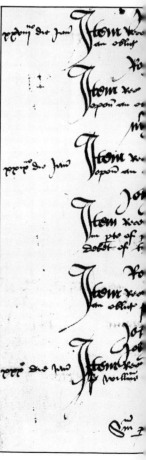

Burghers, or town representatives, were chosen in various ways, usually by the richer merchants and traders of the borough.

The Commons met in the chapter-house or refectory (dining room) of Westminster Abbey until 1547 when they moved to St Stephen's Chapel in the royal palace of Westminster. The modern Houses of Parliament stand near this spot. The Commons debates took place without the monarch. MPs' opinions were then reported to the king by their Chairman, who was therefore called the Speaker. A Speaker was supposed to be chosen by the members. In fact, nobody whom the king disliked would have got the job.

'A king who loved wealth'

An English monarch of the sixteenth century was expected to 'live of his own', that is, to run the country out of his own income. As we have seen, only in times of crisis would his parliaments help him financially. Henry kept a careful eye on royal income; one set of account books for 1504–8 still exist and show that he read and signed every page. Henry was allowed by Parliament to tax certain goods coming into the country. This was known as 'Tunnage and Poundage'. At that time this raised about £39,000 a year – not enough to run the country. Customs duties on wool exports, and fees paid to the king on the death of a lord or the marriage of his children, made the final annual total about £110,000. So Henry also devised some rather unusual taxes. He made his richer subjects loan him money, or give him certain sums out of their love for him!

It was said of the first Tudor that, 'Being a king that loved wealth, he could not endure to have trade sick'. Certainly he tried to help trade with special treaties and laws. One treaty he signed arranged for fairer shares of the English wool trade with the Netherlands. Another, the treaty of Medina del Campo with Spain (1498) gave English and Spanish merchants equal trading rights in each other's countries. At home, Parliament passed Navigation Laws which ordered most merchandise to be imported only in English ships. This was meant to prevent unemployment amongst English sailors and shipwrights.

The treaty of Medina del Campo also arranged the marriage of Henry's eldest son, Arthur, to King Ferdinand and Queen Isabella's daughter, Catherine of Aragon. This took place when they were considered of age, in 1501. When Arthur died soon afterwards, Catherine stayed in England and was engaged to his brother, the future King Henry VIII.

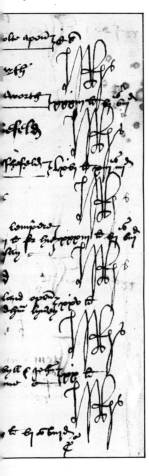

Royal account books for 1506. Henry VII signed each entry

A strong monarchy

Henry VII was respected but not loved. His skill in finance and his efficiency gave him a high reputation at home and abroad. He was less bloodthirsty that his fellow monarchs; Simnel would certainly have been executed had he rebelled against any other king of the time. Even his carefully calculated marriage turned out well. He was a loving husband and was very upset when Elizabeth died in 1503.

Some people called Henry a miser. This is not fair. From his splendid coronation onwards, Henry had the Tudor knack of 'playing the king', and if this meant spending money he was ready to do it. His clothes were always very fine and he even decorated his dogs with silk collars. He also enjoyed expensive meals such as 'perch in jelly dipped', 'peacocks in hackle' and 'castles of jelly'. Yet the impression that Henry was cold and distant remains. Certainly he was cunning and secretive and is said to have kept notes on which people to reward or employ and which to distrust!

Henry died on 21 April 1509 at Richmond Palace. He was buried in Westminster Abbey in a magnificent tomb made by Pietro Torregiano, a Florentine sculptor. It is a fitting resting place for a Renaissance prince.

The full extent of Henry's achievements became clear after his death. His son succeeded without the slightest dispute or disorder.

Sources and questions

1.

Henry's magnificent tomb was made by an Italian sculptor, Pietro Torrigiano. The king is shown lying beside his queen, Elisabeth, who died in 1503. A great deal of the work was done in Henry's lifetime.

(**a**) Using this source as a guide, how do you think Henry regarded his role as king?

(**b**) Why do you think Henry chose an Italian sculptor to make his tomb?

(**c**) What does this source tell you about Henry's attitude to his wife?

(**d**) Is there any evidence in this source to suggest Henry was a religious man? Give reasons for your answer.

2. On 10 May 1509 Henry VII was buried in Westminster Abbey in London. Bishop John Fisher was chosen to make the main speech at his funeral. Here is part of what he said about the dead king.

> His wisdom in governing the country was exceptional, his intelligence always quick and ready, his reasoning substantial, his experience notable . . . his speech gracious

in many languages, his looks good and amiable, his eyes
fair. . . . He made alliances with all Christian princes, his
mighty power was dreaded everywhere. . . . His people
were obedient to him . . . his land many a day in peace
. . . his good fortune in battle marvellous . . . treasure
and riches incomparable, his buildings most goodly.

Source: The English Works of John Fisher, *Vol. I, Early
English Text Society, page 269. Quoted by Millward,
Sixteenth Century Documents, Hutchinson Educational, 1961*

(a) In what ways is this an exaggerated description of Henry
VII and his reign?

(b) What was there about Henry's early life that made it
likely he would speak foreign languages?

(c) Who in the congregation that day would have expected
only good to be said of Henry? How might this have affected
what John Fisher said?

(d) Using this source as a guide, list the qualities expected
of a king in those days.

3. Polydore Vergil was an Italian scholar who came to England
in 1501 to collect taxes for the pope. He became friendly
with Henry, who asked him to write a history of England.
This extract is from Polydore's *Anglica Historia*.

The whole country of Britain (which is called England and
Scotland) in divided into four parts, England, Scotland,
Wales and Cornwall. . . . All these parts are different,
either in language, manner or laws. . . . England is the
largest and is divided into shires which Englishmen call
counties. . . . It is a wealthy land, most fruitful to the
south of the river Humber, for to the north . . . it
abounds in mountains. . . . The ground is marvellously
fruitful and has plenty of cattle, so . . . Englishmen are
more likely to be keepers of cattle than labourers in the
fields. . . . Above all, they have an enormous number of
sheep, which yield . . . quantities of wool of the best
quality. They have no wolves, because they would
immediately be hunted down by the people; it is said,
however, that they still exist in Scotland. . . . London is a
wealthy city . . . in one single street [*Cheapside*] . . .
there are fifty-two goldsmith's shops, so rich and full of
silver objects . . . that in Milan, Rome, Venice and
Florence put together I do not think there would be found
so many.

Source: Polydore Vergil, The Anglica Historia, *translated
by Hay, Camden Series, Quoted by J. D. Mackie,* The
Earlier Tudors, *Oxford University Press, 1952, Vol. 74,
R. H. Society*

(a) Who do you think this book was written for? Give
reasons for your answer.

(**b**) How many parts would Britain be divided into today? What was particularly different about Scotland at that time?
(**c**) What evidence is there in this source that Polydore had probably not visited Scotland?
(**d**) This source was translated into English in 1546. Polydore did not write it in Italian but in another language. Can you guess what language it was, and why Polydore used it? (There is a clue in the title.)

4. This is a 'Tudor rose'. What did Henry hope to do by taking this as his badge? Are there any such roses on old buildings near where you live?

'A VERY ACCOMPLISHED PRINCE': HENRY VIII 1509–20

Henry VIII in his prime – a very accomplished prince

Henry VII was given a memorable funeral. Five horses, draped in black, pulled the hearse which was escorted by archbishops, bishops, lords and barons. The dead king's richly decorated armour and battle-axe, his helmet with gold crown and spear sheathed in black velvet, were carried in the procession. On 10 May 1509 the victor of Bosworth was laid to rest in Westminster Abbey.

He was succeeded by his seventeen-year-old son, Henry VIII. Most paintings of Henry show him when he was fat and middle-aged so it is easy to forget how magnificent 'Bluff King Hal' seemed as a young man. The Venetian ambassador to England in 1509 wrote home:

> His majesty is . . . extremely handsome . . . very accomplished, a good musician, composes well, is a most capital horseman, a fine jouster, speaks French, Latin and Spanish, is very religious . . . He is extremely fond of tennis, at which game it is the prettiest thing in the world to see him play.

No man was better qualified to play the Renaissance prince. In looks and character, Henry resembled his grandfather, Edward IV, who had won the crown through his skill and courage on the battlefield. He was tall and strongly built, an athlete who could hunt, fight and drink with the toughest of his courtiers. Like the Yorkist king, also, he could be ruthless and savage. Henry boasted that there was no head in the kingdom so noble 'but he would make it fly' if its owner defied him. One of his first actions was to execute two of his father's most faithful but hated tax-collectors, Empson and Dudley. One of his last acts was to sign the death warrant of the Duke of Norfolk. The headman's axe and the hangman's rope were never far away in Henry VIII's reign.

Two weeks before his coronation Henry kept a promise made to his father and married Catherine of Aragon, his brother Arthur's widow. This was against Church Law, but Pope Julius II gave special permission.

Battle of the Spurs

Henry VII had been a reluctant warrior at the best of times. He had told his son to avoid war because of the cost. The warlike young prince ignored such wise advice.

Europe offered plenty of opportunities for war. The feud between the Holy Roman Empire (an area covering much of modern day Germany, Czechoslovakia and Northern Italy), Spain, and the Papacy on one side and France on the other was as bitter in 1512 as it was to be a few years later when Luther defied the pope (see Chapter 6). There was not much doubt which side Henry would be on. As a faithful son of the Church he wanted to side with the pope. As an Englishman he regarded France as the traditional enemy. Furthermore, the Holy Roman Emperor Maximilian ruled the Netherlands (now Belgium and Holland), where English merchants sent wool to be made into cloth. Maximilian could, if he wished, cripple this vital industry by banning English wool imports.

It came as no surprise, therefore, when England joined a 'Holy League' consisting of the Papacy, Venice and Spain against France. In the summer of 1513 Henry crossed to France with an army and linked up with Maximilian's forces; the wily emperor had gone to war because he was connected by marriage with Spain. On 13 August the two armies nearly trapped the enemy at Guinegate, near Courtrai (now in Belgium). The French were ordered to escape and fled so quickly that the skirmish became known as the Battle of the Spurs.

Flodden

While the English king was away on the continent with the main English army he missed a far greater victory at home. For centuries France and Scotland had been allies. When war-clouds began to gather, James IV of Scotland promised to invade England if the English invaded France. In August 1513 he kept his promise. The Earl of Surrey gathered northern troops and sent a messenger, challenging the Scots to battle. James accepted the challenge and Surrey swore 'to give the said king battle by Friday at the furthest', that is, 9 September.

James took up a well-defended position on Flodden Hill, not far from Berwick. Surrey split his forces and got round behind the Scottish army. The Scots then began to move towards another hill. Why exactly they did this will never be known because the men who made the decision never lived to tell the tale. It was a fatal mistake. The Scots ranks broke up as they encountered rough and marshy ground. Their pikemen were most effective when attacking in close-packed ranks. Now they were scattered and so became easy targets for the English axemen. There was a fearful slaughter and James and his son died leading a desperate charge into the English army.

The death of King James IV turned a bad military defeat into

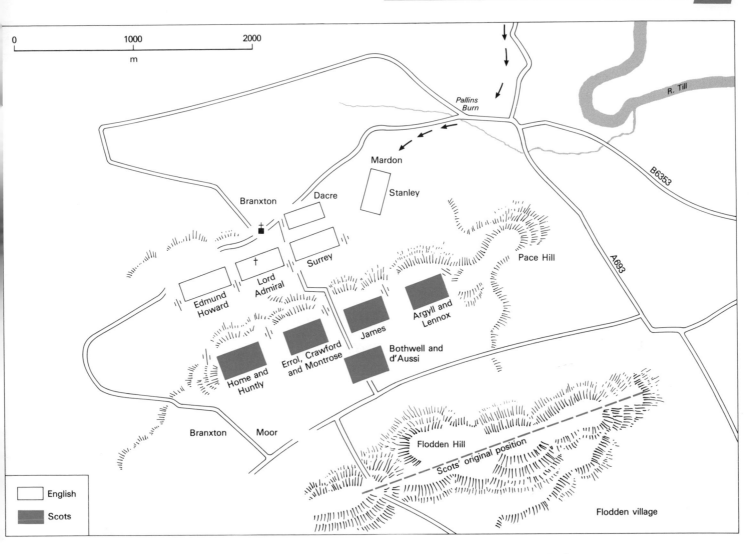

Battle field plan of Flodden Hill, 1513

a political disaster. Scotland mourned not only 11,000 dead; for many years to come it suffered from weak government because it had only a boy-king.

Enter Francis

Henry's Queen, Catherine, sent James's bloodstained coat to Henry, who showed it proudly to Maximilian. The crafty emperor, however, had already started peace negotiations with the French behind Henry's back. Luckily for the English king, Louis of France was more afraid of an English army than of Maximilian's troops. Years before he had paid Henry VII a pension to stop him invading France. Now he offered to double it if Henry went home! He also offered to marry Henry's sister, Mary. The English king returned to a hero's welcome.

It seemed Europe might enjoy peace for a while. Unfortunately, Louis died two months after his marriage to Mary (1515) and was succeeded by his nephew, Francis I. The new king was a typical Renaissance prince. One of his first actions was to invite Leonardo da Vinci to live in France. 'No one in the world knows so much

Francis I, King of France

as Leonardo', boasted Francis. The old man was given a pleasant house and the title 'First Painter, Engineer and Architect to the King'. Leonardo brought two of his finest paintings with him – the 'Virgin of the Rocks' and the 'Mona Lisa'.

At the same time, Francis was most warlike. He was tall and athletic, with a bushy black beard and a long nose. He was also cruel, wildly extravagant and brave to the point of foolishness. Within a year of becoming king, he crossed the Alps, smashed a Swiss army hired by the Italians at the Battle of Marignano, and made himself master of northern Italy. Three years later, when Maximilian died, he swore he would be elected emperor if it cost him millions in bribes. Actually, his greatest enemy, Charles V, spent less and got the imperial crown.

The years which followed were to see large-scale wars between power groups led by these two great monarchs.

Cardinal Wolsey

Thomas Wolsey, 'the glorious peacock'

One of the men who encouraged Henry to interfere in continental affairs was Thomas Wolsey, his chief minister for sixteen years. Wolsey's story is one of 'rags to riches'. He was born in Ipswich, the son of a butcher. He went to Oxford University and then became a priest. In those days a poor man could better himself in the Church, where brains counted as much as wealth or high birth. From the start the ambitious young man looked for powerful friends who could help his career. His ability was soon noticed and he became, first, chaplain to the Archbishop of Canterbury and then to the governor of Calais. (Calais belonged to England in those days.)

Desiderius Erasmus

Few men have risen so quickly. In 1507 Wolsey was appointed a royal chaplain. Two years later he was made dean of Lincoln. After the French war, he became a cardinal, then Archbishop of York and Lord Chancellor. He was never Archbishop of Canterbury because the holder of that office, William Warham, outlived him. In 1518 the pope made him legate, or papal ambassador, in England. By 1520 the butcher's son from Ipswich lived in palaces and dreamed of becoming pope one day.

There can be no doubt that Wolsey was a clever and capable man. On the other hand, there was nothing particularly religious about 'the glorious peacock', as he was called. As a young man he had lived with an innkeeper's daughter, giving her two children. As a cardinal he made himself rich by taking bribes. What probably annoyed people even more was his pride. On ordinary days Wolsey ate alone, like a king. He gave magnificent feasts, dressed in gorgeous clothes and made his personal clergy wear silk. Visitors were nearly always kept waiting, and then made to stand 'an arrow's length' from him. He even carried an orange filled with a sponge of vinegar to keep off the smell of poor people.

In 1519 the Venetian ambassador reported to his government: 'This cardinal is the person who rules both the king and entire kingdom.' This was not correct. Henry knew he had nothing to

fear from a commoner who was so unpopular with people and nobles. Time was to show that the king had made Wolsey and the king could break him.

Thomas More

Henry liked to have educated men about him. His own teachers had been humanists (see Chapter 4) so he welcomed many humanist scholars, both foreign and English, to his court. The most famous English humanist was Sir Thomas More, a lawyer, who was introduced to the king by Wolsey. Henry grew fond of More's witty and educated talk. He would invite him to the royal apartments, or even visit More's pleasant house in Chelsea. There the two would walk and talk together in the pretty garden by the river.

More's most famous book is *Utopia*, which means 'the land of nowhere'. In it, More described an ideal state on an imaginary island 'where no man has property' but 'all men pursue the good of the public'. Utopians fought no wars and built no prisons. Criminals were made to do useful work instead of being tortured and executed. More used the book to condemn many of the evils of his day – war, poverty, greedy landlords and idle monks. He described his island so well that some readers thought it was real. After all, it was an age when new 'discoveries' were quite common.

Erasmus

The most notable foreign scholar to come to England was Desiderius Erasmus (1469–1536), a Dutchman. He gave lectures at Cambridge University which were so full of 'modern' ideas that they caused a stir. Erasmus was a friend of Sir Thomas More. In 1509 he stayed with him and wrote a little book to amuse his friend. It was called *Praise of Folly* and in it 'Folly' condemned the evils of the day. Here is what 'Folly' has to say about monks:

> The whole tribe is so universally loathed that even a chance meeting [*with them*] is thought to be ill-omened – and yet they are gloriously self-satisfied. In the first place, they believe it's the highest form of piety to be so uneducated that they can't even read . . . . Then . . . they bray like donkeys in church, repeating . . . psalms they haven't understood . . . .

'Folly' was disgusted with Pope Julius II's warlike ways and criticised him, although not by name. In spite of these harsh words, however, Erasmus wanted the Church to be improved, not destroyed. For this reason he condemned Luther's actions.

Luther's teachings also shocked Henry and he wrote a book attacking the German reformer. In 1521 a copy was sent to Pope Leo X who was told that the King would like as his reward the title *Fidei Defensor* which is Latin and means 'Defender of the Faith'. The pope agreed, so FID DEF has been engraved on most British coins since then.

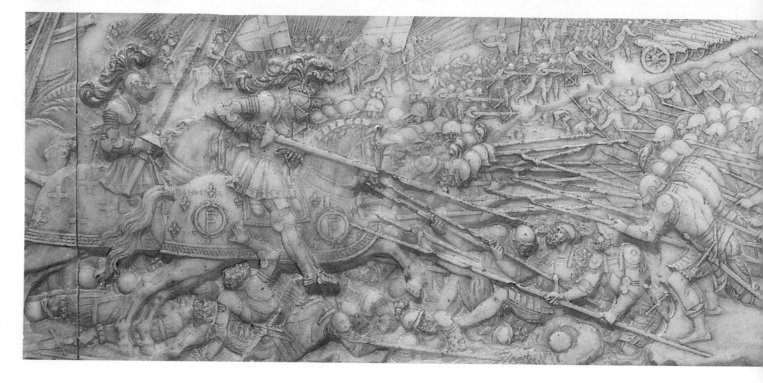

Sources and questions

1. Venetian ambassadors were expected to send very detailed reports back to their governments. Here, Giustiniani has this to say about Cardinal Wolsey.

> He is about forty-six years old, very handsome, learned . . . of vast ability. He, alone, conducts all business, both civil and criminal . . . and all state affairs. . . . He has the reputation of being exceedingly fair: he favours the people exceedingly, and especially the poor . . . he also makes lawyers work free for all paupers. . . . He is in very great repute – seven times more than if he were Pope. He has a very fine palace, where one walks through eight rooms before reaching his chamber, and they are all hung with tapestry. . . . He is supposed to be very rich indeed . . . the Archbishopric of York yields him about 14,000 ducats; the bishopric of Bath 8,000.

Source: Giustiniani, Despatches, *Vol. II, page 314. Quoted by Millward*, Sixteenth Century Documents, *Hutchinson Educational, 1961*

(a) What do you think Giustiniani's government in Venice would have made of this report? How might it have affected the way they dealt with England?

(b) Judging from this source, what particular criticism could be made of the Church at that time?

(c) Why might Wolsey be expected to be kind to the poor?

(d) What evidence in this source suggests that the pope was not popular in England?

(e) Which detail in this source suggests that it was written by a foreigner?

2. On 12–13 September 1515 Francis I won the Battle of Marignano. The carving above shows the battle and is on his tomb at Saint Denis, near Paris.

(a) Why should the sculptor have thought it important to carve *this* battle on the tomb?

(b) Which figure is meant to be Francis? Give reasons for your answer.

(c) What weapon played a leading part in the battle to judge from this source?

(d) What 'modern' weapon was used at Marignano?

(e) To judge from this source, what was the importance of flags in a battle?

3. Imagine you are the Venetian ambassador to Francis. Write a similar report to Question 1, about Francis I.

DOCUMENTS: THE NEW LEARNING

Document 1

In the Middle Ages people learnt as much about religion from what they *saw* in a church as what they heard. Look at these pictures.

Questions

1. Why did medieval people need pictures, statues, etc. to teach them Bible stories?
2. Why would they find it difficult to understand the prayers said in church in those days?
3. Explain what story this 'doom' painting taught the parishioners. Why do you think such paintings were called 'dooms'?
4. Picture B reminded people of the story of Christ meeting Mary Magdalene in the garden after his resurrection. Who would have told them this story in the first place?
5. What is A meant to be a painting of? Why do you think the Church authorities frightened people in this way?

A   'Doom' mural at St Thomas's Salisbury

B   St Mary's Church, Fairford, Gloucestershire

A

B

Document 2

Here is a page from the first printed book, the 'Gutenberg Bible' printed in 1450.

Questions

1. Why do you think the Bible was the first book to be printed?
2. What language is used in this book?
3. Where did the printer get the idea of beginning each section with a very large letter? What was often inside these letters?
4. From the evidence in this source, explain in what way
   (a) This invention would help to spread biblical knowledge more widely.
   (b) Biblical knowledge would still be restricted to a relatively few people.
5. Imagine you are Gutenberg. Write a letter (in English) explaining to a friend how the new invention works.

Document 3

In 1516 Erasmus published a new Latin version of the New Testament translated from the Greek. Until that time, the Church had used a Latin version translated by St Jerome in the fourth century. Jerome's version was known as the 'Vulgate', meaning common or usual. Scholars were horrified that Eramus had dared to 'correct' Jerome. In this letter Erasmus replies to one of them, his old friend Martin Dorp.

> I now come to the third part of your letter concerning my translation of the New Testament. I really do wonder what has happened to you and why you aren't using your brains anymore. You don't want me to make any changes in the Vulgate . . . and you won't admit there are any faults in it. You think it irreligious to pick holes in something which has been approved by so many councils of the Church over the years. If you are right on this point . . . . Why does Jerome himself . . . correct many passages word by word, passages which are still used in our version? . . . You surely can't intend to ignore all this and follow your own text which may have mistakes in it because of a copyist's errors? No one is claiming that anything in the holy scriptures is a lie. . . . Just that there are parts which have been badly translated from the Greek. . . .

Source: Adapted from Letter to Martin Dorp *by Erasmus, Penguin Classics, 1971*

Questions

1. Why did the Church use Latin rather than some other language for its books and services?
2. Which parts of this letter suggest that Dorp and Erasmus were friends?
3. How could 'copyist's errors' be important before the invention of printing?
4. Which sentence in this source explains *why* Dorp and other scholars were afraid of a new translation of the New Testament?

Document 4

Erasmus thought that there should be *vernacular* versions of the Bible. In other words, he wanted Bibles printed in the language spoken by the people as we have today. This was another revolutionary idea which he explained as follows.

> Wisdom . . . may be drawn from these few books [*of the Bible*] with far less trouble than the wisdom of Aristotle which is scattered amongst so many books which are difficult to read. . . . This knowledge, however, is available to everybody. I believe Christ desires that his teachings shall be spread as widely as possible. I should hope that all good wives read the Gospel and Paul's Epistles; that they were translated into all languages; that the farmer sang them while ploughing; the weaver whilst at his loom; that travellers should break the boredom of their journeys by telling such stories . . . .

Source: Adapted from Letter to Martin Dorp, *op. cit.*

Questions

1. Would accuracy in biblical translation be helped or hindered by different versions in different languages? Give reasons for your answer.
2. Although he was very critical of the Church, Erasmus remained a Catholic. Looking at Documents 3 and 4, explain why many Catholics blamed him for influencing Protestants, and spreading Protestant ideas.
3. What great event, starting in 1517, justified the worst fears of the Church about spreading Christ's teaching?
4. Imagine you are a clergyman. Write a letter to a friend defending the idea of using only Latin Bibles, rather than Bibles in different languages.
5. Is Document 1 a better or worse way of learning the Bible? Explain your answer.

'SUPREME HEAD': HENRY VIII 1520–36

In June 1520 Henry VIII of England and Francis I of France met in open fields near Calais. The aim of the meeting, according to the French king, was 'to give laws to Christendom'. For two weeks a 'town' of wood and canvas pavilions, cloth of gold tents and fountains running with wine housed thousands of soldiers, courtiers and ladies. At this 'Field of the Cloth of Gold' both the English and French tried to outdo each other. Each king challenged all comers and beat them, whether on horse or foot. Local peasants came from great distances when they heard there was free wine. They were soon lying in drunken heaps.

It was a tense occasion in spite of all the show. French and English soldiers were more used to meeting each other in battle. They were quick to take offence or laugh at one another. The two young monarchs were proud and jealous. At their first meeting Francis embraced Henry. On another occasion, when Henry playfully put his hand on Francis's neck and said, 'Come, you shall wrestle with me', the French king threw him to the ground. Several courtiers were needed to hold the English king back!

It was the sort of show Castiglione was thinking of when he wrote *The Book of the Courtier* (see Chapter 4). But it was only show. Talk of peace between the two countries was as temporary as the pavilions and tents. No sooner had the meeting ended than Henry met the Emperor Charles V (see Chapter 6). At this conference the two monarchs decided to form an alliance against France. Charles also offered to marry Henry's sister Mary, now a widow because of the death of her husband, King Louis of France. This double-dealing was the sort of politics described by Machiavelli in *The Prince* (see p. 44).

A captured king

The second French war of Henry's reign (1522–5) was unpopular in England. Some discontented Englishmen summed up the general feeling when they remarked that in spite of all the fighting and expense, Henry 'hath not one foot of land more in France than his most noble father had'. This attitude weakened the

The Field of the Cloth of Gold where Henry VIII met the French king in 1520

English war-effort and the country took hardly any part in the dramatic events which followed in Europe.

Francis invaded Italy once again but at Pavia, in February 1525, he was defeated and captured by the imperial troops. Such a devastating victory made Charles feel he was strong enough to do without England as an ally. He dropped the idea of marrying Mary and ignored Wolsey's hint that Henry might now be given the vacant French throne. The Cardinal retaliated by offering France peace in return for an increased pension for the king. In May 1526 the Holy League of Cognac (France, Florence, Venice and the Papacy) was formed against the emperor with Henry as its 'protector'. Francis, meanwhile, gave up his claims to Italy and bought his release.

With Francis free, Charles's triumph did not last long. The French king returned home determined to renew the war. In Germany the Protestant revolt grew worse every day and the Catholics looked to Charles to crush it. In the east the Turks won a battle and threatened Vienna. Even the imperial troops mutinied when they were not paid. For several days they looted Rome, killing people (Sack of Rome, 1527). It was clear that the emperor could not fight all his enemies at once. Although his armies again beat Francis in Italy, Charles gave the French king fair terms by the Peace of Cambrai.

In England people were rioting against a war which might ruin trade. They blamed Wolsey for their troubles. Some people even suggested he should be pushed out to sea in a boat full of holes! Actually, the proud Cardinal was about to 'sink' for a different reason.

The king's 'great matter'

For some time Henry had been thinking of taking a new wife. He wanted a son to rule after his death; of Catherine's seven children, only a daughter, Mary, had lived. By 1527 it was obvious that the Queen was past child-bearing age. Divorce was unknown in those days but Henry remembered that Catherine had first been married to his brother Arthur. Did it not say in the Bible, 'And if a man shall take his brother's wife, it is an unclean thing . . . they shall be childless'? Although Pope Julius II had ruled that the marriage was lawful, was Henry being punished for having broken God's law?

Julius had ruled the marriage lawful because Catherine said that Arthur had not had intercourse with her during their very short married life. Up till that time Henry had believed, indeed probably knew, that this was the truth. Now it suited him to worry about the matter. This problem, called 'The King's Great Matter', was made more urgent by Henry's love for Anne Boleyn. Anne came from a wealthy merchant family related to the Dukes of Norfolk. She spent her early years as a 'maid of honour' at the French court. When she returned to England, her black hair and eyes, pale face and bewitching ways soon attracted the English king.

Henry poured out his feelings in love-letters, nine in French and eight in English. They were written in 1528–9 and are now in the Vatican library in Rome. In one of them he wrote,

> I beseech you now, with the greatest earnestness, to let me know your whole intention as to the love between us two. I must of necessity obtain this answer from you, having been for a whole year struck with the dart of love.

Anne knew all about Henry's ways with women; he had been her sister Mary's lover. She was determined not to be just another royal mistress. She decided to refuse the king until he offered marriage. It was a love-game which was to have important consequences for England.

Catherine of Aragon, Henry's first wife

Wolsey's fall

Wolsey had often boasted of his influence with the pope. The king now expected him to prove it by persuading Pope Clement VII to declare his marriage to Catherine unlawful. The cardinal stood to lose either way. If he failed he would be ruined. If he succeeded, a member of the family who hated him most, the Norfolks, would become queen. In fact, he stood no chance of success. Since the Sack of Rome Clement had been the prisoner of Charles V who happened to be Catherine's nephew. Charles saw the 'divorce' as nothing but a plot against his family. There was no doubt he would never allow the pope to grant it.

The pope decided to play for time by sending Cardinal Campeggio to England to try the case. Campeggio knew his mission was doomed so he took three months to reach England.

When he did arrive, in October 1528, he suggested that Catherine should enter a convent but she refused. At a special meeting in London the following June the queen confronted the king, Wolsey and Campeggio, saying, 'I call God to witness that I have been a true, humble and obedient wife . . . and when you had me first, I take God to be my judge, I was a true maid, without touch of man.' The king could not look her in the eye when she said this. She turned proudly on her heel and walked out, cheered by her ladies-in-waiting.

Nothing could save Wolsey now and his enemies gathered for the kill. He was accused of breaking an old law which forbade English people to obey the pope instead of the king. As a cardinal Wolsey could hardly do anything else but it was enough for the king. The proud cardinal begged forgiveness. He was dismissed from most of his offices although he remained Archbishop of York. He retired to that city and it is possible he might have been left alone. Unfortunately for him, he wrote to the pope begging him to persuade Henry not to marry Anne. When news of this reached the court the king ordered Wolsey to be arrested and sent to the Tower of London.

This time the executioner was cheated. Wolsey was a sick man by the time he reached Leicester Abbey on his journey south. 'Father Abbot,' he told his host, 'I am come to leave my bones among you.' Two days later he was dead (November 1530).

A new queen

Two men, Cranmer and Cromwell, arose to wield Wolsey's power over Church and Parliament.

Thomas Cranmer (1489–1556) was a Cambridge scholar and priest. He first came to Henry's notice when he suggested that the two universities should be asked their opinion about the lawfulness of the king's marriage to Catherine. Henry liked the idea and Cranmer was made a royal chaplain and attached to the household of Anne Boleyn's father. He was also sent to the continent to consult foreign scholars about the problem. While he was there he met several Protestant princes as well as pleading personally with the pope.

Cranmer gained little from his travels. Some foreign professors agreed with Henry and some did not. Yet on his return Cranmer was made Archbishop of Canterbury. Such a swift rise to power was not of Cranmer's choosing. Unlike Wolsey, he was a timid, unambitious man who preferred study to politics. The driving force of a strong-willed king made him famous, and led him from triumph to tragedy.

Meanwhile, the 'King's Great Matter' had ceased to be a subject for scholarly discussion. Anne had at last given in to the king and was pregnant. In January 1533 the couple were secretly married so that if a son was born he would be heir to the throne. Three month's later Cranmer held a court at Dunstable which declared that Catherine had never been Henry's wife in the eyes of the

Anne Boleyn

Church. This meant that the queen was guilty of adultery and her daughter, Mary, was illegitimate! The unfortunate lady retired to Kimbolton Castle in Huntingdonshire where she died in 1536.

Anne Boleyn was crowned queen in Westminster Abbey at Whitsun 1533. Few people liked her for Catherine had been very popular. Many were scandalised that Henry could marry whilst his previous wife was still alive. Of the ceremony, an eyewitness wrote bitterly, 'All the world was astonished, not knowing whether to laugh or cry.' On 7 September the new queen gave birth to a daughter, the future Queen Elizabeth I.

The Reformation Parliament

Cranmer had given the king his 'divorce'. Thomas Cromwell (1485–1540) helped the king destroy the power of the Church in England. Cromwell was a tough man of the world, a 'jack of all trades' who had been at various times a soldier, banker, businessman and lawyer. His path to power had been laid by Wolsey whom he served as a secretary. Cromwell was cold, clever and ruthless. No more suitable person could have been found to shape the 'new' England which began with the summoning of the so called 'Reformation Parliament' in 1529.

The king wanted three things from Parliament. First, the people's help in his quarrel with the pope. Second, the support of the English clergy in this fight. Third, he hoped by his actions through Parliament to persuade or bully the pope into recognising his marriage to Anne. The last was impossible because the pope could not free himself from the emperor (see p. 79). The first two objectives were achieved, partly because some English people disliked papal rule and also because of the brilliant way Cromwell handled Parliament.

The English clergy soon surrendered. Henry discovered, as if for the first time, that priests at their consecration, or appointment, 'make an oath to the pope, clean contrary to the oath they make us [the king], so that they seem his subjects, not ours'. The clergy begged his pardon and were fined £118,000. Then Parliament abolished papal taxes in England. They also agreed that Henry was 'Supreme Head of the Church of England' (by the Act of Supremacy, 1534).

All government officials now had to swear loyalty to the king as the head of the Church. Sir Thomas More refused, so he was beheaded. Thomas More had once said of Henry, 'if my head would win him a castle in France, it should not fail to go'. In the end it was chopped off for 'wrong' beliefs!

A nineteenth century picture of the execution of Sir Thomas More

Sources and questions

1. Here Eustace Chapuys, the ambassador of the Holy Roman Empire in England, answers a question from his friend, Nicolas de Granvelle, 15 November 1535.

> As you desire me to give you a detailed account of secretary [*Thomas*] Cromwell and his origin, I will tell you that he is the son of a poor blacksmith. . . . His uncle . . . was cook to the last Archbishop of Canterbury. . . . . After being some time in prison, he went to Flanders, Rome, and other places in Italy. . . . On his return to England . . . he became a solicitor, and thereby became known to the late Cardinal of York [*Wolsey*] who took him into his service . . . at his master's fall . . . he obtained an audience [*meeting*] with King Henry, whom he addressed in such flattering terms – promising to make him the richest King in the world – that the King at once took him into his service. . . . Since then he has constantly risen in power . . . so that now he has . . . more influence with his master than the Cardinal [*Wolsey*] ever had . . . nowadays everything is done at his bidding. . . .

Source: Cal. State Papers, 1534–5, page 568. Quoted by Millward, Sixteenth Century Documents, Hutchinson Educational, 1961

(a) Why should a foreigner wish to know about Cromwell?
(b) Do you think Chapuys *liked* Cromwell? Give reasons for your answer.
(c) Which of Cromwell's ways of making Henry rich would

have particularly annoyed an official of the Holy Roman Empire?

(**d**) What do you think Chapuys thought of Henry?

2. Here Henry explains his attitude towards Catherine of Aragon to nobles, the Lord Mayor of London, merchants and lawyers gathered at his palace at Bridewell, London in November 1528.

> We have reigned for twenty years with victory, wealth and honour, but, when we remember we must die, then we think that all our doings in our lifetime will be spoilt . . . if we leave you in trouble. For if our true heir be not known at the time of our death, see what shall succeed to you and your children. Great clerks [*educated men*] have told us that we have long lived in sin. Think you my lords that these words touch not my body and soul? If the clergy could say the queen was our lawful wife, we should be thankful for she is of high lineage, if not, we can only lament our misfortune and lack of true heirs. . . . These be the sores that vex my mind . . . and for these griefs I seek a remedy.

Source: Quoted by John Bowle, Henry VIII, *Allen and Unwin, 1965, pages 143–4*

(**a**) Why did Henry think it necessary to explain his actions in this way to a gathering of important people?

(**b**) In what way did Henry think he had lived 'in sin'?

(**c**) Would Henry really have been 'thankful' if the clergy had said his marriage was lawful? Give reasons for your answer.

(**d**) From this source, what do you think the main worry was for Henry and his people?

(**e**) What 'true heir' was Henry ignoring when he made this speech, and why?

3. Imagine you are Henry VIII or Anne Boleyn – whichever is appropriate. Write a love letter dated 1532, showing knowledge of the 'King's Great Matter'.

PILGRIMS, WIVES AND WARS: HENRY VIII 1536–47

Henry now switched his attack from priests to monks. At that time monasteries owned one quarter of England's land. Their annual income was greater than the royal revenue. Since Henry needed money in case his quarrel with the pope led to war abroad and rebellion at home, such wealth was very tempting. Cromwell had helped Wolsey to close several small monasteries so that their income could be used to found colleges at Ipswich and Oxford. Possibly because of this experience he suggested Henry should close all of them.

There was no doubt that monastic reform of one sort or another would please many English people. For centuries monks had been unpopular. Humanist scholars like Erasmus condemned them for their ignorance (see Chapter 8). Clergymen often disapproved of their way of life. Bishops grumbled that they had no power over them. Ordinary people complained that they lived unholy lives. Scandals involving monks themselves were exaggerated by their enemies. Although it was true that unsuitable young people were sometimes forced or persuaded to become monks, many people forgot that the majority lived good lives.

In January 1535 Cromwell was made 'Vicar-General' of Henry's new Church of England. He at once sent teams of lawyers on 'visitations' to monasteries. The questions asked of the abbots were the usual ones for an inspection. The difference was that this time the questioners were interested in closure, not reform. Sure enough, bad reports were not long in arriving – monks with several wives and six or seven children, monks who sold abbey silver, and even a monk who made profits out of piracy.

The 'visitors' discovered what everybody knew anyway: that there were large numbers of 'hangers-on' – stewards, bailiffs, ploughmen – living in monasteries as well as monks. Powerful lords often used monasteries as hotels for months on end. Good works such as teaching, healing, farming and copying books were neglected. The lawyers had found what they wanted. A Parliament which pretended to be surprised quickly ordered 270 monasteries to be closed. Then Henry and his minister waited to see how the English people would react.

The Pilgrimage of Grace

Most of England stayed quiet, although there was a small rising in Lincolnshire which was quickly put down. In Catholic Yorkshire, however, where fifty-three religious houses had been closed, an army of discontented 'pilgrims' assembled, led by Robert Aske. They called themselves the 'Pilgrimage of Grace for the Commonwealth' and marched with a banner showing Christ on the Cross. After capturing York, they moved on to Pontefract Castle where they demanded that Princess Mary, Catherine's daughter, be declared the legitimate daughter of the King. They also wanted 'lord Cromwell' to suffer 'punishment, as the subverter of the good laws of this realm'.

There might have been a major battle with the royal army had it not been a rainy autumn in which 'each side could not come at the other' across flooded countryside. The king's commander, the Duke of Norfolk, was short of men. He decided to play a waiting game, telling the king, 'I beseech you to take in good part whatsoever promise I make to the rebels, for surely I shall observe no part thereof . . . .' The Pilgrim leaders did not know Norfolk was lying to them. When they were invited to come to London to see the king they thought that their 'pilgrimage' had succeeded.

Henry hid his rage and said he would consider the Pilgrims'

Fountains Abbey: ruins of a monastery closed by Henry VIII

demands. But no sooner had Aske disbanded his forces than the king broke his promise. This caused another rising when rebels attempted to take Hull and Scarborough. They failed and were captured. Now the rebels saw a different side to their king. Henry ordered 'dreadful execution to be done upon a good number . . . by hanging them up in trees as by quartering them'. Aske was hanged in chains at York. Over 200 others, including the abbots of some Yorkshire monasteries, were also executed. The most serious rebellion of the reign was over.

'The whip with six strings'

The failure of the Pilgrimage of Grace showed once more the power of the Tudor monarchy. It also signalled the closure of the larger monasteries (1537–9). Most abbots wisely became bishops or retired with pensions. Those at Reading and Glastonbury defied the king and were hanged. All monastic goods became the property of the Royal Exchequer. Cattle were sold and abbey servants sacked with half a year's wages. Monastic land was rented or bought by rich farmers. Between 1536 and 1547 the Crown made £1,500,000 by leasing or selling monastic land.

Although the power of the pope in England had been broken, Henry's Parliament passed the Statute of the Six Articles which maintained Catholic worship and belief (1539). This 'Catholic' Church with a Tudor 'pope' showed where it stood on a day in 1540. Three Protestants who denied Catholic beliefs plus three Catholics who denied the Royal Supremacy were burned together! With such severe punishments it is not surprising that the statute was called the 'whip with six strings'.

Anne of Cleves: the wife rejected by Henry

Jane Seymour, Henry's favourite wife

Wives

Henry had courted Anne Boleyn for six years. His marriage to her lasted only three. The new queen was proud and bossy. She quarrelled with Henry as well as disappointing him by giving birth to a dead boy (January 1536). Her enemy Cromwell managed to persuade the king she had been unfaithful. She was even accused of having an affair with her brother. Following a fake trial, Anne was beheaded (May 1536). A week after a French swordsman had cut off Anne's head, Henry married Jane Seymour, a childhood friend.

Jane was Henry's favourite wife. In October 1537 she gave him a boy, Edward, only to die soon afterwards. Henry was heartbroken. He wrote to the French king, 'Divine providence hath mingled my joy with the bitterness of death.' Two years later Cromwell arranged for the lonely king to marry Anne, sister of the Duke of Cleves in Germany. Whether Henry really called her 'a Flanders mare' when he first saw her is doubtful. But he certainly found her unattractive. 'The King's Majesty upon the sight of her person was not contented', reported the Earl of Southampton. After

six months' marriage Anne and Henry were divorced and Anne was allowed to live in comfortable retirement for the rest of her life.

Henry blamed Cromwell for the affair, which had made him look foolish. Soon afterwards, Cromwell was beheaded on trumped-up charges of 'encouraging heresy', charges master-minded by his enemies, the Catholic Howards led by the Duke of Norfolk. So ended the career of the king's most able minister. Long before his own death Henry regretted this particular execution. The Howards might rejoice but Henry had lost the man who had spearheaded his own 'Reformation'.

Certainly Cromwell would have been against the king's next marriage. Henry's fifth wife was Catherine Howard, a young girl related to the Norfolks. Unfortunately, the king's intense love for Catherine disappeared when he discovered she had had lovers before her marriage and may have been unfaithful afterwards. She suffered the same fate as her cousin, Anne Boleyn, and several of her lovers were slaughtered too. Eighteen months after Catherine's execution, Henry married his sixth, and last, wife, Katherine Parr. She was destined to outlive him.

Final wars

The king's last years were spent in wars with Scotland and France. They plunged England ever deeper into debt and Henry was forced to debase the coinage to pay his bills. Between 1542 and 1547 Henry VIII turned £400,000 of silver coins into coins with a face value of £526,000 simply by having a proportion of base metal put into each one. This meant that he could make more coins out of the same amount of silver. The King, of course, made a profit but the people remarked sadly that these new red-coloured coins were 'blushing with shame' at what the king had done!

The Scots were defeated at Solway Moss in 1542. Their king, James V, died soon afterwards, leaving the throne to his baby daughter, Mary, Queen of Scots. Henry proposed that Mary should be married to his own child, Edward. When the Scots rejected this proposal, an English army raided Scotland, burning Edinburgh and Leith. In 1548 Mary was offered in marriage to the son of the king of France. The French agreed, and the young child was sent to the French court.

The attack on Scotland was to ensure that there would be no 'stab in the back' invasion whilst Henry was away in France. In July 1544 Henry sailed for France for his last campaign. His ally was again the Emperor Charles V. Boulogne was battered with Henry's new sixty-pounder guns and forced to surrender. This triumph was followed by disaster. Charles now made a separate peace with France, leaving England to fight alone.

Henry returned home immediately, for he was afraid Charles's desertion would mean a French invasion of England. The English people rallied loyally when they heard the news, supplying Henry with men and money. The king stationed himself bravely at Southsea where a French landing was expected. In fact, the matter

Katherine Howard

Katherine Parr, Henry's last wife who outlived him

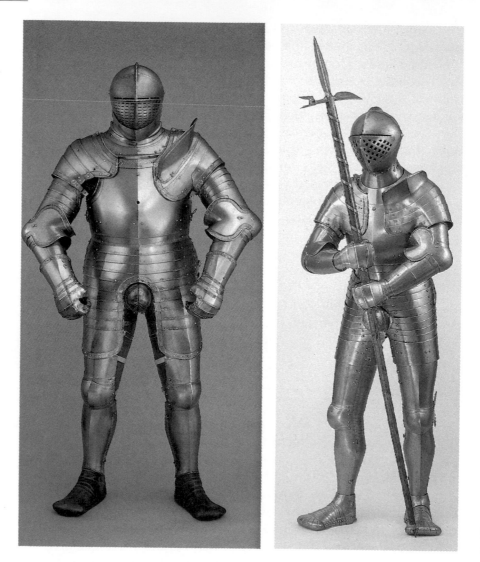

Two sets of armour made for Henry VIII. How are they different?

was decided by confused sea-battles during which Henry's favourite warship, the *Mary Rose* sank when water entered its lower gunports. The French fleet sailed away and England was saved. (In 1982 the wreck of the *Mary Rose* was raised and is now on display at Portsmouth.)

Henry's last years

As Henry's reign drew to a close, the religious problems increased. Had Henry made himself head of a Catholic or a Protestant Church? Henry himself had no doubt of the answer, as his 'whip with six strings' showed. But Protestant ideas were spreading. Henry decided to make a last appeal to his Parliament to stop religious quarrels.

On Christmas Eve 1545, king and Parliament met for the last time. Henry told them, 'no prince in the world more favoureth his subjects than I do you, nor no subjects or commons more love and obey their sovereign lord than I perceive you do me . . . .' Despite all the bloodshed and turmoil, it was probably true.

As Henry's death approached in the winter of 1546, the dark corridors and candle-lit rooms at Whitehall Palace were the scene of a power struggle between the Catholic Howards and the Protestant Seymours, relatives of the dead queen. Thanks to Howard plots the king nearly executed Queen Katherine Parr because of her 'heretical' religious views. She talked herself out of danger and the Howards themselves fell. Surrey, Norfolk's son, was beheaded. Norfolk himself was due to die on 28 January 1547. He survived because King Henry VIII died early that morning.

When Prince Edward was told his father was dead he clung crying to Princess Elizabeth's skirts. Great, terrifying Harry had been replaced by a nine-year old boy.

Sources and questions

1. There are two different accounts of how the *Mary Rose* sank on 19 July 1545. One English account says:

> . . . it was the King's pleasure to appoint Sir George Carew to be Vice Admiral . . . to a ship named the 'Mary Rose' which was as fine a ship, as strong and well equipped as any in the realm . . . . Sir George being entered into his ship . . . and sails hoist but as this was done the 'Mary Rose' began to heel over. . . . Sir Gawain [*Carew's uncle*] passing by the 'Mary Rose' called out to . . . Carew asking him how he did, who answered he had the sort of knaves whom he could not rule . . . it was not long after that the said 'Mary Rose' thus heeling more and more was drowned with 700 men.

> *Source: Archaelogia – narrative eyewitness account of the battle by Sir Peter Carew. Republished in 1979 as a reprint of S. Horsey,* The Loss of the Mary Rose, *Hunnhill Publications, Isle of Wight, page 28*

However, the French admiral wrote this:

> Our galleys had all the advantages of sailing which we could desire to the great damage of the English [*fleet*] who for lack of wind were not able to move [*and*] lay exposed to our cannon . . . hardly a shot missed them while we, with the help of our oars, shifted at our pleasure . . . the 'Mary Rose', one of their principal ships, was sunk by our cannon and 5 or 600 men . . . on board, only 5 and 30 escaped.

> *Source: Lediard,* Naval Records, *recording D'Annebault's version.* Quoted by Rule et al. pages 36–7

(a) Looking at the picture, can you see evidence to suggest that the English account of how the *Mary Rose* sank was probably true?

The Mary Rose *named after Henry VIII's sister*

(b) Do you think the cannons of those days could sink a ship as quickly as the *Mary Rose* sank? What reason might the French admiral have for claiming that his ships had sunk the *Mary Rose*?

(c) What evidence in the first source suggests that all was not well on the *Mary Rose* just before it sank? How might this have contributed to the disaster?

(d) In what details do the two accounts more or less agree?

2. After the Pilgrims captured Pontefract Castle, they took these badges and carried them.

   (a) What was the point of carrying these banners?

   (b) This badge is known as 'the wounds of Christ'. Can you think why?

   (c) How did the Pilgrims feel that Christ had been 'wounded' in England at that time?

   (d) In what ways was the 'Pilgrimage of Grace' not really a pilgrimage at all? Why do you think the Pilgrims claimed that it was?

3. Make up a rhyme about Henry VIII's wives, putting them in correct chronological order and mentioning their fate. (Catherine of Aragon – divorced. Anne Boleyn – beheaded. Jane Seymour – died. Anne of Cleves – divorced. Catherine Howard – beheaded. Catherine Parr – survived Henry.)

DOCUMENTS: THE DISSOLUTION OF THE MONASTERIES

Document 1

This extract is from Simon Fish's *Supplication of Beggars*, written in 1529 and addressed to Henry VIII. When Fish writes of 'tenths' he is referring to a tax of one-tenth of food and other things which had to be paid to the vicar of the parish annually. This was known as a tithe.

> In times . . . past there crept into this realm . . . holy and idle beggars and vagabonds . . . I mean the bishops, prior, deacons, priests, monks and friars. This idle . . . sort have begged so well . . . that they now own more than a third of all the country. The best lordships, manors, lands and territories are theirs. Beside this they are allowed the tenth part of all corn, meadow, pasture, grass, wool, colts, calves, lambs, pigs, geese and chickens. . . . Yes, and they work out their profits so greedily that every poor wife must give them every tenth egg, or else lose her Easter rights to go to church and confess her sins. . . . Who is she that will work for 3d. a day when she may have at least 20d. a day if she is prepared to sleep with a friar, monk or priest?

Source: Quoted by G. M. Trevelyan, English Social History, *Longman, 1944*

Questions

1. Why did Fish address this book to Henry VIII? What sort of reaction did he expect from the king, and why?
2. Why do you think people paid goods, not money to the church?
3. Why was it thought particularly important for a Christian to go to church at Easter?
4. Which would people of the time have regarded as the most serious of these charges:
   (**a**) That monks paid women to sleep with them.
   (**b**) That priests refused a woman the sacraments of the Church if her tithes were not paid.
   Give reasons for your answer.

Document 2

Edward Hall was a member of the 1529 'Reformation Parliament'. He had this to say about MPs' attitudes to the Church in general and abbeys in particular.

> When the commons . . . assembled . . . they began to discuss their grievances at the way clergymen had oppressed them, both contrary to the law . . . and contrary to what was right and fair. . . . [*Hall then lists six causes of discontent of which two concerned monasteries.*] The Third cause was that priests had become surveyors, stewards and officials to bishops, abbots and other spiritual heads. . . . they had taken over farms, granges and grazing lands in every county so that the poor farm labourer could get no benefit from them. . . . The fourth cause was that abbots, priors and spiritual men kept tanneries and sold wool, cloth and all manner of goods, just like ordinary merchants. . . .

Source: Edward Hall, Henry VIII, *ed. C. Whibley, London, 1904. Quoted by Palmer,* Henry VIII, *Longman Seminar Studies, 1971*

Questions

1. Hall says that the clergymen 'oppressed' people. Which Document (1 or 3) supports this claim?
2. Is there anything in this source to suggest that MPs might have benefited from the closing of the monasteries?
3. Imagine you are Henry VIII. Explain why you intend to close the monasteries, outline the reasons why you think the English people will support you.
4. Can you think of a reason why the 1529 Parliament contained so many MPs who were *against* chergymen?

Document 3

Robert Aske, leader of the Pilgrimage of Grace, was questioned during his final imprisonment in the Tower of London, April 1537. This source is compiled from some of his answers.

> The abbeys in the north of England gave great help to poor men and worthily served God. . . . When they were closed . . . the divine service to Almighty God was greatly reduced. . . . The temples of God have been pulled down, the ornaments and relics treated with disrespect. . . .
>
> Many of the abbeys were in the mountains where the people are ignorant of religious knowledge, and whilst the abbeys were there, these people received care for the needs of their bodies as well as religious teachings the monks gave them. . . . The abbeys were one of the beauties of this country. . . they helped the poor with money . . . they educated boys . . . whilst the nunneries taught girls to lead good lives. . . . Monks also repaired the sea-walls and dykes, bridges and roads . . . and did other things for the good of the commonwealth. . . .

Source: Letters and Papers of Henry VIII. Quoted by Fletcher, Tudor Rebellions, *Longman Seminar Studies, 1983*

Questions

1. What evidence is there in this source that the north was not a prosperous part of the country?
2. Document 1 condemned the monks as 'idle'. What parts of Document 3 contradict this charge?
3. The only rising against the closing of the monasteries was in Yorkshire and Lincolnshire. Does this source help to explain why? Give reasons for your answer.
4. Which monastic tasks mentioned in this source might be considered normal and which unusual?
5. What aspects of monastic life mentioned in Documents 1 and 2 are not mentioned in Document 3?

Document 4

Before a monastery could be closed it had to be inspected in what was called a Visitation. Here is the report of three visitors to their master, Thomas Cromwell, on 22 September 1539.

> This is to inform your Lordship that we came to Glastonbury [*Abbey*] on Friday . . . and because the abbot was then at Sharpham, a house of his a mile . . . or more from the abbey, we, without delay, went to the same place, and there questioned him upon certain matters to do with running the monastery. . . . And because his answers were not satisfactory we proceeded that night to search his study for letters and books, and found hidden a book of arguments against the divorce of the Kings's majesty . . . which we take to be a great matter . . . we also found a fair chalice [*cup*] of gold and other parcels of plate. . . .

Source: Three Chapters of Letters relating to the Suppression of the Monasteries, *ed. Thomas Wright, Camden Society No. 26.*

Questions

1. Is there a clue to the life-style of certain abbots in this source? How does it fit in with the complaints in Document 1?
2. The abbot of Glastonbury was hanged for stealing church property. Is there anything in this source to suggest a more likely reason for his execution?
3. What evidence is there in this source that the visitors were already suspicious of the abbot before they reached Glastonbury?
4. What parts of this source suggest that the visitors were anxious to please Cromwell?

Document 5

This is a plan of Battle Abbey in Sussex, built on the site of the Battle of Hastings. Not all these buildings remain today.

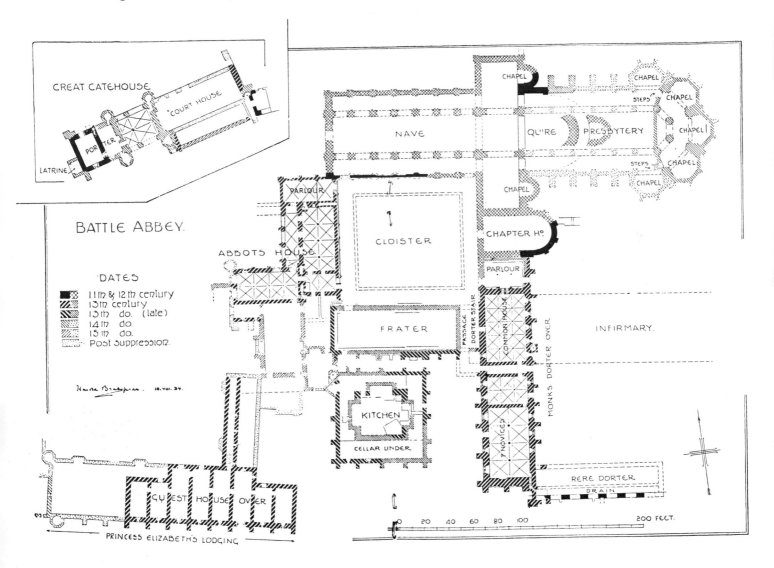

Questions

1. Using this source as a guide, what was the main task of a monk?
2. What evidence is there of other monastic duties?
3. What language did the monks use for reading and study?
4. What evidence is there that the abbot could live very well if he wished?

THE BOY KING: EDWARD VI 1547–55

Henry VIII had been cruel, selfish and arrogant. He defied the pope, forced great changes on England and made the country bankrupt with his wars. He crushed both friends and enemies without pity. No man was a more typical 16th-century ruler, caring little for individuals and behaving as God's representative on earth. The great square figure, legs apart, hands on hips, which stares at us from many of his portraits, casts a long shadow over English history.

In spite of his faults, both rich and poor remembered Henry with affection. He gave England the strong government its people wanted. The beheadings, burnings and hangings which horrify us today were few compared with those ordered by European kings of the time. Neither, it seems, were they resented by a tough and brutal people. When disorders, plots and rebellions followed Henry's death most Englishmen were certain they had lost a great king.

The new ruler was slightly small for his age, with fair hair and grey eyes. He was a rather serious boy who understood Greek and Latin well, and kept a diary. Only once is he known to have laughed publicly, although he seems to have enjoyed parties and games. Of course, he was too young to rule on his own so Henry appointed a Council to rule until he was of age. This was headed by a Lord Protector, the Duke of Somerset, Edward's uncle.

Battle of Pinkie

From the start of Edward's reign, Somerset faced serious foreign dangers. Henry's old rival, Francis I, had died in March 1547. His successor, Henry II, proved to be just as arrogant and troublesome. He demanded the return of Boulogne and Calais, two French towns held by the English. He also plotted with England's enemies in Scotland and Ireland. Scotland, in particular, became almost a French province, with Protestants persecuted and French troops occupying key points in the country.

Somerset was a soldier, so he chose a soldier's solution. In the autumn of 1547 he crossed the border into Scotland with 16,000

The King's School—an Edward VI grammar school in Macclesfield, Cheshire

Henry VIII (the figure in the bed) bestows the crown upon his son Edward VI to the dismay of the Pope

men. The Protector found the enemy entrenched at Pinkie, east of Edinburgh. The Scots' right flank was protected by a marsh, their left by the sea, whilst a river lay in front. These advantages were thrown away by the Scots. Their commander decided to cross the river and attack the smaller but better-armed English forces. In the battle which followed, the Scottish ranks were shattered by gunfire. After nearly 6,000 had been killed, the survivors fled.

When the news of the battle fought on 'Black Saturday' reached the Scots' government they decided to send their young queen, Mary, to France in case the English forced her to marry Edward. Somerset placed English soldiers in Scottish castles, distributed large numbers of Protestant Bibles, in the hope of breaking the Catholic hold on Scotland, and returned home in triumph.

The Prayer Book Rebellion

Even though he was only nine years old, the new king was a keen Protestant, ready to argue with grown-ups about religion. Consequently, Edward's reign saw the birth of an English Protestant Church. The new policy took various forms. Henry VIII's 'whip with six strings', which maintained Catholic worship, was repealed, or cancelled. Chantries – the scheme whereby people left money for priests to 'chant' (pray) for their souls – were dissolved and their funds used to found 'Edward VI' grammar schools in various places. Catholic bishops were imprisoned, and foreign reformers, like those living in Geneva, were allowed to come to England.

In 1549 Archbishop Cranmer issued a revised Prayer Book written in English instead of Latin. The idea was not entirely new. Henry VIII had liked to hear English spoken in church. In 1535, for example, he had given permission for Miles Coverdale's English translation of the Bible to be published. By the time he died, English people were used to hearing the Creed, the Ten Commandments and the Lord's Prayer in their own language. The 1549 Prayer Book, however, had no Latin services.

There were mixed reactions to this new Prayer Book. Some Catholic priests stuck firmly to the old ways, celebrating the full Latin Mass. Protestant-minded clergymen often went to the other extreme. They did not want anything which reminded them of the old church. These men replaced stone altars with wooden tables, removed 'papist' ornaments and statues from their churches and had wall paintings covered up with whitewash. They were also angry that Cranmer's Book still used words which suggested that the bread and wine turned into the body and blood of Christ during the mass. This is what Catholics believed, but it was denied by many Protestants. Such a belief is called transubstantiation.

The people of Devon and Cornwall were particularly angry at these changes. Their discontent was made worse by the arrival of a government agent, William Body, who gave the impression that the new rulers would confiscate church valuables. When he reached Cornwall in April 1547 a mob led by a local priest murdered him. One ringleader announced that West Countrymen would obey *only* the 'laws and ordinances touching the Christian religion' as they were in the time of Henry.

Ordinary people were not only worried about religion. They groaned under the heavy taxes needed to pay for Somerset's Scottish campaigns. What started as grumbling, grew into a protest movement and ended as a full-scale rebellion. An army which rushed to the West Country beat the rebels and relieved Exeter after a six-week siege (August 1549). In Oxfordshire, a smaller rising was crushed easily and discontented priests were hanged from their own church spires.

The front page of a book which caused a rebellion—the Protestant Prayer Book of 1549

Kett's rebellion

Somerset might have dealt more quickly with this Prayer Book Rising, as it became known, had he not had his hands full with another rebellion. This was in East Anglia, where religion was not the only cause of trouble that summer.

Throughout Henry VIII's reign there had been widespread enclosure of farmland so that it could be used to keep sheep. Many landlords preferred sheep-farming because it made good profits as the cloth trade expanded. Flocks of sheep replaced fields of corn in many parts of southern England and the midlands. Richer farmers also joined their smallholdings together to make larger estates, and broke the rule about the number of animals allowed to graze on the village common-land. All these changes deprived peasants of work and homes, because fewer workers are needed for sheep-farming.

Somerset was himself a large landowner, so he knew how country-folk felt about the changes. Like the two Henries before him, therefore, he issued orders forbidding further enclosures. He also put a tax on sheep. Consequently, Norfolk peasants probably thought Somerset would be on their side when they began to break down the fences of unpopular, sheep-owning landlords. A 'sit-in' developed as peasants set up camps in various parts of East Anglia – at Norwich, Ipswich and Bury St Edmunds. The Norwich camp consisted of 12,000 labourers led by Robert Kett who assembled at Mousehold Heath. Kett demanded better treatment for the peasants. He claimed that his men were not rebels, although they captured Norwich after a bloody struggle with the townsfolk.

The sympathetic Protector might have agreed to Kett's demands. But John Dudley, Earl of Warwick, persuaded the Council to declare these gatherings a rebellion. At that moment 1,500 foreign soldiers had landed in England, ready for garrison duty in Scotland. Warwick led these professionals to the Norwich camp. He offered Kett's men a pardon but they refused it because they said they were not rebels. Warwick then attacked and killed many of them. Kett himself was hanged from the walls of Norwich Castle.

Kett, seated under the so-called 'Oak of Reformation', giving orders to the rebels. A drawing made in 1803

The fall of Somerset

Somerset was already unpopular with some people because he had executed his brother, Thomas Seymour, for plotting to marry the fifteen-year-old Princess Elizabeth. The discontent over war-taxes, and the upheavals in Norfolk and Devon, led to his downfall. Warwick was a strong-willed, unprincipled man. He convinced his fellow councillors that neither rebellion would have happened had he been Protector instead of Somerset. The Council were tired of Somerset's disastrous economic policies as well as his arrogance. They forced him to resign. He was promised his life but later he was beheaded on a false charge of conspiracy (January 1552).

Warwick, now the Duke of Northumberland, had been supported by Catholic as well as Protestant lords when he overthrew Somerset. In spite of this he decided the best way to stay in power was to please the king with further doses of Protestantism. For this reason yet another Prayer Book was issued in 1552. This Book moved the English Church further towards Protestantism. The belief behind the Mass, that the bread and wine changed into the body and blood of Christ, was completely denied in the new Prayer Book. The Mass was left out altogether and was replaced by a communion service in remembrance of the Last Supper. This 'communion' service remains the basis of Church of England worship to this day.

The beautiful wording of this Prayer Book was written by Cranmer. He also helped to prepare forty-two Articles of Belief for English Protestants. Genuine reformers were pleased. One even called the unholy Northumberland a 'faithful and intrepid soldier of Christ'. In fact, the Duke's thoughts were far from religion at this time!

Nine-day queen

All Northumberland's plans were soon threatened by Edward's ill health. In January 1553 the young king was troubled by a bad cough. By May he could not sleep and his legs were swollen. It was clear he was dying, probably from tuberculosis. The king's death would mean the end of Northumberland unless he could stop Mary, the Catholic daughter of Catherine of Aragon, from becoming queen. She had been horrified by the religious changes made by her brother's government and was unlikely to show any mercy to the Duke.

Northumberland decided on a wild scheme to save his skin. Edward was persuaded to make a will leaving the crown to the children of Lady Jane Grey, granddaughter of Henry VIII's sister Mary. Henry, of course, had left the crown to Edward, then Mary and finally Elizabeth. To make sure Lady Jane had children she was forced to marry one of Northumberland's sons. Edward's will also stated that Mary and Elizabeth could not succeed to the throne because they were women.

Even this weak excuse was contradicted by events. When it

Lady Jane Grey – the innocent victim of Northumberland's plot. She reigned only nine days

Edward VI's will

became obvious that Edward would die before Lady Jane had a child, the will was altered to give the throne to Jane herself. On this copy of Edward's will you can see the vital alteration from 'Lady Jane's heirs male' to 'the Lady Jane *and* her heirs male'. Some experts think Northumberland himself made the alteration.

'Lady Mary hath the better title'

Only Northumberland's strong personality and military skill gave the plan a chance of success. When Edward died on 6 July 1553 the news was kept secret for three days. Only after the Duke had bullied the Council into agreeing to a monarch who they knew had no right to the throne, was Jane proclaimed queen in London.

The proclamation was received without a cheer. A brave spectator, Gilbert Potter, shouted 'the Lady Mary hath the better title'. For this he was fixed in the pillory so tightly that his ears had to be cut off to release him.

All might still have gone well for Northumberland had he managed to seize Mary. However, his agents let her slip and she fled into Norfolk and Suffolk, two counties dominated by the Catholic Norfolks. From this stronghold she wrote to the Council demanding the throne. Such a bold action ruined Northumberland's plans. He had forgotten that no child of Henry VIII was likely to let the crown be taken away without a fight!

Mary's brave defiance made the timid councillors recover their nerve. As recruits joined her in large numbers at Framlingham Castle, Suffolk, the council declared its loyalty to Mary. By the time Northumberland reached Cambridge on his way to crush Mary's 'rebellion', his troops had deserted in hundreds. There was nothing for him to do except surrender. The Duke was now as humble as he had once been arrogant. He appealed for mercy, claiming that he had always been a Catholic at heart! This last-minute conversion did not save him. He was beheaded in the Tower of London in July 1553.

Mary told her sister Elizabeth to meet her at Wanstead and the two entered London in triumph, riding side by side. At one time or another, Henry had declared both of them illegitimate. Now his two daughters were destined to rule England for the rest of the century.

Sources and questions

1. (a) Henry VIII (the figure in the bed on page 97) is pointing to King Edward as his choice for king. Who is the figure bottom centre, and why is he horrified by the news?
   (b) Can you guess the name of the book which has knocked this figure down?
   (c) Who is standing on Edward's left? Why is he shown as an important man?
   (d) Who are the figures at the bottom of the picture meant to be? Why would they have been unpopular in England at the time?
   (e) What is the drawing (top right) meant to show?

2. Here are some of the demands of the Western rebels in 1549.

   The Articles of us the Commoners of Devonshire and Cornwall in various camps by east and west of Exeter.
   1. First we will have the holy decrees concerning religion of our forefathers obeyed . . . .
   2. We will have the laws of our sovereign lord, King

Henry VIII concerning the six articles to be in use in the churches again . . . .

3. We will have the Mass in Latin, as was before . . . .

8. We will not accept the new service because it is but like a Christmas game, but we will have our old service of Matins, Mass, Evening Song . . . in Latin, not English, as it was before. And we Cornishmen (whereof certain of us understand no English) utterly refuse this new English service . . . .

14. We will have the abbey lands in every man's possession, howsoever he came by them, be given again to establish a place for religious persons . . . .

Source: Transcript from copy in Lambeth Palace Library. Quoted by Anthony Fletcher, Tudor Rebellions, *Longman Seminar Studies, 1968*

(**a**) What do you think the rebels meant by calling the new services 'a Christmas game'?

(**b**) Why did the people think that the *way* they worshipped God was so important?

(**c**) What fact emerges from these demands which nowadays seems surprising?

(**d**) Who do you think is most likely to have written these demands – commoners, knights or priests? Give reasons for your answer.

(**e**) Which part of this source would have infuriated Henry VIII if he had still been alive? Give reason for your answer.

3. Write a letter to Protector Somerset, pointing out his mistakes between 1547 and 1549 and warning him of the dangers if he does not change his policies.

DOCUMENTS: THE BIRTH OF ENGLISH PROTESTANTISM

Document 1

Look at the picture on page 97 which shows Pope Clement VII being crushed by a book. Then answer these questions.

Questions

1. What position has Henry taken from Clement?
2. Why are the monks and priests (right) shown to be unhapppy about this?
3. In what ways do you think a picture, rather than a description, of what had happened in England, might reach a wider audience?

Document 2

Anne Askew (or Ayscough) attended Protestant Bible reading groups in London in the 1540s. As a result she queried the Church's teaching that the bread and wine in the Mass turned into the body and blood of Christ. The following comes from Foxe's *Book of Martyrs* and is supposed to have been written by Anne herself. She is being questioned by Edmund Bonner, Bishop of London.

BONNER   I cannot help you until I know what your conscience is burdened with.

ANNE   My lord, my conscience is clear on all things.

BONNER   Very well, then you force me to charge . . . you that you said that he that doth receive the sacrament [*bread and wine*] from the hands of an evil priest, or a sinner, receiveth the devil and not God.

ANNE   I never spoke such words. What I said to the question and to my Lord Mayor [*at a previous interrogation*] . . . was that the wickedness of the priest cannot hurt me, but that I receive the body and blood of Christ in spirit. . . .

BONNER   What a saying is that! In spirit only!

ANNE   My lord, without faith and spirit I cannot receive Christ properly.

BONNER   Are you saying that after the priest has blessed the holy bread . . . it is still only bread?

ANNE   No, my Lord. When I was asked the question I gave no answer.

BONNER   But you quoted certain passages of Scripture in order to disprove the doctrine of the mass.

ANNE   I only quote St Paul's words to the Athenians in Acts 17: 'God liveth not in temples made with hands'.

Questions

1. Why do you think Anne was trying to avoid answering the questions?
2. In what way was Bonner trying to help Anne?
3. Why did Anne's second answer horrify Bonner?
4. Why would a bishop question Anne about these matters?
5. Where do you think Bonner got his information about what Anne had said?

Document 3

Henry VIII was a Catholic in his beliefs even though he quarrelled with the pope about who was in charge of the Church in England. But in 1539 Henry pleased Protestants when he allowed Bibles printed in English to be installed in churches. However, by 1545 he had begun to wonder whether this had been a good idea, and had this to say to this Parliament.

> And although you have been allowed to read Holy Scripture, and to have the word of God in your mother tongue [*English*] you must understand that I have given you this freedom only to satisfy your own conscience, and to instruct your children and family, and not to . . . make scripture an excuse for arguing and abusing . . . priests and preachers. . . . I am very sorry to know . . . how disrespectfully that most precious jewel, the word of God, is disputed, rhymed, sung and jangled in every alehouse and tavern, contrary to its true meaning. . . . I also hear daily that you . . . clergy preach one against the other, teach one contrary to the other. . . . Alas, how can poor souls live in peace when you preachers set them quarrelling with your sermons and debates. . . they look for light, and you bring them darkness. . . .

Source: Edward Hall, Henry VIII, *ed. C. Whibley, London, 1904. Adapted from Palmer*, Henry VIII, *Longman Seminar Studies, 1971*

Questions

1. In Henry's opinion, what duty had a father to his family?
2. What was the duty of a priest?
3. By what right did Henry claim to permit, or restrict, the reading of the Bible?
4. In what way was this situation unlikely to have arisen in Catholic countries?
5. What evidence is there in this source that women had a subordinate role in English life?
6. Why did people think it important to understand the Bible correctly?

Document 4

Source: The burning of Anne Askew, a drawing from Foxe's Book of Martyrs

Questions

1. To the right of the stake is a figure in a pulpit. Why do you think he was there and what do you think he was doing?
2. Why was Anne Askew burned? Use Document 2 to help your answer.
3. What parts of this source suggest that the authorities regarded this as an important case?
4. Anne would not change her beliefs but she did appeal to Henry VIII to save her life. The king refused. Which source indicates why he did this? Explain your answer.
5. Imagine you are Henry VIII. Explain why you feel that your decision about the Bible in English led directly to the tragedy of Anne's burning.

'TURN OR BURN': MARY 1553–58

The new queen was in some ways the best of the Tudors. Mary had her father's pride and determination without his cruelty. She was more frank and straightforward than Elizabeth, and her courage might have made her as popular as 'Good Queen Bess'. From her mother, however, she inherited two features or characteristics not shared by other Tudors – high principles and a fanatical Catholic faith. Had she reigned before the Reformation this Spanish side of her nature might not have mattered. But it came at the wrong moment in England's history. Mary, alone of Tudor monarchs, was remembered with hatred.

Mary was probably the keenest Catholic in England. She had watched her father's 'Reformation' with horror. After his death much that she loved had been destroyed by Edward's ministers. Now she felt it her duty to restore the old Church in all its power and pageantry. Catholic bishops, imprisoned by Edward, came out of the Tower. They were replaced by Protestant bishops – Hooper, Latimer and Ridley. Thomas Cranmer, Mary's arch-enemy who had helped Henry divorce her mother, was sent to prison. A triumphant Mary ordered Mass to be celebrated in parish churches and both Edwardian Prayer Books were condemned (see Chapter 11).

Parliament prepared to change reluctantly. Few of its members were keen Protestants but fewer still wanted a return to rule by the pope. They would not let Mary give up the title 'Supreme Head of the English Church'. Neither would they give back the monastic lands. It was November 1554 before they knelt with their Queen in Whitehall to beg the pope's pardon for the rift started a quarter of a century before by her father.

The Spanish match

Mary I

It was the Queen's marriage, not her faith, which first caused trouble. Mary had spent a lonely and unhappy childhood parted from her mother and rejected by a father she loved. As a grown woman she had been stopped from marrying, first by her father and then by her brother. She was now thirty-seven years old, with fading good looks and signs of the illness which was to kill her.

To find herself queen increased her loneliness. She felt over-whelmed by the task before her and longed for a husband to help her govern and give her children.

The English people agreed that she should marry. They thought a woman ruler an unknown, freakish thing. However, they expected her to wed an Englishman, possibly Edward Courtenay, a great-grandson of Edward IV. A foreign marriage was out of the question because it would mean in reality a foreign king.

Mary's view was the exact opposite. She was half-Spanish and disliked Englishmen in general and Courtenay in particular. When the Queen decided on Prince Philip, son of her cousin, the Emperor Charles V, and heir to the Spanish throne, the entire country was horrified. Even Catholics were worried at the thought of Mary marrying a Habsburg. The marriages of this family had helped bring the Netherlands and Italy under Spanish rule. Was England to be added to Charles V's world-wide possessions? With Tudor obstinacy, Mary ignored the uproar and instructed her agent to begin marriage negotiations.

Wyatt's rebellion

Some Englishmen did more than protest. Three soldiers, Sir James Croft, Sir Peter Carew and Sir Thomas Wyatt, decided to prevent the marriage by force. They were joined by the Duke of Suffolk, whose daughter, Lady Jane Grey, had been sentenced to death for her part in Northumberland's plot (see Chapter 11). Wyatt was an energetic, restless man. He claimed that his actions were not directed against the queen. 'We seek no harm to the queen, but better counsel [advice] and councillors', he proclaimed. In fact he detested Spaniards and may have wished to replace Mary with Princess Elizabeth so as to restore the Protestant Church.

The conspirators tried to rouse the country with rumours of a Spanish invasion. They were not very successful. The Duke of Suffolk found that people living in the Midlands did not take such a threat seriously. Carew was too unpopular to get much support in the West Country because he had taken a leading part in crushing the 1549 rebellion. Only Wyatt raised an army, mainly because he came from Kent where foreigners were known and disliked. When he told the Kentish men that 'hundreds' of Span-iards were landing at Dover he quickly recruited 4,000 men. The old Duke of Norfolk, Mary's chief general, was sent to fight against him. Norfolk was forced to retreat when 500 of his men deserted to Wyatt.

Mary again proved herself a Tudor. She knew that some Londoners might open the city gates to Wyatt so she decided to meet the City Council at Guildhall. 'What I am ye right well know,' she announced proudly, 'I am your Queen, to whom at my coronation . . . you promised allegiance'. Then, in a clear, deep voice she condemned Wyatt and his followers as 'rank traitors'. She cunningly reminded her rich audience of what would happen if the rebels let loose a mob upon the city. 'And now, good subjects,' she concluded, 'pick up your hearts, and like true men, stand fast against these rebels.' The assembly, we are told, 'wept for joy to hear her speak.' When the rebels arrived on 3 February 1554 they found the gates of London shut.

Wyatt swung west and crossed the Thames at Kingston. He managed to enter the suburbs through Knightsbridge. At first all went well. He beat off an attack by royal soldiers at what is now Hyde Park Corner. But when he reached Ludgate he found it firmly closed. There was nothing to do except retreat. As he did so his troops were scattered by a cavalry charge. Wyatt himself was surrounded in a narrow street where he fought desperately before surrendering.

Mary and Elizabeth

There was the usual end to such an adventure. The Tower was soon full of rebels awaiting execution. Gallows were put up in various parts of the City so that as many people as possible could see what happened to traitors. Suffolk's part in the rising led to the death of his innocent daughter, Lady Jane Grey, who was beheaded, aged sixteen. With so much rebellion in the air, Mary could no longer afford to ignore the threat posed by the so-called 'Nine-day Queen'.

Wyatt was tortured to find out if Mary's sister, Elizabeth, was involved in the plot. It emerged that he had written to the princess. Elizabeth was now in great danger. She wrote to her sister, desperately.

> I humbly crave to speak with your Highness which I would not be so bold to desire if I knew not myself most clear as I know myself most true. And as for the traitor Wyatt, he might peradventure write me a letter, but on my faith I never received any from him.

Mary refused to see her and she was sent to the Tower. As Elizabeth was rowed along the Thames and through the Traitor's Gate, she must have remembered her mother's execution. Once ashore she sat on the steps in the pouring rain and refused to move. The Lieutenant of the Tower said 'you had best come in, Madam, for you sit here unwholesomely'. 'Better sit here than in a worse place,' replied Elizabeth – but she did go in.

The Spaniards wanted Elizabeth dead and Mary herself had no love for Anne Boleyn's daughter. But without proof of guilt she would not have Elizabeth executed. It was a decision which would hardly have been made by Henry VIII in similar circumstances. He had never been worried about proof! Elizabeth was sent from the Tower to Woodstock Palace near Oxford under what we would call 'house-arrest'.

By the time Wyatt himself died in April, heads, bodies, legs and arms were rotting in the London streets. But Mary herself did not like such barbarity. As soon as she could, she pardoned 400 rebels who were brought to Whitehall Palace with ropes around their necks. Four months later she married Philip in Winchester Cathedral – it was considered too dangerous for the prince and his Spanish followers to appear in London where so many people were Protestants who favoured Princess Elizabeth. The day chosen for the wedding was 25 July, the feast-day of St James, patron saint of Spain.

Nobody was very happy about the marriage for it tied England to Spain. Parliament had ruled that Philip could never be king of England but what if the pair had a child? The French king predicted that the marriage would drag England into Spain's long war with France. This is in fact what happened in 1557, when Calais, England's last possession on the continent, was captured by the French. It was a blow to every Englishman's pride and many must have wished Mary had been less courageous four years before!

Holy bonfires!

In 1554 Mary invited her cousin, Cardinal Reginald Pole, to return to England as papal legate, or ambassador. Pole was of royal blood, for his mother had been a niece of Edward IV. She had been executed by Henry VIII, whilst Pole had fled from England during the arguments about the 'King's Great Matter'. In Rome he had became an important churchman. He had helped Pope Paul III organise the first Council of Trent (see Chapter 6) and was nearly elected pope himself in 1550.

Neither Philip nor Charles V wanted Pole in England. To them he was an unworldly scholar who, according to one cardinal, did not 'understand the first thing about the conduct of affairs'. This was not correct. Pole knew a great deal about 'the conduct of affairs' but after twenty-five years' absence he was out of touch with the religious mood in his homeland. At first, Mary, too, was reluctant to let him come back. Later, however, she changed her mind and it was Pole who strengthened her belief that burning was the only proper end for a Protestant.

Philip did not object to burning heretics in his own country. Nevertheless, he was worried in case religious executions sparked off another rebellion in England. He told Mary that most heretics could, in fact, be executed for conspiracy or treason. Cranmer, for example, had been involved in Northumberland's plot. Mary and her cousin did not heed such advice. In their opinion, the English must be saved from religious error. Better to burn a few bodies and so save thousands of souls from the far worse flames of hell. It was Mary and Pole who gave Protestants the grim choice either to 'turn or burn'.

The Book of Martyrs

The Marian Persecutions, as they are called, began with the burning of John Rogers, editor of a Protestant Bible, on 4 February 1554. Five days later, Bishop Hooper suffered at

The burning of Thomas Hawkes in Coxehall, Essex, 10 June 1555 – from Foxe's Book of Martyrs

Gloucester. Bishops Latimer and Ridley were burnt at Oxford. Here is how John Foxe described their end:

> Then they brought a faggot, kindled with fire and laid it down at Ridley's feet. To whom Latimer spake in this manner. 'Be of good comfort, brother Ridley, and play the man; we shall this day light a candle by God's Grace in England as I trust shall never be put out.

Two years later, Cranmer went to the fire. He was very frightened of such agony and had several times confessed himself to be wrong. But when his enemies demanded a public confession in St Mary's Church, Oxford, Cranmer stood up and proclaimed his Protestant faith, saying, 'I renounce and refuse, as things written with my hand, contrary to the truth which I thought in my heart, and written for fear of death and to save my life . . . .' The two descriptions come from John Foxe's *Book of Martyrs*. Foxe was a Protestant clergyman whose account of these burnings was set up in almost every parish church after Mary's death. So the tales became part of English folklore, giving many English people a hatred of Catholicism which changed the course of British history on several occasions.

Mary's death

Mary's marriage brought her little happiness. Philip stayed in England for only eighteen months and returned again in 1557. After he became King of Spain in 1556 he showed even less interest in his unhealthy wife. Her love was not returned, and the child she longed for never came. In August 1558 she moved to St James's Palace, a dying woman. Philip did not come to England to comfort her. Instead, he told his ambassador to negotiate secretly with Elizabeth, her successor to the throne.

Philip and Mary

News of Mary's last illness caused only relief and joy in London. The citizens called the day before she died 'Hope Wednesday'. The sad queen, who burnt nearly 300 Protestants, was dreaming of 'seeing many little children, like angels' as she passed away on 17 November 1558. Reginald Pole died the same day. Their policy of 'turn or burn' died with them.

Sources and questions

1. Rowland Taylor, a Suffolk clergyman, had tried to prevent the Catholic mass being celebrated in his church at Easter time. For this he was sentenced to be burnt. Taylor was a doctor of divinity, not medicine.

> When Dr Taylor with the Sheriff and his escort . . . came to Hadleigh bridge . . . a poor man with five children . . . cried out, 'O dear . . . Dr Taylor, God help thee, as thou hast many times helped me and my poor children!' The streets of Hadleigh were crowded on both sides . . . with men and women from both town and country . . . who wanted to see and bless him. . . . Then they bound him with chains, and having set up the firewood, one Warwick threw a log at him, which struck him on the head and cut his face, so that the blood ran down. Then said Dr Taylor, 'O friend, I have enough troubles, did you need to do that? . . .' . . . At last they lit the fire, and Dr Taylor, holding up both hands called upon God and said, 'Merciful Father in Heaven! . . . receive my soul into Thy hands!' So he stood still without either crying or moving, with his hands folded together, until Soyce, with a halbert [a spear with an axe-head] struck him on the head . . . and the corpse fell down into the fire.

Source: Foxe's Book of Martyrs (The Acts and Monuments), *Vol. II, ed. Rev T. Pratt, Philadelphia, 1858, pages 351–2. Quoted by Robert Tittler*, The Reign of Mary I, *Longman Seminar Studies, 1983*

(a) Were the authorities right to regard Taylor as an important figure in the resistance to their Catholic policies? Give reasons for your answer.
(b) Why were such executions carried out in public? Do you think this was wise in Taylor's case? Give reasons for your answer.
(c) Why were men like Rowland Taylor so much against the Catholic mass? What service would they have put in its place?
(d) Using this source as a guide, what were the qualities which had made Taylor so popular?

(e) Why do you think Foxe felt it necessary to write this, and other accounts, when Queen Mary was dead and her Catholic laws cancelled?

2.

The young Elizabeth is arrested after Wyatt's rebellion. This was painted on a door at the Manor House, Little Gaddesdon, Herts.

(a) Why is this not likely to have been painted during Mary's reign?

(b) What do you think the owner of the house was trying to show by having such a painting?

(c) Do you think the artist had ever seen Elizabeth? Give reasons for your answer.

(d) Can you think of any reason why this was painted on a door, rather than on canvas?

(e) The rose was a badge of the Tudors, and also a symbol of purity. What is the significance of showing Elizabeth wearing it at a time when she was not queen?

3. Make up a play dealing with the more important incidents in Cranmer's life.

THE ENGLAND OF ELIZABETH

'A TRUE, LAWFUL AND RIGHT INHERITRESS' 1558–1603

On the afternoon Mary died, bells rang in London steeples and the citizens feasted from tables set up in the streets. It was a date long celebrated by Protestants as the 'Birthday of the Gospel'; that is, the day England became a Protestant country. Within hours Parliament was told of 'a true, lawful and right inheritress to the crown . . . which is the lady Elizabeth'. Anne Boleyn's daughter was queen at last.

The pale young woman with red hair and lively, expressive eyes who now ruled England had many qualities necessary to make a successful sixteenth-century monarch. 'Young Bess' had grown up in a hard and dangerous world (see Chapter 12). Her experiences had made her careful, cunning and cautious. She was not cruel like her father but she shared his royal courage, interest in learning and love of showmanship. A few days before Mary died, Count Feria, the Spanish ambassador, reported to his master, Philip II:

> It appears to me that she is a woman of extreme vanity, but acute. She seems greatly to admire her father's system of government . . . . She is much attached to the people and is very confident that they are all on her side (which is indeed true); in fact she says it is they who have placed her in the position she at present holds as the declared successor to the throne.

The next forty years were to show just how right Feria had been.

'The realm exhausted'

There were plenty of problems for the new queen. A court official described England's condition in 1558 like this:

Queen Elizabeth: the so-called 'Rainbow' portrait

'The Queen poor; the realm exhausted . . . divisions amongst ourselves; wars with France and Scotland; the French king bestriding the realm, having one foot in Calais and the other in Scotland.'

It was a situation to worry an experienced ruler let alone a young woman just released from virtual imprisonment. It was not helped by the French king proclaiming his daughter-in-law, Mary Stuart, Queen of England. This was because Henry's marriage to Anne Boleyn had been unlawful in Catholic eyes. In their view the Catholic great grandaughter of Henry VII had a better claim to the English throne. European history for the next thirty years was to be influenced by the struggle between these two women and their supporters. Some of the 'exhausted realm's' troubles were soon over. The French government faced near civil war between its own Catholics and Protestants. It had little time to concentrate on affairs abroad. French forces in Scotland were blockaded by the English fleet off Edinburgh and forced to surrender. The Treaty of Edinburgh (1560) began nearly a century of peace between England and Scotland. One reason for this was Scotland's own Protestant Reformation which started at this time. Scottish Protestants, led by John Knox, closed their monasteries and set up a Presbyterian (Calvinist) State Church. They were unlikely to keep 'the auld alliance', as it was called, with a Catholic France.

The middle way

By 1560 the English government had tried to settle its own religious problems. The 'holy bonfires' of Mary's reign had turned many men and women Protestant. Even those who remained Catholic sometimes regarded the pope as a foreign prince, allied to England's enemies. Elizabeth told Feria that her own wish would be 'to restore religion as her father had left it'. In other words, she wanted a Catholic Church independent of the pope. This was no longer possible. The pope also supported Mary's claim to the throne. Elizabeth had no choice but to form a Protestant Church. And because so many members of Parliament were keen Protestants, she was forced to form it more quickly than she wished.

Even if the people had not loved Elizabeth, the only alternative to her was a Catholic monarch. The painful memories of Mary's reign made this impossible. For better or worse, the Lords and Commons had to accept Elizabeth. An Act of Supremacy (1559) was hurried through Parliament, declaring Elizabeth 'supreme governor in all spiritual and ecclesiastical things'. So Elizabeth, not the pope, became the head of the Church in England. At the same time, an Act of Uniformity ordered a new Prayer Book, based on the 1549 and 1552 Prayer Books (see Chapter 11), to be used in churches throughout the land.

For Elizabeth these Acts represented a 'middle way' which she hoped would satisfy her subjects. Catholics, for example, could still believe that the bread and wine of the Communion turned into the body and blood of Christ if they wished. The new Church was still administered by bishops, whom Catholics regarded as spiritual descendants of St Peter, one of Christ's disciples.

Moderate–minded Christians were happy with the new 'Church of England'. Other, equally sincere believers, were not satisfied. Devout Catholics would not accept a service book without the Mass. They held private services at home and so became 'recusants' who were fined for not attending their parish church on a Sunday. Some Protestants, nicknamed 'puritans' by their enemies, aimed to 'purify' the new Church of all traces of Catholic worship. They wanted to abolish the position of bishop and set up a Calvinist-style church in England.

The Dutch revolt

On the continent there was rarely a middle way where religion was concerned. In France a struggle raged between Huguenots (French Protestants) and their Catholic government, led by Catherine, Queen Mother of France. Huguenots often lived together in fortified ports or towns. They were well-disciplined Calvinists, ready to fight and die for their faith. On St Bartholomew's Day (24 August), 1572, Catherine took advantage of an assembly of Huguenots in Paris to let loose the Paris mob in an orgy of murder. About 3,000 Huguenots were killed, and the war between the two sides became even more bitter.

The massacre of St Bartholomew from a drawing made at the time

In the Spanish Netherlands, Protestantism took root in the northern provinces (now Holland) but not in those of the south (now Belgium and parts of northern France). By 1560 Dutch Protestant worship went on in open defiance of the Spanish governor. Catholic statues and shrines were damaged or destroyed by Protestant mobs. Philip II was unlikely to tolerate this. The Spanish king once told the pope he would rather lose both his life and his crown than rule Protestants. He regarded himself as the leader of the military forces of the Counter-Reformation (see Chapter 6).

In 1567 Philip sent a large army to the Netherlands. Its commander, the Duke of Alva, had orders to crush the rebels. At first he was successful. The Dutch were defeated and their leader, William of Orange (also known as the Silent), driven out of the country. But Alva's cruel ways annoyed both Protestants and Catholics who knew their political freedoms were threatened by the Spanish. First, an 'underground movement' began against Alva's forces. It was spear-headed by Dutch pirates, the so-called 'sea beggars', who roamed the Channel attacking Spanish ships. In 1572 these 'beggars' captured Brill, an ideal base for their operations. Such a success sparked off a general revolt.

William re-entered Holland to lead the fight. He faced a new Spanish commander, the Prince of Parma. Parma was a brilliant soldier. He captured one town after another from the rebels, killing those citizens who dared to resist. By 1585 most of the south was back in Spanish hands. Only the northerners were undefeated.

Undeclared war

Elizabeth did not want to fight Spain but circumstances gradually drove the two countries apart. The queen knew that if Philip beat the Dutch he would probably attack England as part of his crusade against Protestantism. With the cloth trade ruined owing to the war, England no longer had any commercial reasons to remain friendly with Spain (see Chapter 7). Elizabeth had hoped that the French would defeat Spain. When France became distracted with civil war there was nothing for it but to commit herself. In 1585 Elizabeth sent English troops, led by her favourite, the Earl of Leicester, to fight alongside the Dutch.

Actually, an undeclared war had raged between English and Spanish sailors for many years. In 1568 two English captains, Sir John Hawkins and his cousin, Francis Drake, were trading African slaves with the Spanish colonists at San Juan de Ulua (now Vera Cruz in Mexico). The Spanish governor was happy to obtain fresh workers, although his government had forbidden him to trade with foreigners. Suddenly a Spanish fleet appeared. Hawkins could have stopped it entering the harbour but that would have been an act of war. When the Spanish admiral promised to be friendly, his ships were allowed to sail in.

A few days later the Spanish attacked without warning. After a fierce fight, only Drake and Hawkins escaped with their ships. Many English sailors were killed or captured. Drake never forgot San Juan and spent the rest of his life taking revenge. In 1572 he landed in Panama, South America, joined with runaway negro slaves, and captured a Spanish mule-train carrying treasure worth £20,000. This exploit was followed by his voyage round the world, during which he raided Spanish settlements in South America, captured a Spanish treasure ship and brought back a fortune (1577–80).

Sources and questions

1. In 1576 King Philip of Spain appointed his half-brother, Don John of Austria, as Governor-General of the Netherlands. Don John was a famous and successful soldier. He had this to say when given the job.

> The true remedy for the Low Countries [*Holland*] in the opinion of everybody is that England be [*put*] under the authority of a person devoted to . . . Your Majesty, and, if this is not done, people are convinced that they [*the Low Countries*] will be . . . ruined and lost to the [*Spanish*] Crown. It is rumoured in Rome and everywhere that, with this idea, Your Majesty and His Holiness [*the pope*] have thought of me as the best instrument you could choose for . . . carrying out your purposes, incensed [*angry*] as you are by the evil proceedings of the Queen of England and the wrong she has done to the Queen of Scotland . . . in supporting heresy in Scotland against her will.

Although for this or anything else I do not believe myself as capable as Your Majesty would wish . . . may it please Your Majesty to permit me to kiss your hand for so high a favour.

Source: L. P. Gachard, Correspondence of Phillippe II, *Vol. III, pages 429–32. Quoted by Sir Philip Petrie*, King Philip II, *Eyre and Spottiswoode, 1964*

(a) What did Don John mean by his first sentence? How might Philip go about putting England under such an authority?

(b) What parts of this source indicate that Don John was a Catholic?

(c) What parts of this source suggest that Don John was of very high rank? (Remember to whom he was writing.)

(d) Do you think Don John was keen to take the job? Give reasons for your answer.

(e) Don John writes of Elizabeth's 'evil proceedings' and the 'wrong' she had done Mary, Queen of Scots. What do you think he had in mind?

2.

(a) In this Dutch painting of around 1580, King Philip of Spain is shown sitting uncomfortably on a cow. Can you guess which country the cow is meant to be?

(b) Why is the Duke of Alva sitting on the ground milking the cow? Is this a suitable way of illustrating what he did?

(c) Why are William of Orange and Elizabeth shown standing *together?*

(d) Both Elizabeth and Philip are holding similar objects in their hands. What are the objects, and why are they shown holding them?

(e) Why do you think the artist chose an agricultural scene for his picture?

DOCUMENTS: DRAKE'S WORLD VOYAGE 1577–80

In 1581 Queen Elizabeth ordered a weatherbeaten ship to be brought ashore and put on show at Deptford, near London. The ship was Francis Drake's *Golden Hind* in which he had become the first Englishman to sail round the world. Some of the men who sailed with Drake left accounts of the voyage. From these sources we can build up a picture of this famous seaman during his greatest voyage.

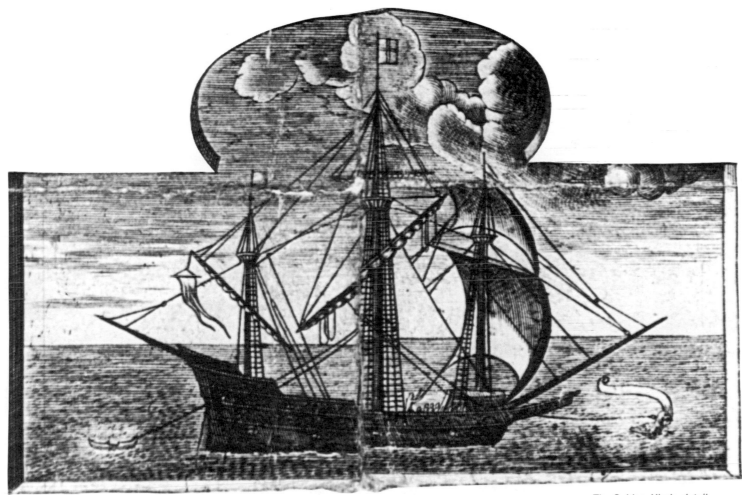

The *Golden Hind; detail from a world map engraved around 1590*

Document 1

Francis Fletcher was Drake's chaplain on the voyage. He kept a journal which was later published under the title, *The World Encompassed*. Here he sums up his feelings about the voyage.

> The main ocean by right is the Lord's alone, and by nature left free for all men to sail in . . . and large enough for all men's trade. And, therefore, that valiant enterprise, accompanied with happy success, which that rare and worthy captain, Francis Drake, achieved in first turning up a farrow about the whole world, doth surpass, in many respects, the mighty victory of the noble mariner, Magellan . . . . But hereof let future generations be the judge. . . .

Source: Hakluyt Society, 1854. Quoted by E. Bradford, Drake, *Hodder and Stoughton, 1967*

Questions

1. Why was it necessary for the English to claim that the ocean was free to all men? Who might have disputed this claim at the time?
2. What does 'turning up a farrow' mean? Why might you expect a writer of the time to use such an expression?
3. In what way was Drake the first man to sail round the world, rather than Magellan?
4. Why might a chaplain be more likely to have kept a journal than other sailors on the voyage?

Francis Drake

Drake's voyage around the world, 1577–80. A map drawn soon after the circumnavigation

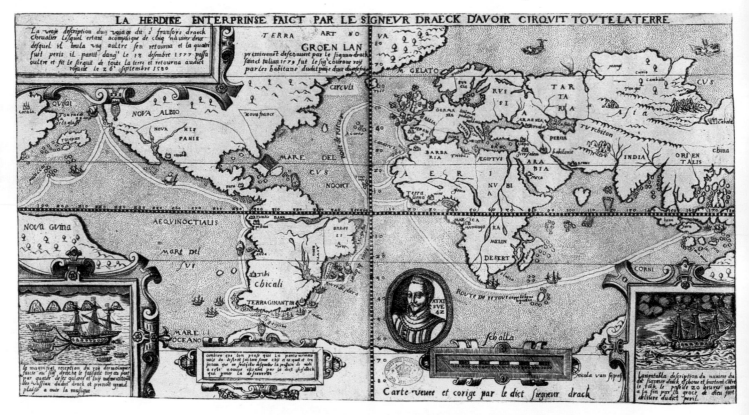

Document 2

During his voyage Drake captured a Spanish merchant ship. Its captain, Francisco de Zarate, wrote this report to the Viceroy of New Spain, after his release.

> This Drake is a cousin of John Hawkins, and the same man that looted and damaged Nombre de Dios five years ago. He seems to be about thirty-five years old. . . . He is of middle height and thick-set. He is one of the greatest sailors in the world, both in his skill and his command of men. His ship is a war vessel . . . . She is a good, fast sailing vessel, and has a crew of about one hundred skilled men, all of them well-trained and young. He treats all his men with affection, and they treat him with respect. He has also nine or ten gentlemen with him . . . who are members of his council. On every occasion, however unimportant, he calls them together and listens to what they have to say before giving his orders – although, in fact, he pays no real attention to anyone. Drake has no special favourite, and the gentlemen I mention are all equally invited to his table . . . . Drake is served his meals . . . on silver plate, all of which is engraved with his badge. . . . He says Queen Elizabeth herself gave many of these things to him . . . .

Source: Bradford, op. cit.

Questions

1. Why do you think Drake was anxious to show Zarate that he was in favour with the Queen?
2. Zarate says Drake knew how to control his crew. What examples of good leadership does he give?
3. Why might the Viceroy of New Spain, the leading Spaniard in America, wish to know as much as possible about Drake?
4. Why should Zarate's opinion of Drake as a seaman be more reliable than that of other men?
5. How important and reliable is this assessment of Drake by one of his enemies?

Document 3

Early in the voyage Drake sentenced one of the gentlemen, Thomas Doughty, to death for trouble-making. After the execution, he had this to say to his men.

> By the life of God it doth take my wits from me to think of it! Here is such quarrelling between sailors and gentlemen, and such stomaching between gentlemen and sailors, that it doth make me mad to hear it. But . . . I must have it stopped. For I insist that the gentlemen haul and draw [*work*] with the mariner and the mariner with the gentlemen. . . . Let us show ourselves to be united in one company and let us not give our enemies a chance to rejoice at our disunity. I would know the name of him that would refuse to set his hand to a rope, but I feel sure there is not such a man here. . . .

Source: Bradford, op. cit.

Questions

1. What exactly was the difference between a gentleman and a sailor in the eyes of the people of that time? What are the two groups likely to have quarrelled about?
2. How does this speech help to reinforce some of the opinions in Document 2?
3. In what ways did Drake treat gentlemen and sailors differently? (See Document 2.)
4. From this source, describe the sort of work done on a ship in those days.

Document 4

Another well-treated prisoner on the voyage was a Portuguese pilot named Nuno da Silva. Da Silva was on board for 15 months before being released near Panama in April 1579. Here he is writing about Drake and his men. When he calls *The Golden Hind* a French ship he means that she was of French design; some experts think she was made in France.

Drake's ship is very stout and strong with double sheathings on the hull. . . . She is a French ship, well-fitted with good masts, and is a good sailing ship, answering the helm well. . . . She is very water-tight when sailing with the wind behind her, but in a rough sea she lets in a lot of water. . . . Drake himself lives well, carrying for his pleasure . . . expert musicians. . . . His furniture is rich and costly so that . . . the magnificence of his native country might be admired by all nations . . . . Francis Drake kept a book in which he wrote all his navigations and in which he drew birds, trees and sealions. He is skilled at painting and so is his nephew John who is a great painter. When they both shut themselves up in his cabin they are always painting. . . .

Source: Bradford, op. cit.

Questions

1. Why might Drake wish to have a Portuguese pilot on board in southern waters?
2. Drake drew coastlines, etc. for a practical as well as an artistic reason. Can you think what it was?
3. What parts of this source suggest that the writer was knowledgeable about ships?
4. Write a character study of Drake based on these sources. How far does it back up the 'sea-dog' and 'pirate' image of him?
5. Which parts of this source suggest that Drake was patriotic?

Coconut Cup. This cup is traditionally said to have belonged to Sir Francis Drake.

DOCUMENTS: RALEIGH AND THE QUEST FOR EL DORADO

Sir Walter Raleigh (1552–1618) was a soldier, sailor, poet, historian, merchant and courtier. Yet his most lasting claim to fame probably rests on his attempts to found colonies in America. These failed, but he lived long enough to see a successful colony established at Jamestown, Virginia in 1607. He also led expeditions in Central America to find the jungle kingdom believed to be ruled by 'El Dorado' – the golden one.

Document 1

In 1584 Elizabeth granted her favourite, Raleigh, this patent or licence. It was to last for six years.

> Elizabeth by the Grace of God of England, France and Ireland, Queen, Defender of the Faith etc . . . greeting . . .
>
> Know ye . . . we have given and granted . . . our trusty and well-beloved Walter Raleigh . . . and to his children . . . for ever, free liberty . . . to discover, search, find out, and view such remote, heathen and barbarous lands . . . not actually possessed by any Christian prince, nor inhabited by Christian people. . . . He may have, hold, occupy and enjoy any such lands. . . . In witness thereof, we [*she means herself*] have caused these letters to be made Patents. Witness our signature, at Westminster the five and twenty day of March, in the sixth and twentieth of our reign.
>
> Elizabeth

Source: Hakluyt's Voyages, *Vol. VIII, page 289. Quoted by Quinn,* The Roanake Voyages, *2 volumes, 1955*

Questions

1. Why can we regard this as a reliable source?
2. What does this source suggest about the attitude of Europeans to other parts of the world?
3. What parts of this source suggest that Elizabeth was anxious not to annoy other European countries?
4. What part of this source suggests *why* Elizabeth thought she had the right to take over foreign countries?
5. Imagine you are a local chieftain in Central America. What would your (peaceful) answer be to Englishmen who claimed your land because of this patent?

Document 2

In 1595 Raleigh led an expedition to Guiana (now Venezuela) to find El Dorado (the kingdom had become known by the nickname of the king). He failed to find this land which was thought to be like the Aztec or Inca empires, and just as rich in gold. Back home, he wrote *The Discovery of Guiana*. This extract describes his meeting with an Indian chief called Topiawara.

> After this old king [*Topiawara*] had rested a little while in a little tent that I caused to be set up, I began, through my interpreter, to talk with him . . . asking him about the Spaniards, and before I went any further, I told him why I had come hither, whose servant I was, and what the Queen wanted, which was that I should undertake the voyage for the Indians' defence, and to deliver them from the tyranny of the Spaniards. . . . I talked at length . . . about her Majesty's greatness, her justice, her charity to all oppressed nations. . . . Topiawara listened to this attentively and seemed to admire what I said. . . . Then I began to ask him questions about Guiana, and its condition. . . .

Source: Quoted by Norman Lloyd Williams, Sir Walter Raleigh, Eyre and Spottiswoode, 1962

Questions

1. Why was Raleigh anxious to make friends with Topiawara?
2. Which parts of this source suggest that it was written to please people in England?
3. Had Raleigh undertaken the voyage for the Indians' defence? Explain why you think Raleigh had gone to Central America.
4. Compare Documents 1 and 2. Does anything in Document 1 justify what Raleigh said about the queen in Document 2?

Document 3

In this extract from his *History*, Raleigh describes Guiana.

> The West Indies were first offered to her Majesty's grand-father by Columbus, a stranger, in whom there might be deceit and whose stories of so many islands and regions never written of before, seemed hard to believe. . . . However, this Empire is now made known to her Majesty by her own servant [*Raleigh means himself*]. . . . In Guiana . . . the face of the earth hath not been torn, nor the goodness and salt of the earth exhausted . . . the graves have not been opened for gold, nor the mines broken into, nor any statues pulled down from the temples. . . . Any common soldier who goes there, can pay himself with plates of gold half a foot broad, not pence. . . .

Source: Lloyd Williams, op. cit.

Questions

1. In what way had Columbus 'offered' the West Indies to Henry VII?
2. From this source, explain how you think Raleigh felt about foreigners.
3. In what ways does this source criticise the Spanish without naming them?
4. What did Raleigh hope to achieve by writing books about Guiana? There is a clue in the last sentence of this source.

Document 4

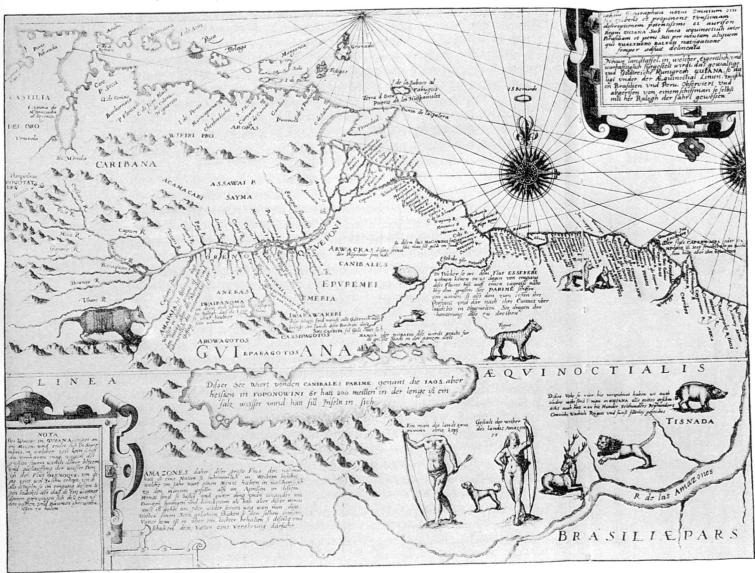

An early seventeenth-century map of Guiana

Questions

1. Raleigh believed that the kingdom of El Dorado was in Guiana. Does this map suggest that he had found it? Give reasons for your answer.
2. What sort of information was used to draw this map?
3. Give examples of where this map is reliable/unreliable.
4. Why do you think the explorers called the river in the right-hand corner 'the Amazon'? There is a clue in the map.
5. What dangers and difficulties likely to be encountered by colonists in Guiana are *not* mentioned in Document 3 but are in this source?

QUEEN TAKES QUEEN

Even before the news of San Juan reached England in 1568, a diplomatic crisis had blown up between England and Spain. Some Spanish ships, carrying 450,000 ducats (about £100,000) to the Netherlands to pay Spanish soldiers, took shelter in Southampton after being chased by French Huguenot raiders. Philip demanded the return of the money but Elizabeth refused. She was afraid it would be used to finance an invasion of England. Philip was furious. He ordered all English property in the Netherlands to be seized. He even considered declaring war but decided against it in case the English fleet cut off his Channel supply routes.

As an alternative he began to think of encouraging Elizabeth's enemies to drive her from the throne. After all, had not Mary Stuart, Elizabeth's rival, just reached England?

Mary, Queen of Scots in 1573

Knox and Darnley

A dramatic story lay behind Mary's arrival in England. During her upbringing in France Mary had married Francis, then the French Dauphin or heir to the throne. When he died in 1561 she returned reluctantly to her Scottish throne. But a greater prize, the crown of England, was never far from her thoughts, as this letter she wrote to Elizabeth in 1562 shows.

> We know how near we are descended of the blood of England, and what devices have been attempted to make us as it were a stranger from it! We trust being so near your cousin, ye would be loth we should receive so manifest an injury as all utterly to be debarred from that title which in possibility may fall unto us . . .

Such remarks were hardly likely to please the English queen!

Mary found a far different country from the one she had left as a child. Mary was a Catholic but large numbers of Scots had turned Protestant, led by John Knox. Knox detested all Catholics and had suffered for his faith, spending eighteen months as a galley slave on a French warship. He had written a book condemning the idea of women rulers, called *First Blast of the*

John Knox

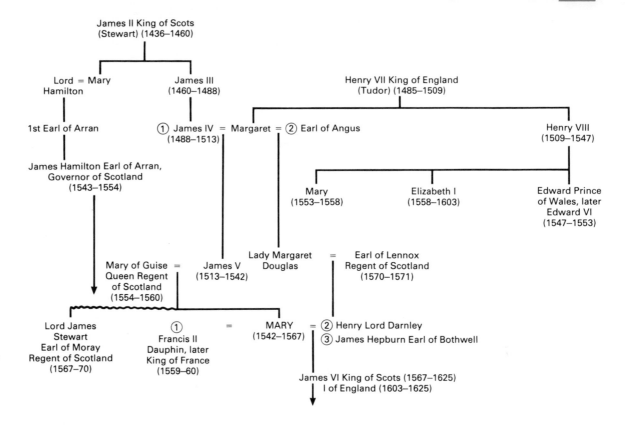

This family tree shows how many of the Tudor royal family and Scottish Stuart royal family were related

Trumpet against the Monstrous Regiment [rule] of Women. Clearly, Knox did not like Mary's faith, her French blood or her sex!

At first, Mary accepted the situation. Knox was allowed to organise his kirk, or church, of 'true believers' without interference. Protestants as well as Catholics were appointed to her royal Council. A happy and peaceful reign seemed possible. Then Mary married Henry, Lord Darnley, a grandson of Henry VIII's sister, in July 1565. This union strengthened her claim to the English throne, thus annoying Elizabeth. It brought Mary herself little happiness.

Darnley was said to be the 'lustiest, best-looking lad' in Scotland. Unfortunately, he was also spoilt, a drunkard and fond of other women. He resented not being made king and neglected his official duties as well as his wife. A lonely and unhappy Mary turned to her Italian secretary, David Riccio, for company. Darnley grew jealous.

Murder at Holyrood

In March 1566 Mary was sitting in her bedroom in Holyrood Palace, Edinburgh. She was attended by her ladies-in-waiting and one or two friends including Riccio. Suddenly Darnley appeared in the doorway, drunk and angry. Behind him loomed a Scottish lord, armed with a sword and wearing armour and a helmet. The two men rushed at Riccio who threw himself at the queen's feet for protection. In the uproar tables were overturned and candles blown out. Riccio was dragged screaming from the room and stabbed to death on the stairs.

Mary was afraid this murder might be the signal for an uprising against her. That night she fled from Holyrood and persuaded a sober and repentant Darnley to go with her. Once the fuss had died down, the royal pair returned to Edinburgh. Whatever her real feelings, Mary kept them hidden. Even in private she seemed fond of her husband, especially after their son James was born in June. Behind the scenes, however, she was falling in love with 'a glorious, rash and hazardous young man', the Earl of Bothwell.

In 1567 Darnley fell ill with smallpox. He was brought to his house at Kirk O'Field near Edinburgh to recover. The queen visited him almost every day. On 9 February Mary cut short one of her visits to return to the city for a wedding. At two o'clock next morning an explosion wrecked the house. Darnley and a manservant were found dead in the garden. It seemed a tragic accident until it was discovered that they had been strangled.

If it was murder, who had done it? Mary announced, '. . . the murderers will shortly be discovered . . . . We hope to punish the same with such rigour as shall serve for example of this cruelty to all ages to come.' These were fine words. But when it became clear that Bothwell was responsible for the explosion, Mary staged a trial which found him not guilty. Worse still, she married Bothwell three months later. This move turned the Scots people against her. Why Mary did it is still a mystery. Perhaps she had fallen deeply in love with Bothwell. Maybe she was frightened of him, or had suffered a nervous breakdown following the murders of Riccio and Darnley. Whatever the reason, this marriage soon ended her reign.

Within a month a rebellion of Scots nobles had led to her defeat and imprisonment in Lochleven Castle. Mary was forced to abdicate in favour of her baby son, James. Bothwell escaped abroad where he eventually died, insane, in a Danish prison. Mary made a daring escape from Lochleven. Possibly she might have got a ship to France where she would have got a warm welcome from her French relatives. Instead, she rode hard for the English border, crossing it in May 1568.

Had the lure of another crown, of 'that title which . . . may fall unto us . . .', made her do this?

The Northern Rebellion

Elizabeth refused to meet a woman suspected of murdering her husband. A Court of Inquiry was ordered to investigate Darnley's murder. 'When you are acquitted of this crime, I will receive you with all honour; till this is done I may not', Elizabeth told Mary.

Mary's enemies brought to the Court eight letters, two marriage contracts and other documents which, if genuine, proved the queen guilty. Mary claimed that these Casket Letters, named after the box they were found in, were forgeries. Nobody has ever discovered the truth. What was more certain was the effect of Mary's arrival in England. Those who were afraid that she would become the centre of plots against Elizabeth were proved right.

The political situation in England increased the danger. Eliza-

Places mentioned in this chapter

beth's secretary of state, Sir William Cecil (later Lord Burghley) was engaged in a struggle with the Norfolk family. They represented the old Catholic England that was passing. Burghley was typical of the new class to whom Henry's Reformation had given power and influence. He stood for the new Protestant England, the England of expanding overseas trade. The Norfolks feared that this expansion would lead to war with the Catholic powers of Europe, particularly Spain.

The Norfolks also resented Burghley's high position. They hoped to ruin him just as their ancestors had ruined another 'upstart', Thomas Cromwell, nearly thirty years before. As a first step they demanded that the queen recognise Mary's right to the throne, after her own death. When Elizabeth refused they plotted to marry the fourth Duke of Norfolk to the Scots queen. It was a dangerous scheme and when Elizabeth found out she sent the Duke to the Tower.

Norfolk's arrest sparked off a rising of those dissatisfied with Tudor rule. In particular, it roused northern Catholics who hated the government's 'new found religion and heresie' (Protestantism). When the mighty Earls of Northumberland and Westmorland joined in, their troopers and horsemen seized towns and burned the homes and crops of Protestants. At Durham they rushed into the cathedral, tore up the new Bibles and Prayer Books and openly celebrated the Mass.

Government agents managed to carry Mary away before Northumberland's men could reach her. Then a large royal army moved into action. It found little to do. Few of the northern rebels were well-armed. Many were poor men who had merely followed their lords out of loyalty. They were reluctant to fight when they realised the queen was against them. The only serious skirmish was at Carlisle. Elsewhere rebel forces faded away as quickly as they had gathered. Northumberland was captured and beheaded. Westmorland fled abroad. A grim Elizabeth ordered the death of at least one man from each rebellious village.

When she took no action against Mary, Knox wrote to her, 'If you strike not at the root, the branches that appear to be broken will bud again with greater force.'

Execution of Mary

There were no more rebellions after this. But the plots continued. All of them seemed to lead to Mary who sat, spider-like, at the centre of every web uncovered by Elizabeth's spy-master, Sir Francis Walsingham.

Had Elizabeth been a wife and mother there would have been less danger. But the queen's determination that there should be 'a Mrs but no Mr in England' meant that Mary was heir to the throne. In 1571 Norfolk became involved in a wild scheme to dethrone Elizabeth and assist Spanish troops to land in England. The man behind the plot, Roberto Ridolfi, escaped abroad but Norfolk was beheaded. Fifteen years later the Spanish ambassador in London encouraged a plan by Anthony Babington and other Catholics to kill Elizabeth. This plot was discovered and Babington and his friends were executed.

The Babington Plot involved a secret correspondence between Mary and Babington. Coded letters were smuggled in beer barrels in and out of Chartley Hall in Derbyshire, where Mary was imprisoned. The idea of the beer barrel letters had been Walsingham's. He hoped that Mary would make a mistake and write letters encouraging the plotters. His plan worked. The documents showed clearly that the Scots queen had known of the plot and had written to Babington. She was put on trial at Fotheringay Castle, in Northamptonshire, found guilty and sentenced to death.

Burghley, the royal Council and Parliament demanded that the sentence be carried out. Elizabeth was in a dilemma. All her political instincts told her that the Scots queen must die. On the other hand, she was terrified at the thought of killing a close relative and a fellow monarch. Her state of mind is shown by her reply to Burghley and the others.

> I protest . . . for my own life, I would not touch her. Neither hath my care been so much bent how to prolong mine as how to preserve both, which I am right sorry is made so hard, yea, so impossible . . . I have not used over-sudden resolutions in matters that have touched me so full near . . . and as for your petition, your judgement I condemn not . . . but pray you to accept my thankfulness, excuse my doubtfulness, and take in good part my answer – answerless.

The execution of Mary in 1587

Even when Elizabeth did sign Mary's death warrant she changed her mind and refused to send it to Fotheringay. Finally, Burghley and the Council sent it without her permission. On 8 February 1587 Mary went bravely to her death in the hall of the castle.

King Philip was not over-worried by Mary's death. Since he had at last decided to conquer England, it would be better if a Spaniard sat on the English throne!

Sources and questions

1. After the Northern rebellion, the Earl of Northumberland was examined about the reasons for the uprising and said this.

> We first began to talk of these matters [*the rebellion*] when the Duke [*of Norfolk*] went in displeasure from court to his house in London, and it was rumoured in Yorkshire that the Council was . . . divided about the succession [*to the English throne*] . . . so I sent to the Duke and assembled my friends, to know their inclinations [*opinions*]. I . . . intended to join the Duke, if the quarrel were for the reformation of religion or naming a successor, but not to risk my life for the marriage [*of the Duke of Norfolk and Mary, Queen of Scots*]. . . . Our first object was the reformation of religion and preservation of . . . the Queen of Scots as next heir, failing [*there*] being issue [*children*] of her Majesty. . . . I hoped my Lord Leicester, and especially Lord Burghley . . . had by this time been blessed with godly inspiration to discern [*tell*] chalk from cheese.

Source: Cal. S. P. Domestic, 1566–79. *Sir Cecil Sharp*, Memorials of the Rebellion of 1569, *London, 1840. Quoted by Fletcher*, Tudor Rebellions, *Longman Seminar Studies, 1968.*

(a) What sort of changes had the Earl in mind when he talked of the 'reformation of religion'?
(b) Can you think why the Earl might not have wanted the Duke of Norfolk to marry Mary?
(c) Do you think the Earl liked Burghley or Leicester? Give reasons for your answer.
(d) Why do you think Elizabeth would not name Mary as her successor?

2. The sketch of the Kirk O' Field explosion and death of Darnley (next page) was sent to William Cecil (later Lord Burghley) from Scotland.
(a) Why do you think Cecil's agent thought it necessary to send him this sketch?
(b) The baby in the left-hand corner is saying 'Judge and

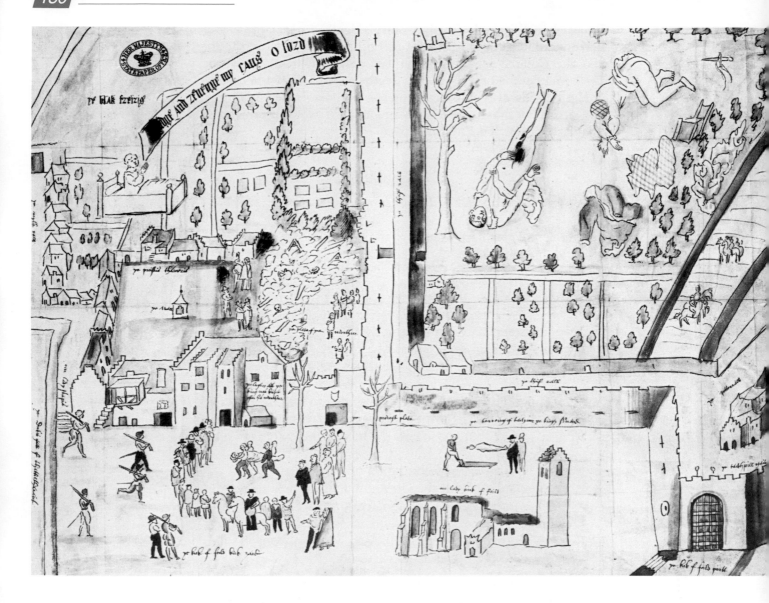

avenge my cause, O Lord'. Who is this meant to be, and in what way had the baby been wronged?

(c) What parts of this sketch would have been of interest to Cecil? What parts were unnecessary?

(d) Look at the sketches of Darnley and his servant. Do you think the artist was an eyewitness or had talked to an eyewitness? Give reasons for your answer.

3. Queen Elizabeth and Mary, Queen of Scots never met. Act out a meeting between the two. What do you think they might have said to each other?

GOD'S OWN CAUSE: THE DEFEAT OF THE ARMADA 1588

Philip of Spain planned to invade England, overthrow Elizabeth and replace her with a Catholic. He felt it was his duty as leader of the Counter-Reformation (see Chapter 6). His memories of England when he was Mary Tudor's husband made him certain that its people were still Catholic at heart. He believed that once his armies had landed the English would flock to support the new government.

The pope was not so sure. It was true that since 1570 Elizabeth, condemned as 'pretended queen of England', had been excommunicated by the Church. A later pope had gone further and pardoned in advance anybody who might murder 'that guilty woman of England'. Nevertheless, the papacy was worried about a conquest which would make the power of Spain even greater. Consequently, the pope gave Philip's 'crusade' his blessing without much enthusiasm.

Philip's military and naval experts insisted that the only hope was to take England by surprise. The king knew that preparations for such an expedition could not be kept secret. He was proved right in April 1587 when Drake sailed into Cadiz harbour and set fire to Spanish ships and supplies. This daring raid, which the English called 'singeing the King of Spain's beard', delayed the Spanish fleet – the Armada – for more than a year.

Phillip II of Spain

'God Will Help Us'

After the raid on Cadiz, Philip began building ships at Lisbon, a port which even Drake could not attack. Early in 1588 Spain's best admiral, Santa Cruz, died. This was a severe blow to Spanish hopes. His replacement as commander was the Duke of Medina Sidonia, a cousin of the king. Medina was not a sailor. He did not want the command and remarked, 'I possess not one qualification for this post'.

It would have been difficult and dangerous to transport all the soldiers needed for the invasion from Spain. So the Armada was to carry only enough troops to seize Margate as a bridgehead. Parma's troops in the Netherlands could then be ferried across to complete the conquest. Parma himself was doubtful about the whole enterprise. He did not control a large port on that part of the coast. The waters off the sandy shores were too shallow for a warship to float safely. A link between the Armada and Parma was impossible unless a good port was captured from the Dutch.

Philip ignored this vital point. To him the expedition had become a personal crusade. Spain's astrologers had warned that 1588 would be a year of disaster. Philip did not believe them. God was on his side. How could he fail? The English felt the same: John Hawkins told Elizabeth, 'God will help us, for we defend the chief cause, our religion, God's own cause'.

Fight in the Channel

The Armada sailed from Lisbon on 20 May 1588*. It consisted of 130 ships, carrying 19,290 soldiers, 8,350 sailors, 2,080 galley-slaves and 2,630 guns, according to the English. About half the ships were genuine warships; the remainder were merchantmen loaded with supplies. Spanish galleons were not necessarily bigger than English ships, as is often claimed. In fact, the largest ship on either side was the English *Triumph*. Neither was there much difference in number, for the English could call on 102 warships of various sizes.

Bad weather delayed the Spanish fleet and, when its food supplies began to rot, the whole fleet put into Corunna on the northern coast of Spain. Because of this the English fleet sent to intercept them found nothing and returned to Plymouth. The Armada finally appeared off Cornwall on 19 July. It was time to light the beacon fires which flashed their warning from hilltop to hilltop. At Plymouth the English fleet was trapped in harbour by contrary winds. Years later, a Spanish writer commented, 'their commanders were at bowls upon the Hoe at Plymouth'. Even if this was true, they had plenty of time to finish their game!

When the English fleet put to sea it was to the windward (rear) of the enemy ships. When they opened fire their light cannon-balls did little damage. The Armada was formed in a crescent, whose powerful ends could close in like the jaws of a trap. In this way, the warships protected the merchantmen in the centre. The darting English ships resembled dogs snapping at a bull; they could hurt but not cripple their opponent. On 23 July Hawkins' *Ark Royal* and Medina Sidonia's *San Martin* exchanged shots. Neither was damaged. So far the most serious injury to the Armada was accidental. One galleon was wrecked by an internal explosion. Another collided with a sister ship and had to be abandoned.

On 25 July there was a confused battle off the Isle of Wight. By now the Spanish ships were beginning to show signs of wear and

---

* In 1588 two calendars were in use. The Spanish had changed to the Gregorian; the English kept to the Julian or Old Style. Consequently there was a difference of ten numbers between Spanish and English dates for the Armada; for the Spanish it began on 29 July, for the English it was 19 July. In this chapter the Old Style dates have been used.

The Resolution of the Council of War of the English Commanders to fight against the Armada: '1 August, 1588. We whose names are hervnder written have determyned and agreede in counsaile to folowe and pursue the Spanishe ffleete vntill we have cleared oure owne coaste and broughte the ffrithe weste of us, and then to returne backe again, as well to revictuall oure ships (which stand in extreme scarsitie) as alsoe to guard and defend oure owne coaste at home; with further protestatione that, if oure wantes of victualles and munitione were suppliede, we wold pursue them to the furthest that they durste

tear. There had been severe casualties on the crowded ships, rigging and sails were torn and the hulls damaged. Yet the crescent shape could not be broken and when the fleet came to anchor at Calais it was still in good order. Medina Sidonia sent messengers to Parma, asking him what he intended to do. The prince replied that he was helpless. His troops had been unable to capture a large Dutch port. Not one of his soldiers could get to the waiting ships.

The Spanish seamen had done their best. They had brushed the English fleet aside and sailed up the Channel. But it needed more than courage and skill to make an unworkable plan work.

Hellburners

Meanwhile, outside Calais, the English Commander-in-Chief, Lord Howard of Effingham, called a Council of War. Howard was an important court official, not a sailor. Elizabeth had chosen him for the same reason Philip had chosen Medina Sidonia – he was of sufficient rank to keep quarrelsome 'seadogs' like Drake, Hawkins and Raleigh in order. Howard asked his experts what he should do next.

The best plan seemed to attack with fireships. These were usually old, empty ships filled with tar and gunpowder and set

A contemporary chart of the Armada

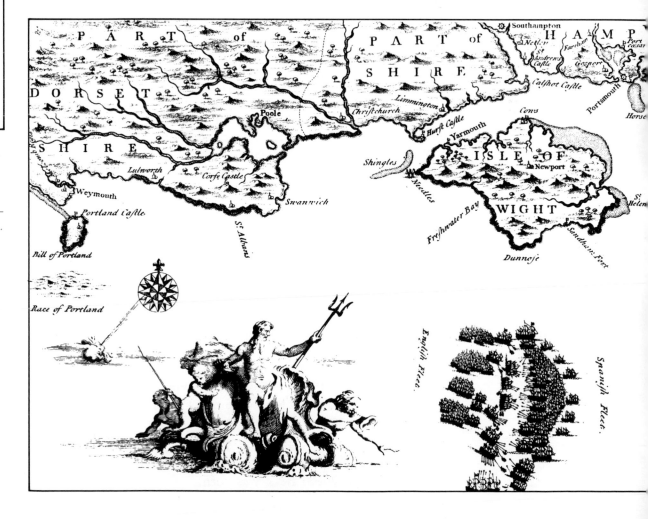

alight. There was no time to send to England for old vessels so fighting ships had to be sacrificed. On 28 July eight of these 'hell-burners', as they were called, were sighted by Spanish lookouts, drifting towards them, 'spurting fire and their ordnance [guns] shooting which was a horror to see'. It was the crisis of the battle.

Medina Sidonia had expected fireships. He had stationed sailors in small boats to push them away with long poles. These 'hellburners', however, were much larger than usual. The frightened sailors rowed away, leaving the fleet unprotected. The result was panic. No danger was more dreaded in the days of wooden ships than fire. Spanish commanders cut their anchor cables, rather than waste valuable time pulling them up, and headed for the open sea. In the confusion one galleon was driven aground and wrecked.

Now that there was no crescent-shaped shield the English seized their chance. A fierce, six-day battle developed off the French port of Gravelines. The Spanish fought heroically, dying in hundreds amongst the flames and wreckage. As the ships rolled over, blood dripped down their sides; some left a red trail behind them. The fighting stopped only as ship after ship ran out of ammunition. The battered Armada drifted north. By now Medina Sidonia had lost eight large galleons and many smaller ships. His battered unseaworthy ships were crowded with wounded and dying men. Soon Catholic Europe would mourn, and Protestant Europe rejoice, at the news of the Armada's defeat.

Good Queen Bess

For a time a strong wind threatened to drive the Spanish fleet on to the Zeeland sand-banks. At the last moment Spanish prayers were answered. The wind changed and the fleet disappeared into the haze of the North Sea. The English followed as far as the Scottish coast and then turned back because they were short of ammunition and food.

Many Spanish galleons were wrecked on the long, hard voyage round Scotland and Ireland. It was September before the first survivors reached Spain. Fifty-three ships and a third of the men never returned. By contrast, the English had suffered very few battle casualties. Their problem was disease, which had spread like wildfire.

Elizabeth had addressed her troops at Tilbury whilst the battle raged in the Channel. She said:

> I am come amongst you at this time, not for recreation or sport, but being resolved in the midst and heat of battle to live and die amongst you all . . . I know I have the body of a weak and feeble woman, but I have the heart of a king, and a king of England too, and think foul scorn that Parma or Spain . . . should dare to invade my realm.

It was the sort of speech Tudor Englishmen loved to hear. At Tilbury Elizabeth reached the crowning point of her reign. The legend of 'Good Queen Bess' was born.

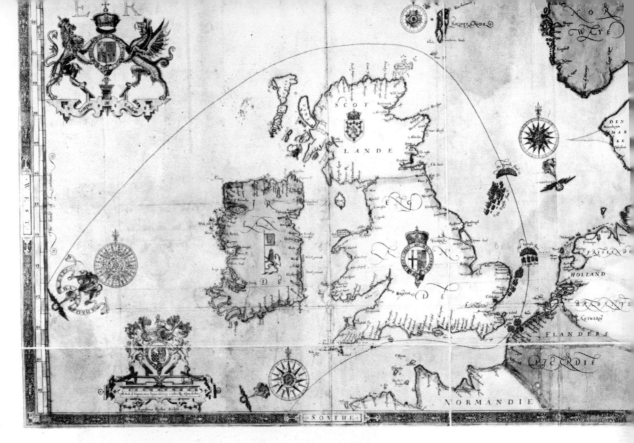

The route of the Armada shown in a map of the time

Sources and questions

1. Before the Armada sailed, King Philip gave this instruction and advice to its commander, the Duke of Medina-Sidonia.

    > Since victories are in the hands of God, to give and take away as he sees fit, and since our cause is . . . His . . . if this is not undeserved by sinfulness, great care must be taken that no sailor commits a sin, and in particular that no blasphemy is uttered . . . . [Y]ou will leave immediately for the Channel. You will sail up the Channel as far as Cape Margate, where you will rendezvous [*meet*] with my nephew, the Duke of Parma . . . in order to cover his army's crossing. . . . Do not fail to let every man know that the enemy has the advantage in artillery and with his superior firepower will try to fight us at long range. The aim of our men must . . . be to bring the enemy to close quarters and grapple with him.

    Source: Sir Philip Petrie, Philip II of Spain, *Eyre and Spottiswoode, 1964, page 283*

    (a) Why did Philip believe that God was on Spain's side in the war?
    (b) What experiences led Philip to believe that the English fleet would have superior firepower?
    (c) What parts of this source might have been given by a modern naval commander, and what parts are most unlikely to have come from such a person?

Elizabeth addressing her troops at Tilbury, 1588

(**d**) Why did Philip think it necessary to give such detailed instructions to Medina-Sidonia?

(**e**) How do you think the Spanish soldiers would have felt about the battle strategy outlined by Philip?

2. The map on the previous page shows part of the route taken by the Armada. It was drawn soon after the battle.

(**a**) Compare this map with a modern one. In what ways is it less accurate?

(**b**) What do we call the lands marked 'Picardei' today?

(**c**) Which country was not at war with Spain in 1588? How does the map indicate this?

(**d**) How does the map-maker suggest that England claimed to rule Ireland?

(**e**) How far is this map an accurate guide to what happened to the Armada? Give reasons for your answer.

3. Write a folk song telling the story of the Armada. Either set it to an existing tune or make up one of your own.

4. Find out more about attempts to salvage Armada wrecks. There have been several of these, including the work in Tobermory Bay, Scotland, and the discovery of the *Gerona* off the coast of Northern Ireland in 1967. Try to work up a group or individual project on such a topic, using the title 'Buried Treasure'.

Elizabeth at a hunting picnic, from a book published in 1573

THE REIGN OF GOOD QUEEN BESS: COURT, CITY AND COUNTRY

We have seen that the English people liked Elizabeth even before she was queen. As the years passed her popularity grew until the mature queen was treated more like a goddess than a woman. Courtiers praised her beauty and goodness. Poets called her 'Gloriana', meaning a sort of fairy queen. Painters showed her as a magnificently dressed doll. Composers wrote pretty tunes for a monarch who loved music and dancing.

Elizabeth boosted this image by never missing a chance to show herself to her people. Londoners saw her frequently, of course, and countryfolk met her when she went on summer tours, called 'progresses'. The Spanish ambassador went on a progress in 1568. Here is part of what he wrote:

> She was received everywhere with great acclamations [cheering] and signs of joy . . . whereat she was extremely pleased and told me so, giving me to understand how beloved she was by her subjects and how highly she esteemed this . . . . She ordered her carriage sometimes to be taken where the crowd seemed thickest and stood up and thanked the people . . .

During these tours the queen spent days, even weeks, at the houses of her courtiers. These lords went to a great deal of trouble and expense to please her. At Kenilworth Castle in 1575 the Earl of Leicester staged a famous entertainment in her honour. There were plays, pageants and dancing for days on end and all sorts of other delights for the queen. When the Earl of Hertford knew she was coming to his country estate in 1591 he got 300 workmen to build extra rooms and dig a lake in the garden.

'Female Sun'

Elizabeth was a woman in a man's world, ruling over a court designed for a king. Most of her subjects believed that God chose the children of royalty. So even though she was a woman Elizabeth had to be obeyed since she was the last surviving child of a king. Nevertheless, people of the time thought it strange for a woman to rule over men. At first, Parliament and country thought Elizabeth

Elizabeth receiving foreign diplomats

would marry and so benefit from a husband's advice. Had not her sister Mary done just that? Elizabeth, however, refused to marry.

If Elizabeth had been timid or stupid she might have become a puppet of her Council. But the proud daughter of Henry VIII was as strong-willed, clever and well-educated as her father. Her personality gave her a strong grip on government affairs. Her education meant that she could meet men on equal terms. For example, the queen spoke Latin, French and Italian. This was very useful because no ambassador to England during her reign spoke English. So she was able to deal directly with these envoys instead of relying on what her ministers told her.

A Renaissance court was like a magnet, attracting men and women eager to find fame and fortune. Such courtiers used flattery when dealing with a king. Elizabeth's court was unusual because its 'sun' was an unmarried woman and its 'planets' ambitious men. So at the court of the 'Virgin Queen' there was an extra ingredient; the flattery was spiced with romance. The queen probably never slept with any man. But she certainly loved the Earl of Leicester and had other favourites, notably Sir Christopher Hatton and Sir Walter Raleigh. These men 'courted' the flirtatious queen who revelled in such love-games.

Favourites and statesmen

Elizabeth was not as cruel as her father. It was fourteen years before she beheaded a nobleman whereas Henry sent two important men to the block in the second year of his reign. However, she inherited her father's temper as well as his charm. Elizabeth was moody and liable to tantrums. During these fits of anger she would shout, throw things and box the ears of anybody who annoyed her. As Christopher Hatton, her Lord Chancellor, remarked: 'When she smiled it was pure sunshine that everyone did choose to bask in if they could, but bye and bye came a storm from a sudden gathering of clouds and the thunder fell in wondrous manner on all alike.' A young nobleman who dressed well, behaved properly and said witty things might well be rewarded by the queen. He might get presents or gifts of land or a well-paid job. These rewards could make a man rich overnight, so there was plenty of competition for her favour.

Three of the most important jobs were Master of the Horse, Lord Treasurer and Lord Chancellor. Leicester was made Master of the Horse as soon as Elizabeth came to the throne. Hatton became Lord Chancellor in 1587. But when it came to appointing her chief political adviser the queen forgot about flattery and favourites. She chose William Cecil, Lord Burghley, as Lord Treasurer. Burghley was a brilliant statesman and very clever at foreign affairs. He had served both Edward and Mary and it is possible that his advice helped save Elizabeth's life during the Wyatt Rebellion crisis (see Chapter 12). Elizabeth's loyalty to Burghley never wavered, and when he lay dying she nursed him with her own hands.

London

Elizabeth ran the country from London, England's capital. She owned thirteen palaces within a day's ride of the city and two, Whitehall and St James, were quite near. Most Londoners must have seen her at one time or another, particularly when she was rowed up the river in the royal barge. During her reign London's population rose from 90,000 to 100,000 – this in a country of about 4,000,000 people. This rise had been even steeper in the middle years of the 16th century and by Elizabeth's time the city was spilling out into the surrounding countryside.

In earlier times a lot of city land had been owned by the monasteries. For example, there was a priory at Whitefriars and an abbey at West Smithfield. When Henry VIII closed the monasteries such property was bought by rich Tudor 'developers'. These men turned chapels into churches, converted the larger buildings to make palaces for themselves, and sold large areas to builders who put up tenements, inns and shops. A great deal of open space inside the city was used up in this way.

London was governed by rich and powerful merchants. The City Council was elected from the ranks of the twelve London guilds – mercers, grocers, drapers, fishmongers, goldsmiths, skin-

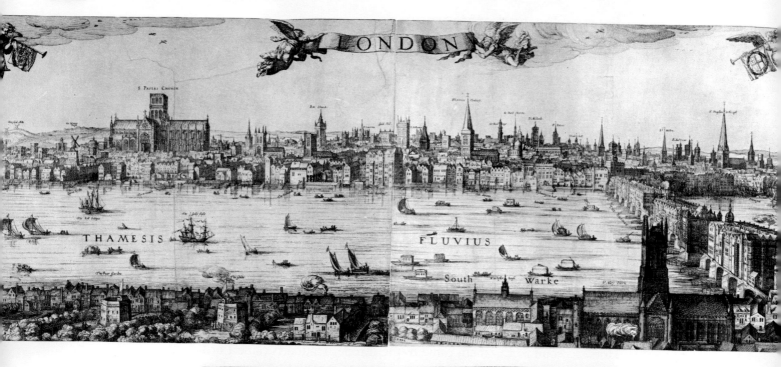

Above: Visscher's long view of Tudor London
Right: Watermen on the Thames at London Bridge

ners, merchant-taylors, clothworkers, haberdashers, salters, iron-mongers and vintners. Some of these trades were not as ordinary as they sound. The leaders of each guild often dealt in banking, foreign trade and insurance. Each year a Lord Mayor was chosen from a different guild.

The City had three famous landmarks: St Paul's Cathedral, the Tower of London and London Bridge. St Paul's towered above the streets, shops and houses. Its spire was 160 metres tall, although it was burnt down in 1561. St Paul's was half-church, half-market place. Here printers sold their books, labourers were hired, lawyers saw their clients and lovers arranged to meet. Sermons and executions took place outside in the churchyard.

London Bridge was 300 years old in Elizabeth's day, a ramshackle structure which was repaired so often that it was the subject of the famous rhyme, 'London Bridge is Falling Down'. It was the only bridge across the Thames near London and its shops and houses made it a tourist attraction. As a travel-writer, John Lyly, remarked,

> . . . and among all the strange and beautiful shows [*in London*] there is none so notable, as the Bridge which crosseth the Thames, which is in the manner of a continual street, well replenished with large and stately houses on both sides, and situated upon twenty [*actually there were nineteen*] arches whereof each one is made of excellent . . . squared stone . . .

The bridge's narrow arches dammed the river, and at times each opening became a flood with a steep drop. One torrent was used to drive a wheel which supplied the citizens with water. There was one grim attraction. The heads of traitors were stuck on poles over the southern gateway. This ghastly 'pin-cushion' served as a dreadful warning. In 1592 a German visitor counted thirty-four heads.

The Thames was London's southern boundary, while a medieval wall circled it to the north, from the Fleet Ditch to the Tower of London. This Tower had been started by William the Conqueror (1066–87), partly to defend the city, partly to frighten the citizens into obeying him! It had many uses. It was a palace where foreigners could be entertained, a prison for important offenders, an armoury for weapons, a safe place for the crown jewels, and a mint. There was even a zoo which had been started by Henry VII.

Outside the walls lay Moorfields and Spitalfields. These were open spaces which Londoners used for sport and recreation. This was where young men were supposed to practise archery in case there was a war. This became difficult as the population grew and lines of shops and houses sprawled over the fields. A famous London writer of the time, John Stow, complained that such 'enclosure' left them no room to shoot so that they crept 'into bowling alleys and ordinary dicing houses'. One wonders what he would have thought of modern London.

Country life

Ploughing in Tudor times. Note the oxen

Most Elizabethans lived in the country and worked on the land. People of the time spoke of three kinds of farmers: yeomen, husbandmen and labourers. This division was based on wealth. A rich yeoman might own as much as 50 hectares. Husbandmen had less land, whilst a labourer divided his time between working his own few acres and serving a yeoman. Village land suitable for crops (arable) was arranged in three very large fields. These fields, in turn, were divided into furlong strips which were shared between farmers. A family's strips might be far apart; this was so that each got a fair share of good and bad soil. Each year, one field was left unused (fallow) to increase its fertility.

Ways of working were centuries old. Oxen, not horses pulled the ploughs. Seeds were scattered on the ground, or 'broadcast'. Teams of four men and a boy would harvest the main crops in August. A good team could cut and stack about 1 hectare of corn a day. Women or young children walked behind each team, gathering up every precious scrap of wheat. This was called gleaning. The wheat was then threshed with a flail – two pieces of wood loosely fixed end-on with a leather strip.

There were many other jobs to be done: firewood to be cut, ditches to be cleared, tools to be sharpened, fruit to be picked and meat to be preserved in salt for the winter. Few families could afford to feed all their cattle through the winter so lots of animals were slaughtered in the autumn; our word 'bonfire' comes from the fires made from their bones. The farmer's wife lived a busy, hard life. She had to bring up the children, cook and preserve food, brew beer and make clothes and candles.

Agriculture needed essential 'back-up' work from craftsmen. There was the blacksmith who made tools as well as shoeing horses, the miller who ground corn, the cooper who made barrels to preserve food and drink, the wheelwrights who made wheels for the waggons and carts, the thatchers and masons who built houses and the carpenter who made furniture. Villages had to 'make do and mend' in this way because shops were few and far between. Only occasionally would countryfolk be able to go to a market or fair to buy some expensive item like a plough or a cooking pot.

England's population was rising during the sixteenth century and more mouths to feed meant higher prices for the farmer. It has been worked out that by 1600 a farmer was getting four times the price for his wheat and barley that his grandfather had got a century before. This improved country people's standard of living. Here is what some old peasants told William Harrison. Harrison was a clergyman who wrote *A Description of England* in 1577.

'There are old men yet dwelling in the village . . . which have noted three things to be marvellously altered within their . . . remembrance . . . . One is the multitude of chimney . . . whereas in their young days there were not above two or three . . . . The second is the great amendment [*improvement*] of lodgings, for (said they) our fathers, yea, and we ourselves also, have lain oft upon straw pallets, on rough mats covered only with a sheet . . . and a good round log under their heads for a bolster . . . The third thing they tell of is the exchange of vessel, as of treen [wooden] platters into pewter, and wooden spoons into silver or tin . . . .

Sources and questions

1. (a) The old peasants (see quote above) remarked that there were many more chimneys than when they were young. Does this suggest improvements in housing? Give reasons for your answer.
(b) In what way do you think 'lodgings' had improved since their younger days?
(c) What does the change from wooden to pewter, tin or silver plates and spoons suggest?
(d) Imagine you are William Harrison. Suggest what answers the peasants would have given to the question, 'Why was England in 1577 a richer place than in their parents' day?'

2. In the portrait on page 112 the queen holds a rainbow, symbol of peace after storm. But this picture of 'Gloriana' also contains clues as to what the artist, and most English people, thought about their queen.

(a) In what ways was the England of 1600 experiencing peace after the storm? Why was this not entirely true?

(b) Why are there eyes and ears painted on the queen's dress?

(c) To the Elizabethans the serpent was a symbol of a human quality. It is painted on the queen's sleeve. Can you guess what the artist is saying about the queen?

(d) Find out, if you can, what the queen's fantastic ruff represents, also the spring flowers painted on her bodice.

(e) Do you think the queen ever had a dress like this? If not, why did the artist paint her in this way?

3. (a) Name the main London landmarks shown in the pictures on page 140.

(b) Were the three people being rowed across the river well-to-do or poor? Give reasons for your answer.

(c) Why are no boats shown passing under the bridge?

(d) What was the function of the object shown on the extreme left of the bridge?

(e) Why do you think artists were so fond of drawing London Bridge?

THE REIGN OF GOOD QUEEN BESS: 'THE FOURTH SORT'

Noblemen and gentlemen

The life story of an Elizabethan gentleman – Sir Henry Unton. Various scenes depict his birth, Oxford University, travelling in Italy, soldiering in the Low Countries, on his deathbed, feasting with his family, watching a masque (a play with music and dancing), his funeral procession

Strong rule by the Tudors had put a curb on the power of the nobles. The days when powerful lords could topple a king from his throne were over. Henry VII had forbidden them to keep the sort of private armies which had caused so much trouble during the Wars of the Roses. Henry VIII had been merciless to any nobleman who dared to defy him. When dukes rebelled they were crushed easily, as in the case of the Northern Rebellion (see Chapter 14). Even nature seemed to be against such families, because between 1485 and 1547 half of them failed to produce a boy, so their titles died out. The new men given such titles were not likely to quarrel with the monarch who had appointed them.

Henry VIII had chosen men of humble birth such as Wolsey, Cranmer and Cromwell as his chief advisers. He allowed noblemen to serve him if they were loyal and hard-working, not by right of birth. Henry also rewarded many of his supporters by selling them church property. Many famous English families date their fame, fortune and titles from the closing of the monasteries.

Elizabeth followed her father's example as far as her ministers were concerned. It became the custom to give high office to gentlemen, that is, men who owned property and were entitled to a family coat-of-arms. Tudor power was based on the support of this class of people, especially those gentlemen who were unpaid Justices of the Peace. These men kept law and order in their districts, an important matter in the days when there was no organised police force.

In Elizabethan England, the ownership of land brought with it power and status, so even rich merchants bought estates to show their success. At the same time noblemen were often pleased to marry their daughters to sons of merchants. A good example of this was Anne Boleyn, whose mother was a daughter of the Duke of Norfolk, while her father was a rich London merchant.

'A ragged rabblement'

One Elizabethan writer divided English society into four – gentlemen, citizens, yeomen and 'the fourth sort of men who do not rule'. This 'fourth sort' had certain rights under English law but, apart from that, they were expected to keep quiet, work hard and obey their 'betters'. Nobody thought they needed a say in governing the country, first because they owned nothing of value, and second, because the queen, Council and Parliament knew what was best for them.

Elizabeth's governments did not ignore such people. The authorities tried to organise trade and industry so as to get the most from working people. The Statute of Artificers (1563) graded work in order of importance. Farming came first, followed by its necessary crafts. The cloth trade was placed third, with men of the professional classes – priests, lawyers, doctors – last. Skilled jobs were scarce and it was difficult to get into crafts or professions. In most cases a seven-year apprenticeship was compulsory for craftsmen, whilst university students, whose families had to own property anyway, took seven years to get their Master of Arts degree.

Those who had regular jobs were lucky. Throughout the sixteenth century the numbers of people out of work increased steadily. There were lots of reasons to explain this unemployment. Many blamed enclosures, for, as one 'expert' wrote:

> Who will maintain husbandry [*farming*] which is the nurse of every county as long as sheep bring so great gain? Who will be at the cost to keep a dozen [*workers*] in his house to milk kine [*cattle*], make cheese, carry it to the market, when one poor soul may by keeping sheep get him greater profit? Who will not be

contented for to pull down houses of husbandry so that he may stuff his bags full of money?

Others thought unemployment was caused by the closing of the monasteries. From earliest times the Church had taught that it was a Christian's duty to help the poor. The giving of alms or charity, either food, clothing or money, was one of a monk's main duties. Now this kind of poor relief was swept away.

> For, although the sturdy beggars got all the devotion of the good charitable people from them, yet had the poor . . . creatures some relief of their scraps, whereas now they have nothing. They had their hospitals, and almshouses to be lodged in, but now they lie and starve in the streets. Then [*before the closures*] was their number great, but now much greater.

Some people thought the increased poverty was due to the debasement of the coinage, higher prices, poor harvests and the importing of too many foreign goods. A few old men thought it was the result of lazy habits which had been unknown in their youth!

There was probably some truth in all these explanations. Nevertheless, there was a deeper cause which could not be blamed on kings or landowners, dishonest ministers or greedy merchants. Everyone in England, indeed the whole of Western Europe, was gradually changing their ways of life and work, as trade increased and industry grew in importance. Above all, the population was increasing. The 'ragged rabblement of rakehells', as one writer called them, who infested the towns and countryside, begging and thieving, were often the results of these changes.

The Norwich experiment

By Elizabeth's reign the number of poor people had increased so much that many had to live on Christian charity. Such desperate men and women turned easily to crime. Tudor towns were full of every type of ruffian and trickster. They had picturesque names. There were 'Abraham-men' who pretended to be mad to get money, 'Clappendogens' who tried to get sympathy by making out they were crippled, 'Dummerars' who pretended to be dumb. There were 'Prygmen' who stole poultry and 'Priggers of Prancers' who stole horses. A female criminal type, called a 'Bawdy Basket', pretended to sell goods from a basket whilst picking the customer's pocket. The authorities hit back with severe punishments. Death was a common end for law-breakers; in Devon alone seventy-four people were hanged in one year of Elizabeth's reign.

Beggars were usually whipped and branded, not hanged. The problem was to find work for the genuine unemployed and to look after the old and sick who could no longer work. In 1549 the Town Council of Norwich discovered that some of Kett's rebels were beggars (see Chapter 11). This terrified them and they decided that citizens must be forced to help the poor. Anything was better than a rebellion. They appointed local 'overseers of the poor' whose job was to collect an annual 'poor rate'. This money could then be used to care for the sick and old and supply work for fit people.

The 43rd Elizabeth

The government and many other towns copied Norwich. The so-called Great Poor Law which Parliament passed in 1601 was really a collection of schemes for poor relief tried out over the previous fifty years. The poor-rate system, with its local overseers, was applied to the entire country. The town councils used the money collected to give work, build workhouses and hospitals and help the old and sick in each parish. If a parish was too small to look after its own poor it was helped by a larger parish nearby. Of course, there was still room for private charity, and kind individuals were encouraged to found their own almshouses and hospitals.

The Great Poor Law became known as the '43rd Elizabeth' because it was passed in the 43rd year of the reign of the queen. It remained the chief way of dealing with poor people for the next 200 years. The poor rate became the basis of all later local taxation (rates).

Sources and questions

1. Edward Hext, Justice of the Peace in Somerset, wrote this to Lord Burghley on 25 September 1596, concerning the increase in rogues and vagabonds in his county. It was a time of food shortages and riots.

> And this year there assembled 80 [*rogues*] . . . and took a whole cart load of cheese from one countryman and drove it to a fair and shared it out amongst them, for which some of them have endured long imprisonment . . . . [T]hey say that the rich men have got it all in their own hands and will starve the poor. . . . I say that the large number of idle, wandering people and robbers of the land are the chief cause of the [*food*] shortage, for they do not work . . . [*but*] lie idly in ale-houses day and night eating and drinking excessively. . . . And when these people are put in jail, the poor country people they have robbed are forced to feed them. . . . The most dangerous are the wandering soldiers . . . of these sort . . . there are three or four hundred in the country.

> *Source: R. H. Tawney and E. Power,* Tudor Economic Documents, 3 vols, *London, 1924, Quoted by J. Pound,* Poverty and Vagrancy in Tudor England, *Longman Seminar Studies, 1971*

(a) Why did Hext think it necessary to report to the queen's chief minister? Why would Burghley have been interested in such matters?

(b) In what way is this source what you would expect a Justice of the Peace to say about the causes of riots and disorder? Do you think there was any truth in what the men who stole the cheese said?

(c) Why were so many ex-soldiers wandering about? Why were they thought to be the most dangerous?

(d) From this source, would you say Hext was sympathetic towards the poor people of Somerset? Give reasons for your answer.

2.

This picture comes from a book published in 1592. It is possible it was written by a Justice of the Peace. It warns law-abiding citizens of the ways of thieves and other criminals.

(a) List the different kinds of robbery shown in this drawing. Which ones are unknown today?

(b) Why are the thieves shown as animals?

(c) What clue is there to the most severe punishment for criminals?

(d) Who is the figure shown at top right? What was his job?

3. Make up a play about the Somerset men who stole the cheese.

THE REIGN OF GOOD QUEEN BESS: PARLIAMENT AND EDUCATION

Elizabeth ruled the country with the help of a royal council of ministers. She did not call Parliament very often; it met for a total of only 104 weeks in a forty-four year reign. In those days the ruler summoned Parliament for two reasons: to pass new laws or to raise extra taxes. Henry VIII's Reformation Parliament, for example, met to make the king head of the Church in England. Elizabeth called Parliament at the start of her reign to reverse Mary's Catholic policy and to found the Church of England. As far as money was concerned, Elizabeth was a good 'housekeeper' who usually managed to make ends meet. She only needed extra taxes in an emergency.

Royal income rose from about £200,000 a year to £300,000 during her reign. With this money Elizabeth ran her court and government. However, she could not manage if there were wars or rebellions; the Northern Rebellion in 1569 cost £93,000 to suppress. From the defeat of the Armada until her death in 1603 Elizabeth fought a war with the greatest power of the time, Spain. This huge expense could only be paid for with Parliament's help. Consequently, from 1588 the queen faced parliaments which met more often and grew more influential with every year that passed.

Members of Parliament knew why they had been summoned. They made it clear they expected some reward in return. An MP usually arrived with some grievance; his constituents wanted this or that matter put right. For the first time it became possible to disagree with royal policies without risking a traitor's death. The queen found herself treated in a way which would have astonished her father. In 1596, for example, the Commons debated for twenty-four days whether to grant another war tax.

Elizabeth did not give in without a fight. She told MPs that they could discuss anything except the succession to the throne, religion, foreign affairs and her possible marriage! This did not please the Commons, and in 1572 a puritan member, Peter Wentworth, complained about these royal hints, which he said arrived in the form of 'rumours' from her officials.

Elizabeth was annoyed with Wentworth for criticising her and he was put in the Tower for a time. It was, she said, 'monstrous that the feet should direct the head'. Fifteen years later she was just as angry when another MP, Sir Anthony Cope, asked for changes in the Prayer Book. He, too, went to the Tower.

The queen's personality charmed even those who disagreed with her. In her last speech to Parliament in 1601 she said, 'Though God hath raised me high yet this I count the glory of my crown, that I have reigned with your loves.' She was then old and wrinkled, with blackened teeth and a red wig, so weak that she nearly fainted under the weight of her grand clothes. Yet an eyewitness wrote, 'Her apt and refined words so learnedly composed did ravish [delight] the sense of the hearers with admiration.'

Grammar and public schools

Most of the men who listened to the queen that day were well-educated and knew a good speech when they heard one. An Elizabethan gentleman's desire to 'get on' showed clearly in his determination to get the best education for his children. Before Henry VIII's time most boys of well-to-do families were schooled either in the household of a great lord or in a monastery. When the monasteries closed, their educational work was continued in grammar schools; the title 'grammar' refers to Latin and Greek, not English. In Edward VI's reign chantry money (see Chapter 11) was used to found 'Edward VI grammar schools' which in some cases survive to the present day.

This Tudor thirst for knowledge also led to the founding of famous public schools such as Repton (1553), Rugby (1567), Uppingham (1584) and Harrow (1590). Tudor pupils learnt their lessons by heart, in a dull and uninteresting way. Young children were taught the alphabet with textbooks; one reader begins with 'A for Apple' but cheats with 'X for Expensive'! The alphabet and the Lord's Prayer were printed on a hornbook – a piece of wood shaped like a bat and covered with a sheet of transparent horn. Each pupil had one of these and he sometimes used them to play ball games. The boys wrote with a goose quill (feather) which needed to be scraped a lot so that the ink would not stick.

School hours were long, and holidays far less frequent than today. One Tudor school had eighteen days at Christmas, thirteen at Easter and nine at Whitsun. Most pupils worked six days a week, with ten hours lessons each day. Discipline was very strict and boys were flogged for quite trivial offences. One old man remembered that when he was young he had once received fifty-three strokes of the cane at the same time. Some Tudor school badges even showed boys being beaten and one had a design of birches.

There were no girls' schools in those days. Great ladies like Elizabeth herself or Lady Jane Grey were educated at home by private tutors. Mary Tudor had both English and Spanish scholars to direct her studies. Elizabeth studied with some of the finest humanist scholars of the age, including William Grindall and Roger Ascham. Consequently she received exactly the same education as a male student at Oxford or Cambridge.

Queen Elizabeth opening Parliament in 1586. The lords and bishops are seated to left and right. Members of the Commons are standing (front foreground)

Poor children of either sex, of course, rarely had much schooling. The lucky ones might get a few lessons from the village school-master or parish priest. As one ordinary man remarked, 'This is all we go to school for – to read Common Prayers at Church and set down common prices at market'. Even this amount of learning was rare among the 'fourth sort of people who do not rule'.

Universities

There were only two English universities, Oxford and Cambridge. Each one consisted of a small number of semi-independent colleges which had developed from 'halls' or hostels for the students to live in. Oxford was the oldest, for its earliest college had been founded in 1248. Cambridge's oldest 'hostel' was Peter-house which dates from 1284.

A student studied for four years for the degree of Bachelor of Arts and a further three years to become a Master. The chief subjects were religion, law, Greek philosophy, medicine, dialectic (debating), geometry, astronomy, Greek and Hebrew. Law students often went on to special colleges in London – Grays Inn, Lincoln's Inn, the Inner Temple and the Middle Temple. All examinations in those days were oral. The candidate answered questions put to him in Latin. The final disputation, as it was called, was the scholar's 'masterpiece' which, if approved, gave him his Master's degree.

Elizabeth took a keen interest in university education. She gave her support (though not her money) to the founding of Jesus College, Oxford in 1571. Her visits to both universities were great occasions, marked by feasting, plays, speeches and music.

Physicians and surgeons

Most Tudor physicians were university-trained. Each medical student had to cure at least three patients to get his degree. Doctors battled with most of the diseases known today except cancer. Two of their greatest enemies were bubonic plague and a deadly fever known as the 'sweating sickness'. Plague reached England between 1349 and 1351. It is carried by fleas on black rats. One of the symptoms is swellings on the body called 'buboes', hence the name 'bubonic'. It was usually fatal. Sixteenth-century doctors suspected that rats might be responsible in some way, though they did not know how. A cure was not finally discovered until 1894.

Elizabethan cures were rather different from modern ones. Whereas a modern doctor might prescribe a course of pills or a bottle of medicine, a Tudor physician would probably suggest as many as a hundred treatments. These varied from pleasant things like milk and apples to horrible mixtures of crabs' eyes, buttered live spiders, ants' eggs and even powdered human skull. Blood-letting was thought to help. So was 'taking the waters', that is, going to spas like Buxton to sit in baths of strong minerals. Some experts also believed

Tudor school scene

that the stars affected people's health, so a medical student might be tested on his knowledge of astrology and astronomy.

In the Middle Ages the crafts of barber and surgeon had been mixed up. A barber might do simple operations as well as cutting hair and trimming beards. During the sixteenth century surgeons started to go up in the world. They were encouraged by the pioneer work of Andreas Vesalius, a Belgian professor at Padua University in Italy. Vesalius broke new ground in surgery when he dissected a human body. Before his time students had used only dead animals, but Vesalius knew that their bodies are not exactly similar to those of humans.

An Elizabethan surgeon demonstrating how to dissect a body

In 1543 Vesalius published *On the Structure of the Human Body*. This book was a true Renaissance creation, beautiful as well as accurate. Its 277 woodcuts showed bones, muscles, the heart, arteries and veins in a way Michelangelo would have loved. And because of printing the book was soon being studied by medical men all over Europe. It became the essential guide for surgeons for many years.

Sources and questions

1. Peter Wentworth, an MP, asked these questions during a Parliamentary debate in 1578 – and was sent to prison by the queen. Remember that the Speaker, or chairman of the House of Commons, was then the monarch's representative in Parliament.

   Is not this Parliament a place for any member to speak freely on any subject concerning the worship of God, the safety of the prince, and this noble realm? Is there any other council which can make, add or detract from the laws of the realm other than Parliament? . . . Can the Speaker interrupt any member . . . when he is speaking?. . . . Is it not against the liberties of the House of Commons to receive messages from the Queen which forbid us from doing something? . . . Can any Prince or State . . . be governed properly without this council of Parliament?

   Source: Adapted from Somers Tracts (1809). *Quoted by Millward*, Sixteenth Century Documents, *Hutchinson Educational, 1961*

   (a) Why do you think this speech in particular was thought worth writing down?
   (b) Which questions do you think were most likely to have annoyed the queen?
   (c) What had led the House of Commons to become more powerful in the sixteenth century?
   (d) On what grounds did MPs claim extra privileges?

2. (a) How many different lessons seem to be taking place in the classroom opposite?
   (b) What language are the boys likely to be translating to the teacher in front on the right?
   (c) What happened to boys who could not learn their lessons?
   (d) Why are there no girls in the picture?
   (e) From this source, explain the methods of teaching used in Tudor times.

3. You are an Elizabethan doctor. Choose a patient, give him a disease, and prescribe a few 'Tudor' remedies.

THE REIGN OF GOOD QUEEN BESS: GOD AND THE DEVIL

The Renaissance world was so full of great art and learning, of new discoveries and inventions, that it comes as a surprise to find so much ignorance and superstition as well. For, though God may have been on people's minds, so was the devil. A child might be frightened by tales of 'an ugly devil having horns on his head, fire in his mouth and a tail, eyes like a basin, fangs like a dog, claws like a bear and the voice roaring like a lion'. This is what one boy was told, and it was the sort of vision which haunted men and women during the often gloomy days and black nights of a candle-lit world.

People believed that evil took many forms – witches, urchins, elves, hags, fairies, satyrs, dwarfs, giants and imps. They 'saw' troublesome spirits like 'Robin Goodfellow' and 'Tom Thumb' in fields and woods. They thought that ravens croaked to warn of death, and sea-voyages should only be started on 'lucky' days. The devil was always at work, causing accidents, illnesses, floods and storms.

Witches

The person most likely to do the devil's work was a witch. Most witches were women. One German said this was because they were the more wicked sex! Witches killed or injured man and beast, sank ships and destroyed crops. There were two sure ways to tell if a woman was a witch. First, the devil had always put a special mark on their bodies, so any sort of birthmark or deformity was suspicious. Second, every witch had a 'familiar' which could do her work for her. This was usually an animal – a cat or a toad. Any old lady living alone and talking to her pet might be accused of being a witch.

Not everybody who believed these tales was ignorant or stupid. John Jewel, Bishop of Salisbury, preaching before the queen, had this to say in 1572:

These [*my*] eyes have seen most evident and manifest marks of their [*the witches'*] wickedness. Your Grace's subjects pine away even unto death, their colour fadeth, their flesh rotteth, their speech is benumbed, their senses are bereft. Wherefore your poor subjects most humble petition until your Highness, is, that the laws touching such malefactors [*wrong-doers*] may be put into execution.

The good bishop need not have worried too much. The 'laws touching such malefactors' were often put into action by the malefactors themselves. People accused of being witches often boasted of their powers. Ursley Kemp claimed she had four cats working for her. They were called Tyffin, Tittey, Piggen and Jacket. Two were used for injuring people and two for killing them. Witches who pleaded not guilty were tied hand and foot and thrown into a river or deep pond. If they floated they were guilty and if they sank it was usually too late to save them.

Male witches, called warlocks, were also punished if convicted. In 1590 in Scotland a Doctor Fian was burned for trying to sink a ship in which James, the Scots king, was voyaging to Denmark. Actually, hanging was the more usual punishment for witches in England. Sometimes a warlock would escape by claiming he was a sorcerer. Sorcerers were thought to be scholars skilled in a kind of 'respectable' magic which might work for good rather than evil.

An expert in the 'black art', as it was called, claimed to be able to summon up devils. He might 'control' as many as seventy-nine of

The end of a witch in 1571

these spirits, from Marbas, who could cure all diseases, to Asmodai, who found buried treasure and made people temporarily invisible. Of course, a sorcerer had to be careful because he might be accused of using devils for evil. It was difficult for people of the time to know what was magic and what was science. After all, many modern scientific marvels would have seemed magic to them.

The Church year

Witchcraft and sorcery were remnants of old pagan beliefs driven underground by Christianity. This is why churchmen were so much against any form of witchcraft. Yet the early Church had mixed pagan and Christian customs, as when pagan gods were replaced by saints, or the Roman feast of Saturnalia by Christmas. In this way, old customs did not have to be wiped out.

Elizabeth founded a new Protestant church but she was quite happy that people should enjoy the old festivals they had known before the Reformation. So each year was marked by religious events. The feast of Christmas went on for twelve days. During this time rich men entertained servants and friends in their mansions, where jesters told jokes and posed riddles, jugglers and acrobats gave displays and minstrels sang their old tales. Children played 'Blindman's Buff' or 'Kiss in the Ring', and each year every town chose a 'Boy Bishop'. This lad was allowed to play practical jokes,

Old customs: morris dancers at Richmond

and on Holy Innocents' Day (28 December) he preached a sermon in church. Two pagan customs, the hanging up of mistletoe and the burning of a 'yule' log, were as popular then as they are now.

Candlemas (2 February) was a day to celebrate the return of the 'light' of spring. Houses and churches were decorated with candles to represent this light. It was also the date to start spring sowing. People made long and serious preparation for Easter. It began on Shrove Tuesday when everybody went to church to confess their sins and be forgiven, or shriven. The next day was called Ash Wednesday. At a special service the priest made the mark of a black cross on each person's forehead to remind them that one day they would be turned to dust. During the forty days of Lent which led up to Easter every Christian made some small sacrifice in memory of Christ's own sufferings in the wilderness.

On Maundy Thursday, the day before Good Friday, the queen and her bishops washed the feet of a few poor people. This imitated Christ's washing of His disciples' feet at the Last Supper. Afterwards, food, clothing and money were shared amongst them. The number of men and women depended on the queen's age that year. A similar ceremony still takes place today when the present queen gives out specially minted 'Maundy Money'. She no longers washes feet!

On Good Friday all church statues were covered with black cloth. This was a way of mourning Christ's death on the cross. A solemn service and perhaps a play about the crucifixion marked the day in most parish churches. Easter Day was the most important church festival of the year. There were many services and ceremonies to celebrate Christ's resurrection. Seven Sundays later, the coming of the Holy Spirit to Christ's disciples was remembered on White (now Whit) Sunday. This was also an important holiday, marked with feasting and plays. In medieval times it had been one of the three occasions (Christmas and Easter were the others) when the king 'wore his crown', that is, entertained his nobles at court, received oaths of loyalty, and asked them their advice on important matters.

May Day

Such religious holidays were mixed up with pagan ideas about the 'rebirth' of the earth at spring time. We have already seen this at Candlemas. Easter comes from Eostre, the Saxon goddess of dawn. At the other end of the year bonfire festivals came from the pagan idea of keeping the earth 'warm' during the winter.

The most popular non-religious festival was May Day – the First day of May, when people celebrated the coming of summer. Here is how Philip Stubbes described preparations for the day:

> All the young men and maids, old men and wives run gadding over night to the woods and groves, where they spend the night in pleasant pastimes and in the morning return, bringing with them branches of trees to deck their houses.

In fact, their chief task was to find a tree-trunk suitable to be made into a maypole. When this had been cut down and trimmed it was carried to the village or town green and set up so that people could dance round it.

On May morning the villagers or townsfolk chose a pretty girl as 'May Queen' and a popular young man as 'Lord of Misrule'. She spent the day dancing and receiving gifts. He spent the day being a nuisance, frightening people with bells or rattles, chasing girls for kisses and riding a wooden hobby-horse. Here is Stubbes talking about him:

> My Lord of Misrule chooseth twenty, forty, a hundred lusty
> lads like himself and decketh them in his liveries [*uniforms*] . . . .
> They bedeck themselves with scarves, ribbons and laces,
> hanged all over with gold rings and jewels . . . . Then have they
> their hobby-horses, dragons and other antics, together with their
> pipers and thundering drummers to strike up the devil's dance.

Stubbes was a puritan. He hated all these old customs, as the last two words of this quotation show. In later years puritans did their best to stamp out such festivals. They were unsuccessful. Consequently, although Elizabeth's parliaments and fleets, her beggars and witches, are no more, it is still possible to celebrate Easter, Whitsun or May Day in a way the great queen would have recognised.

THE REIGN OF GOOD QUEEN BESS: TUDOR SUNSET

Nowhere did Elizabethan England's light shine so brightly as on the stage. Elizabeth's playwrights were every bit as famous as her sailors or courtiers. By the sixteenth century, as well as mystery and miracle plays at festival times, people could enjoy entertainments provided by travelling actors. These companies were small, often no more than four men and a boy. The boy played women's parts because it was not thought respectable for a female to appear in public. These groups moved from place to place, giving shows in town halls, inn-yards and large houses.

The first permanent theatre in England was built by an actor, James Burbage, in 1576. He called it the Theatre because it was the only one. Soon other playhouses were built. The most famous was the Globe but there was also the Swan, Curtain and Rose. These buildings were designed like the inns in which the companies had so often played. The show was presented in its 'yard'; the audience sat around the stage or watched from the balconies. They were all open to the sky to give good lighting. A trestle stage called the Scaffold was partly covered by a roof called the Shadow or Heavens. This got its name from the sun, moon and stars painted on it. The stage was above ground level. This gave everybody a good view, and meant that actors could hide underneath or drop down through a trapdoor.

William Shakespeare

'The upstart crow'

The most famous playwright of the time was William Shakespeare (1564–1616). He was born in Stratford-on-Avon, Warwickshire, and came to London to seek his fortune in the 1580s. It was a new and exciting time for drama. Before that time most of the plays had been written in Latin. Now it became fashionable to watch plays in English. Tragedies and comedies were in great demand and a favourite playwright was Christopher Marlowe (1564–93).

Although Marlowe had been to university he did not write in Latin. Instead he wrote exciting dramas in English. They had plenty of action to please the spectators. *Tamburlaine* is the story of a cruel Asiatic conqueror. *Dr Faustus* is about a man who sells

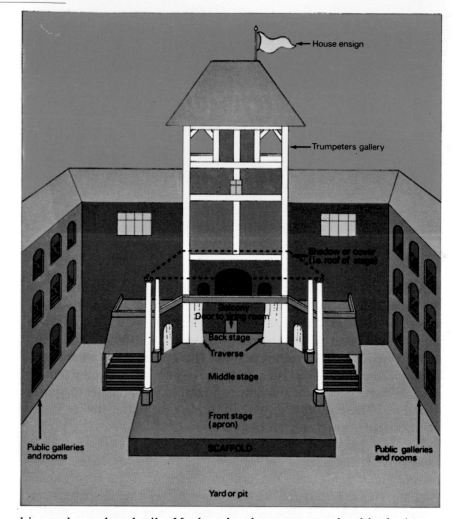

Labels on diagram:
House ensign
Trumpeters gallery
Shadow or cover (i.e. roof of stage)
Balcony
Door to tiring room
Back stage
Traverse
Middle stage
Front stage (apron)
SCAFFOLD
Public galleries and rooms
Public galleries and rooms
Yard or pit

An Elizabethan theatre

his soul to the devil. Marlowe's characters spoke blank (non-rhyming) verse which the actors shouted rather than spoke. Such poetry, delivered with waving arms and violent gestures, is known as 'Tudor rant'. Marlowe lived a wild life and was killed in a tavern fight. Shakespeare knew Marlowe and admired his plays.

In 1592 Shakespeare took the unusual step for an actor of writing a blank verse play of his own. We are not sure which one, but it was either *Love's Labours Lost* or *The Comedy of Errors*. This annoyed university-trained playwrights who thought they were the only people educated enough to write plays. Robert Greene, for example, wrote all his stage directions in Latin just to show off his knowledge. Two Latin words, 'exit' and 'exeunt' (when more than one person leaves the stage), are still used today. Greene's plays were failures so he became very jealous of Shakespeare. Just before he died, Greene wrote this. It refers to a fable about a crow who dressed up in the feathers of a more colourful bird:

> . . . there is an upstart crow, beautiful with our feathers, that with his tiger's heart wrapped in a players hide, supposes he is well able to bombast out a blank verse . . . and in his own conceit [*opinion*] is the only Shake-scene in the country.'

It was clear that Greene was talking about Shakespeare. In fact, the 'upstart crow' became England's greatest dramatist.

'Enemies of the Gospel'

Elizabeth's last years were not all glory. The 'fairy queen' lived in a real, hard world. The war with Spain dragged on, becoming a battle for profit rather than the glorious fight for survival it had been in 1588. English sailors were less successful because the Spanish had learnt from their mistakes. The days when Drake could find a rich galleon sailing alone were over; now such a treasure ship was protected by a small fleet. Even a successful English attack on Cadiz in 1596 did not produce as much plunder as its leaders had expected.

At home, puritanism continued to spread. In 1588–9 pamphlets were published in London by a writer calling himself Martin Marprelate. It was obvious this was not his real name but a disguise to escape punishment. The 'letters' were very rude about the Church of England in general and bishops in particular. In one letter bishops were described as 'petty antichrists, proud prelates, intolerable withstanders of reformation, enemies of the gospel'. The authorities were furious and set out to find Martin Marprelate. Government agents discovered an illegal printing press which had been used to produce the pamphlets at the home of Sir Richard Knightley, a Northamptonshire gentleman. He was arrested and spent some years in jail. A certain John Penry became suspect number one for Martin himself. He fled to Scotland but when he did return to England he was accused of trying to start a rebellion and hanged.

The Marprelate affair showed how dissatisfied puritans were becoming with the Church of England. It was no longer a matter of improving the Church but of changing it altogether. Separatists or Independents, for instance, did not want the Prayer Book used in services. Presbyterians wanted a Calvinist-style church with elected elders. Elizabeth, for her part, was sure that the Church of England established in 1559 was the right one for England. In 1589 she told Parliament that she was:

> . . . most fully and firmly settled in her conscience, by the word of God, that the estate and government of this Church of England, as it now standeth in this reformation, may justly be compared to any church which hath been established in any Christian Kingdom since the Apostles' time.

Ireland: 'grant and plant'

There was a serious crisis in Ireland during the final years of Elizabeth's reign. Ireland had been claimed by England since 1155, when Pope Adrian IV granted King Henry II 'overlordship' of the island. This meant that Irish kings and lords were supposed to obey him. But when Henry's barons started the 'Norman Conquest' of Ireland they were not very successful. Ireland was a picturesque wilderness. Its people were 'will o' the wisps' who attacked suddenly and disappeared just as quickly into marshland

Robbery and destruction in sixteenth-century Ireland. A drawing of the time

and forest. English troops often ran out of food and supplies. Only Dublin came under direct English rule. Its defensive wall and ditch, The Pale, gave its name to the whole area. Elsewhere the English ruled by making alliances with Irish chieftains.

In Henry VII's time Irish lords backed the claims of both Lambert Simnel and Perkin Warbeck (see Chapter 7). This did not help Irish relations with the first Tudor. Under Henry VIII matters grew worse. Henry claimed to be King of Ireland, not just overlord. He ignored the fact that the Irish elected their own 'High King'. Then came Henry's Reformation when the Irish monasteries were closed and many holy places destroyed. This offended a Catholic people and made it certain they would never become Protestant. So by Elizabeth's time the Irish had a religious as well as a political quarrel with the English.

In 1577 it was estimated that the English only controlled one twentieth of Ireland. To try to solve the 'problem' the English government set out on a ruthless policy called 'grant and plant'. It involved driving the Irish from their land and giving it to English settlers to farm. The idea was to colonise Ireland, taking it away from the Irish as surely as the Spaniards had taken America from the Aztecs and Incas. Actually, these 'plantations' were difficult to defend against a hostile people. No sooner were the invading troops withdrawn than the Irish began a sort of underground war against the settlers. Every now and again this flared up into a rebellion, with farms burned and settlers murdered.

A crisis arose when Elizabeth's war with Spain encouraged the Irish to join together to throw the English out. After all, was not Spain the champion of the Catholic cause? Would they not help the Irish to get rid of the 'heretics'? In 1595 two important Irish chiefs, O'Neill and O'Donnell, led a full-scale rebellion. At first Elizabeth was reluctant to spend more money on another war. But when O'Neill appealed for Spanish help she sent 17,000 men led by the Earl of Essex – the largest army to leave England in the 16th century.

Fall of Essex

Essex had been Elizabeth's chief favourite since the death of Leicester, his stepfather, in 1588. He was an ambitious, spoilt young man who took full advantage of his high position as a sort of adopted 'son' of the queen. But by the time he left for Ireland his arrogance had annoyed Elizabeth; once when he dared to turn his back on her she boxed his ears! When he failed to defeat O'Neill and signed a truce with the rebel instead, she had him arrested. Released after a short while, he staged a hopeless rebellion and was beheaded (February 1601).

His successor in Ireland was Lord Mountjoy who was rather an unusual general. He wrapped himself in three waistcoats against the cold, slept in the afternoon and dined for hours on end. But he stood bravely with his common soldiers when the enemy appeared and marched his men through thick snow to surprise rebel strongholds. In December 1601 he severely defeated the Irish and their Spanish allies at Kinsale. Two years later the Spaniards had gone home and O'Neill was glad to come to terms. For the first time in its history Ireland was controlled by the English.

The death of Essex made the queen more lonely than ever. Burghley had passed away in 1598. Drake and Hawkins had both died at sea. As her end approached, Elizabeth still refused to name her successor, although everyone knew it must be James VI, son of Mary, Queen of Scots. She also refused to take any medicine or go to bed 'because she had a persuasion that if she once lay down she would never rise'. When her new minister, Sir Robert Cecil (1563–1612), Lord Burghley's son, said she must do so, the old queen murmured, 'The word "must" is not to be used to princes.'

In the end Elizabeth could not speak. A messenger stood at the gates of Richmond Palace, Surrey, waiting to gallop to Scotland with the news of her death. Between two and three o'clock on the morning of 24 March 1603 lights flickered at a window as a signal. The horseman rode away as the last Tudor monarch lay dead.

Sources and questions

1. The English government saw the problem of Ireland as one of civilising a barbarous people. In 1571 one English governor, Sir John Perrot, issued these orders for the people of Munster, an Irish province.

   The inhabitants of cities and towns shall wear no mantles,

shorts, Irish coats, or great shirts, nor allow their hair to grow long . . . but they are to wear gowns, jerkins, and some civil garments; and no maid or single woman shall put any great roll or linen cloth upon their heads, neither any great smock with great sleeves, but they are to put on hats, caps, French hoods . . . or some other civil attire upon their heads . . . .

All bards, rhymers, and common idle men or women within this province making rhymes . . . are to be deprived of their possessions . . . and they are to be put in the stocks, there to remain until they shall promise to leave their wicked way of life.

Source: J. B. Black, The Reign of Elizabeth, 1558–1603, *Oxford University Press, 1959, pages 473–4*

(a) Do you think the governor banned certain clothing because he thought it ugly or unsuitable, or just because it was Irish? Give reasons for your answer.

(b) What sort of stories would rhymers and bards be likely to tell? Why might the English dislike such tales?

(c) Which part of these regulations would be most difficult to enforce? Give reasons for your answer.

(d) What does this source tell us about Anglo-Irish relations?

2.

A portrait painted after Elizabeth's death

(a) Why was this portrait painted?

(b) The figure on the queen's left is Death. Can you guess who the figure on her right is meant to be?
(c) Why is there a sandglass in this picture?
(d) Compare this portrait with the 'Rainbow' portrait on page 112. What different aspects of people's attitudes to her do they illustrate?

3. This is part of Elizabeth's final speech to Parliament in 1601. It is known as the 'Golden Speech'.

> And though God hath raised me so high, yet this I account the glory of my crown, that I have reigned with your loves. . . . I do not so much rejoice that God hath made me a Queen, as to be Queen over so grateful a people. . . . Mr. Speaker, you give me thanks, but I am more to thank you, and I charge you, to thank the House of Commons for me; for, had I not been kept informed by you, I might have fallen into error for lack of true information. When I heard of a possible grievance, I could not rest until I had reformed it. . . . Mr. Speaker, I pray you, that before these gentlemen depart to their counties, you bring them all to kiss my hand.

> *Source*: Somers Tracts (1809), *Vol. I, page 244. Quoted by Millward*, Sixteenth Century Documents, *Hutchinson Educational, 1961, pages 92–3*

(a) What evidence is there in this source of the reason why MPs – and the English people – liked Elizabeth?
(b) What part of this source is not strictly true regarding Elizabeth and her Parliaments?
(c) What parts of this source explain the Speaker's role in a Tudor Parliament?
(d) What other parts of the country, besides counties, were represented in Parliament?

KING AND PARLIAMENT

'THE WISEST FOOL': JAMES I 1603–25

James I

Robert Carey was the messenger who left Richmond to tell the King of Scotland the news. He rode the 640 kilometres to Edinburgh, the Scottish capital, in 60 hours, arriving 'tired and sore, be-blooded with great falls and bruises'. James was delighted to become King of England. He asked Carey if he had letters from the English royal council. Carey said no, but showed the king a ring which James had once given Elizabeth as proof that she was dead.

The first Stuart king of England was neither heroic nor attractive. He was small and plump, with thin legs, rolling eyes and an over-large tongue. He suffered from piles, catarrh, diarrhoea and a blood disease called porphyria. All these ailments made him seem older than his thirty-seven years. Some people thought he was a coward because he wore extra padding in case anybody tried to stab him. Yet no man rode more boldly at the Scots king's favourite sport, hunting.

James had been king of Scotland for most of his life owing to his mother's flight and imprisonment (see Chapter 14). His childhood had been lonely and unhappy – left without parents, beaten by his teachers, bullied by lords who struggled for power and clergymen who wanted to rule the country through their General Assembly. Slowly, more by cunning than force, James got the better of both lords and priests. It was centuries since Scotland had been as well-governed as it was by James.

James was very well educated. He was an expert on the Bible, and had written books on monarchy, witchcraft, sport and smoking. Here he is condemning the new-fangled habit of smoking in his book, *A Counterblast to Tobacco*, written in 1604:

A custom loathsome to the eye, hateful to the nose, harmful to the brain, dangerous to the lungs, and in the black, stinking fume thereof, nearest resembling the horrible . . . smoke of the pit that is bottomless . . . .

It was easy to laugh at James and many people did find him funny. He was called the 'Wisest Fool in Christendom', meaning that he was clever in academic subjects but had no common sense. This was not fair. James had many faults. He was lazy, conceited and a bore. But he was generally kind, often witty, sometimes tolerant and always peace-loving.

Conference at Hampton Court

Puritans in the Church of England felt hopeful when James became king. Elizabeth, as we have seen, refused to change Church of England ceremonies and beliefs. Perhaps a monarch brought up as a Calvinist would be more helpful? This is what a number of puritan clergymen hoped when they met James at Hampton Court Palace in 1604.

James was pleased at the opportunity this conference gave him to show off his biblical knowledge. He knew all about the religious quarrels of the old queen's reign, and his beliefs were nearer to those of Elizabeth than to the puritans. Of course, in those days the word 'puritan' covered many different opinions and beliefs. Sometimes it was used to describe anybody who protested at an injustice or felt sorry for the poor. When referring to religion, it could mean all sorts of people from extremists who wanted to abolish the church to those who wanted merely to 'purify' it of certain 'popish', that is, Catholic customs.

On his way from Scotland to London in 1603 James had been presented with the so-called Millenary Petition. It got this name because it was said to have been signed by a thousand clergymen (*mille* is the Latin word for thousand). The petition asked for a number of minor changes in the Church. For example, it wanted clergymen to be allowed to marry. It also suggested purging the Church of such 'popish' customs as using the ring in the marriage ceremony and making the sign of the cross. James had enjoyed reading the petition. Unlike Elizabeth, he believed there were ways in which the Church of England could be changed for the better.

All went well until a Dr Reynolds mentioned the word 'Presbytery'. This brought to the surface James's intense dislike of the Scottish Presbyterian Church which had annoyed him so much when he was a young king. A Scottish Presbytery, he told the conference,

as well agreeth with a monarchy as God with the devil. Then Jack and Tom and Will and Dick shall meet and at their pleasure censure [*criticize*] me and my council and all our proceedings. Then Will shall stand up and say, it must be thus; then Dick shall reply and say, nay . . . but we will have it thus. No bishop, no King, as before I said . . . .

In other words, James's objections to this kind of church were

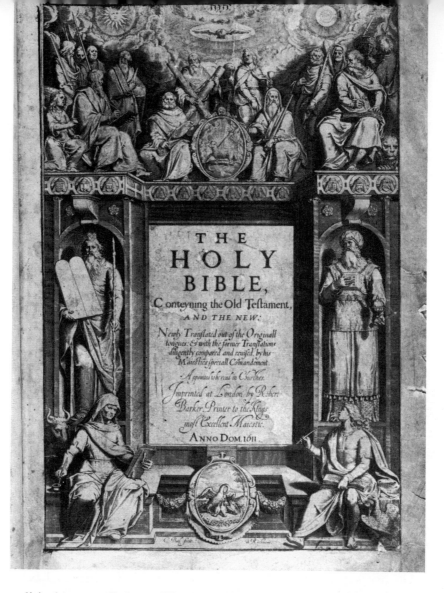

The title page of the 'Authorised Version' of the bible

political, not religious. He was not prepared to be told what to do by clergymen, and his famous slogan, 'No bishop, no King', meant that he believed that the next step after abolishing bishops would be to abolish the monarchy.

Extreme puritans felt that if they could not change the Church they would have to leave it. Unfortunately for them, this was a crime under English law. James knew this and said, 'I shall make them conform themselves, or I will harry [*drive*] them out of the land'. In later years many puritans did leave England, going first to Holland and then on to America.

One long-term result of the Conference was a new translation of the Bible into English. It was called the 'Authorised Version' because James approved of it. This Bible was published in 1611. No book printed in the English language has been more influential or popular.

Parliament and money

The Hampton Court Conference showed that James did not always see eye to eye with his clergy. But such disagreements were nothing compared with his heated arguments with Parliament. The root cause of the trouble was money.

James needed more money than Elizabeth to run the country. His income was less than in Tudor times, prices were still rising and, unlike the queen, he had a wife and a family to support. To make matters worse, however, James was very extravagant; as he once admitted, 'My heart is greater than my rent'. James showered money and gifts on his wife and children, his courtiers, favourites and servants. For example, whereas Elizabeth had spent £9,535 a year on the royal household, James spent £36,000!

On the other hand, Parliament often kept him short of money in order to force him to do what it wanted. In 1610 James suggested that all his income from rents, fees and dues should be turned into a regular annual payment of £200,000. This plan was called the Great Contract. It was what happened later in the century but in 1610 members of Parliament eventually turned it down because their constituents thought it was too much. So James had to depend on non-parliamentary ways of raising money.

The most famous of James's schemes was the creation of a new honour, baronet. Like the title baron, this entitled a man to put 'Sir' in front of his name and have a coat-of-arms. James decided that this 'honour' could be bought for a fee which was originally set at £1,000 but which was reduced as the years went by. A more important source of income was the selling of monopolies. A monopoly gave the person who bought it the sole right to make, buy or sell a certain article or commodity. Traders and customers disliked this system because it put up the price.

Monopolies were not new. Elizabeth had sold them. James knew they were unpopular and said he was against them. Yet in twenty years he granted another 108, whereas only 100 had been sold during the previous fifty years. By 1621 the prices of 700 articles were said to be higher because of this system. Most well-to-do families were affected. English people lived in houses built of monopoly bricks and heated by monopoly coal. They ate monopoly butter, currants and herrings, smoked monopoly tobacco and played with monopoly dice. Ladies travelled in monopoly coaches pulled by horses fed on monopoly hay. Men's breeches were held up by monopoly belts and buttons. Even mice were caught in monopoly mousetraps.

James inherited many financial problems from Elizabeth but he made them worse by his extravagance. Parliament deliberately kept him short and when he invented his own taxes they protested. James once remarked that he would have been a happy king if it had not been for money shortages. This was probably true.

Divine right

Most seventeenth-century men and women believed a monarch was chosen, or at least favoured, by God. They also thought that rule by one person was the best way to govern a country. But in England at least, a monarch was expected to take the advice of his Lords and Commons. James did not do this very often. He preferred to take the advice of favourites whom the Commons disliked. His first choice, Robert Carr (or Ker), Earl of Somerset, had to retire when convicted of murder. His second, George Villiers, Duke of Buckingham, attracted the king because of his good looks, dark hair and blue eyes which reminded James of a painting of St Stephen. James called him 'Steenie' for this reason.

Such choices showed how little James cared for his Parliament's opinions. His long rule in Scotland, where conditions were very different from England, had made him think he was an expert on monarchy. In 1598 he had written a book called *True Law of Free Monarchies*. In this book he made remarkable claims about a king's powers. These theories caused a stir when he came to England. 'The state of monarchy,' he told Parliament in 1610, 'is the supreme thing upon earth . . . . As to dispute what God may do is blasphemy, so it is treason in subjects to dispute what a King may do.' This idea became known as the Divine Right of Kings.

Many loyal men and women were worried about Divine Right. It seemed to suggest that a king could do no wrong. Of course, an English monarch was above the law in one sense; there was no way he could be legally tried for an offence. Nevertheless, most English kings and queens had been careful not to defy the law openly. James broke no more laws than the Tudors. He certainly never behaved with the ruthless arrogance of Henry VIII. But he talked more than the Tudors had done about his rights. 'A good king will frame his actions according to the law, yet he is not bound thereto', he announced. This privilege, known as the Royal Prerogative, meant that a monarch had the right to set aside a law in a particular case. The Tudors had done this but they had not talked about it so much as James!

James was king of two countries, England and Scotland. This union of the crowns, as it was called, led him to hope that they would eventually merge as one state, Britain. English people took a different view. The Scots were their traditional enemies. To them James was a foreigner who might introduce Scottish laws into England. This distrust led them to go to their law books to find an answer to Divine Right. As the years went by, members of Parliament talked about 'the common laws of the realm' as though these, too, had been chosen by God! They demanded that their assembly should have the same rights of free speech as their talkative monarch. The stage was set for a showdown in the next reign.

Sources and questions

1. In 1584 a Frenchman named Fontenoy wrote this to Mary, Queen of Scots's secretary. He was referring to James, her son, who was then eighteen years old and King of Scotland.

   I have noticed in him three defects that may handicap his government . . .: he does not estimate correctly his poverty and unimportance as king of Scotland but is over-confident and scornful of other princes; his love for favourites is not hidden and takes no account of the wishes of his people; he is too lazy and indifferent about political affairs, too fond of pleasure, and allows all business to be conducted by others. Such things are excusable at his age yet I fear they may become a habit.

Source: Quoted by D. Willson, James VI and I, Jonathan Cape, 1956

(a) Why might Mary value the opinion of a Frenchman?

(b) Why were people so interested in the characters of kings and queens in those days?

(c) Can you think of aspects of James's character not mentioned by Fontenoy? Do you think Fontenoy was fair to the Scots' king?

(d) What part of this source became irrelevant later in James's life?

(e) Which defect of the young James do you think most serious in a king?

2. Anthony Weldon wrote a book called *Character of James I*. Here is a well known passage from that book.

He [*James*] was naturally timid, which was the reason he wore quilted doublets . . . his eyes were large, ever rolling at any stranger that came into his presence . . . his beard was very thin; his tongue too large for his mouth. . . . He was very witty, and had as many . . . witty jests as any man living, at which he would not smile himself, but speak them in a grave and serious manner. . . . He was very crafty in petty things . . . so much so that wise men would say they believed him the wisest fool in Christendom, meaning him wise in small things, but a fool in important affairs. . . . He was peaceful, but more out of fear than conscience.

Source: Quoted by Houston, James I, Longman Seminar Studies, 1973

(a) In what ways did James's characteristics, mentioned in the last two sentences of this source, affect his conduct as king of England?

(b) Weldon called his book *Character of James I*. What parts of this source are not about his character at all?

(c) Do you think Weldon knew James well? Do you think he liked him? Give reasons for your answer.

(d) To judge from this source, what side of James's character had really impressed Weldon?

3. Imagine you are King James I. Write a letter to your son, Charles, warning him of the problems he might encounter with Parliament and suggesting ways of dealing with them.

TREASON AND PLOT

At the beginning of his reign James promised to abolish the heavy fines paid by Catholics for not going to church on Sundays. When he was told that this money was needed to reward courtiers he changed his mind. Most Catholics accepted this, knowing that to fight back would only make matters worse. Then, in November 1605, the country was horrified to learn of a Catholic plot to kill both king and Parliament.

The official story of the plot is contained in the *King's Book*. It is called this because James is supposed to have written it. In fact, he did not write it, but he read it very carefully and made changes here and there. According to the *Book*, in 1604 a desperate group of Catholics, led by Robert Catesby, Thomas Percy and Thomas Winter, decided to blow up the king and lords when they met for the state opening of Parliament. Thomas Winter's confession, written in the Tower of London, says this:

> He [*Catesby*] said that he had bethought him of a way at one instant to deliver us from all our bonds, and without any foreign help to replant the Catholic religion; and withal told me in a word, it was to blow up the Parliament-house with gunpowder; for said he, in that place have they done us all mischief, and perchance God hath designed that place for their punishment.

It seems likely the conspirators planned to seize the royal children, make James's younger son Charles king, and overthrow the government. If so it was a crazy scheme, worked out by men already known to the government as troublemakers.

Tunnel and cellar

The plotters tried to tunnel under the House of Lords from a house just outside the walls of Westminster Palace. The going was slow and difficult, and came to a stop when they reached the 3-metre-thick foundations of the building itself. Percy then rented a cellar under the House of Lords chamber and hid thirty-six barrels of gunpowder there. Here is how Guy Fawkes explained the change of plan in his confession:

. . . it was about Christmas [*1604*], when we brought our mine [*tunnel*] unto the wall, and about Candlemas [*2 February 1605*] we had wrought the wall half through; and whilst they were working I stood as sentinel [*guard*] . . . . As they were walking upon the wall, they heard a rushing in the cellar, of removing of coals; whereupon we feared we had been discovered, and they sent me to the cellar, who finding that the coles [*coals*] were a selling, and that the cellar was to let . . . . Percy went and hired the same for a yearly rent.

With this job done, the plotters lay low in the country, waiting for the opening of Parliament in November. For seven months, according to the *King's Book*, the gunpowder lay undiscovered under piles of firewood. In October a new conspirator, Francis Tresham, joined the gang. He offered to help with money on condition he could stop his brother-in-law, Lord Monteagle, from going to Parliament on the fatal day. The plotters agreed to Tresham's request and so he sent an unsigned letter to Monteagle.

The gunpowder plotters

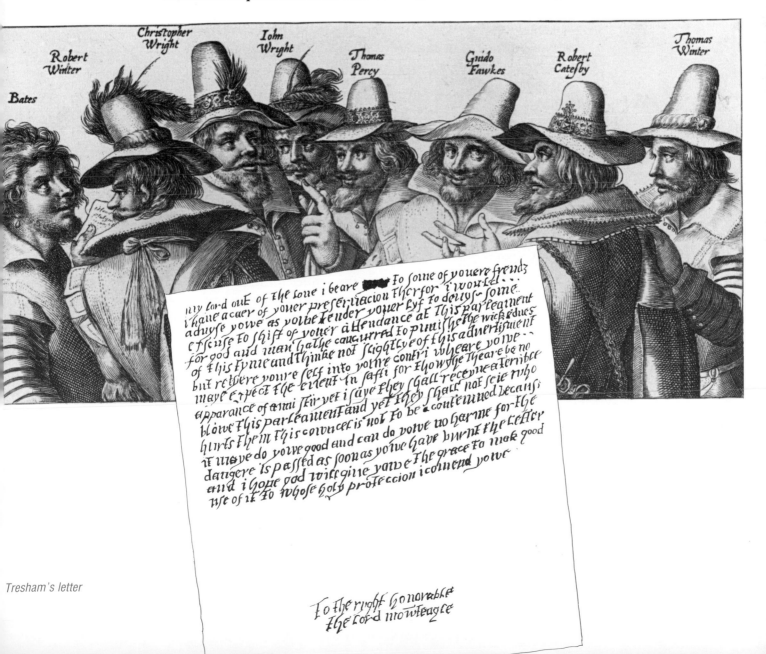

Tresham's letter

It was delivered as the lord sat at dinner with friends in London. Rather strangely, his lordship told a servant to read it aloud.

Among several sinister sentences came this, 'I say they shall receive a terrible blow this Parliament and yet they shall not see who hurts them'. Monteagle was puzzled. Later he passed the letter on to Sir Robert Cecil, the king's chief minister. When James saw the letter he decided that 'the terrible blow' which the Commons would not see meant gunpowder. Afterwards he claimed that God guided him to this conclusion.

The king's questions

Just before midnight on 4 November 1605 guards arrested Guy Fawkes as he came to hide in the cellar. Fawkes was a Yorkshire Catholic who had served as a soldier with the Spanish army in the Netherlands. He had been brought in because he was an expert on explosives. Fawkes said his name was 'Johnson', a servant of Mr Percy.

James was very curious about 'Mr Johnson'. In a letter dated 6 November he told his Privy Council to question him very closely, and suggested these sorts of questions:

> Ask what he is (for I can never yet hear of any man that knows him).
> Where was he born?
> Where hath he lived?
> How hath he lived and by what trade of life?
> How he received those wounds in the breast?
> How he came in Percy's service, by what means and at what time?
> If he were ever a papist, and if so who brought him up in it?

Finally, James added this grim postscript:

> If he will not otherwise confess, the gentler tortures are to be first used unto him, et sic per gradus af ima tenditur [*and so by degrees until the ultimate is reached*]. And so God speed your good work.

It seems probable that Cecil could have answered one or two of the king's questions. Certainly he knew far more about the plot than he would admit. For example, although Guy Fawkes was horribly tortured he did not tell on his friends until 9 November. Yet a warrant for their arrest, naming nine of them, was issued two days before.

Cecil also seemed to know where the plotters were because on 8 November armed men surrounded them at their hideout, Holbeache House in Staffordshire. There was a fierce fight. Catesby and Percy were killed by the same bullet. The man who fired the shot was given a pension of two shillings a day for life, a large sum for those days. Sir Thomas Lawley, who commanded some of the king's men during the battle, wrote this afterwards:

> Upon the 8th day of the present month [*November*], I . . . did

attend Mr Sheriff of Worcestershire into a place called Holbeach, and there did my best endeavour for the apprehending [*capturing*] of the Traitors there assembled, one of my servants being the first man that entered upon them, and took Thomas Winter alive, and brought him unto me . . . and thereupon hasted to revive Catesby, Percy and the two Wrights, who lay deadly wounded on the ground, thinking by the recovery of them to have done his Majesty better service than by suffering them to die. But such was the extreme disorder . . . that, while I with my men took up one of the languishing traitors, the rude people stripped the rest naked; their wounds being many and grevious, and no surgeon at hand, they became incurable, and so died.

Of the thirteen conspirators, eight survived to be brought to London for trial and execution. A committee was set up to suggest a special punishment for them. Eventually it was decided that hanging, drawing and quartering was fearful enough. The convicted men were executed in this way in January 1606.

Unanswered questions

There are lots of questions to be asked about the Gunpowder Plot.

The execution of the plotters from a drawing published in 1795

If a tunnel was dug, why was it never shown to anybody? How did the plotters obtain such a large amount of gunpowder? Why was the cellar rented in the name of Percy, a discontented Catholic known to Cecil and his spies? Were Catesby and Percy killed because they were in the pay of the government? Some historians have even suggested that Percy and Cecil thought up the plot and then Cecil double-crossed Percy! Above all, how much did Cecil know about the plot before he received the letter?

The letter remains at the heart of the mystery. Did Tresham write it, or was it forged by Cecil to give him an excuse to 'find out' about a plot he had already discovered? Almost everybody agrees that the handwriting is disguised. Some think Cecil wrote it. Others claim that Anne Vaux, a Catholic and friend of the conspirators, wrote it to Tresham's dictation. What was its real purpose? Tresham, of course, may have meant to force his friends to give up a hopeless plan. It is possible that Tresham was in the pay of the government. He was never brought to trial but died in prison soon afterwards. Monteagle, too, seems to have known more about the plot than he ever admitted.

It was 1859 before a special 'Gunpowder Treason Service', thanking God for James's safe deliverance, was taken out of the Church of England Prayer Book. It took almost as long for the hatred of Catholics inspired by the plot to die out in Protestant England. Some Catholic historians claim that Cecil invented the plot and tortured and hanged innocent men, just to make Catholics unpopular. If he did he was very successful.

Guy Fawkes's lantern

James the peaceful

James was a peace-loving monarch. He stopped the war with Spain and refused to join in European religious struggles. Even when Frederick of Bohemia, husband of his daughter Elizabeth, was deprived of his crown by Catholic armies, James ignored Parliament's demand for a Protestant 'crusade'. His usual excuse was lack of money. 'A King of England has no reason but to decline a war', he once said. 'The sword is in his hand; the purse is his subjects.' In fact, his puritan Parliaments might have granted a war tax. The real reason for the King's inaction was his love of peace.

When James died on 27 March 1625 he had been pushed into war with Spain by his son Charles, and by Buckingham. Even so, it was true to say of the 'Wisest Fool' that 'he lived in peace . . . and left all his kingdom in a peaceable condition'.

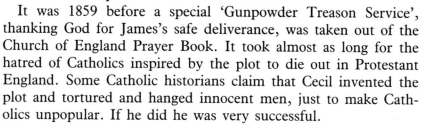

Sources and questions

1. On 9 November 1605 Sir Robert Cecil, the King's chief minister, sent this letter to Sir Charles Cornwallis, ambassador to Spain.

It hath pleased Almighty God out of his goodness to bring to light the most cruel and detestable conspiracy against His Majesty and the whole state of this realm . . . . [T]here was intended not only the extirpation [*wiping out*] of the King and his children, but the downfall of this country. . . . The means to have carried out this great act was by secretly carrying a great quantity of gunpowder to a vault under the House of Lords's chamber, and so to have blown up all . . . . [T]he principal undertaker of it was one Johnson [*actually Guy Fawkes*].

It remaineth that I add something of how this matter came to be discovered. About 8 days before Parliament met the Lord Monteagle received a letter . . . without name or date, and in a hand disguised; whereof I send you a copy. . . . I showed the letter to the Earl of Suffolk to ask his opinion; whereupon, carefully reading it, and observing the words (that the blow should come without knowledge who hurt them) we both decided that the plot could be done with powder.

Source: The King's Book

(a) Why should Cecil have been anxious to explain the government's story to the Spanish? What might they have thought about this plot?

(b) Although Catesby and Percy were known to the authorities, Guy Fawkes's identity seems to have puzzled both the King and Cecil; Cecil still refers to him as 'Johnson' five days after his arrest. Why was this?

(c) How could Cecil and Suffolk know the handwriting of Tresham's letter was disguised?

(d) What did Cecil mean by 'the downfall of this country'?

2. Although this is always known as Tresham's letter, it was probably dictated by him and written by Anne Vaux, a keen Catholic and friend of some of the conspirators. The idea may have been to prevent his handwriting being recognised.

. . . my lord [*Monteagle*] out of the love I bear to some of your friends I have a care of your preservation therefore I would advise you as you value your life to make some excuse not to attend this Parliament, for God and man hath decided to punish the wickedness of this time. Think not lightly of this warning, but retire yourself into the country where you may expect the event in safety for though there be no appearence of any stir yet I say Parliament shall receive a terrible blow and yet they shall not see who hurts them.

(a) What to the plotters was 'the wickedness of the time'?

(b) Compare the first paragraph of Source 1 with Source 2. What details in Cecil's letter are not in Tresham's warning? How do you think Cecil knew these extra details?

(c) Three reasons have been suggested for Tresham sending such a letter. They are,

 (i) To save a friend from injury or death.
 (ii) To force the conspirators to abandon the plot.
 (iii) To betray the conspirators.

Which do you think the most likely explanation? Give reasons for your answer.

3. (a) Do you think the artist had ever seen the conspirators when he drew the picture on page 173? Give reasons for your answer.

(b) Explain why the artist could not have seen Catesby and Percy with the other plotters.

(c) How does the artist indicate that Bates was a less important person than the other conspirators?

(d) Which is most likely? That this was drawn

 (i) To show people what the conspirators looked like?
 (ii) To tell people something about the plot.
 (iii) To stir up hatred and fear about the Gunpowder Plot.

Give reasons for your answer.

4. For many years effigies of the pope, not Guy Fawkes, were burnt on 5 November. Why was this? Can you think why the pope is not 'burnt' these days?

5. Make up a play about the Gunpowder Plot. It could be in four scenes: the digging of the tunnel; the renting of the cellar; Monteagle receiving the letter and going to Cecil; and the arrest of Fawkes and fight at Holbeache.

Bonfire night celebrations at Lewes, Sussex

THE MARTYR KING: CHARLES I 1625–49

Petitions and prayer books

Charles I, who succeeded to the English and Scottish thrones, was the youngest son of James I; his elder brother Henry had died in 1612. At the time of his accession he was rather immature for his age, a quiet, shy young man who stuttered if he grew excited. Charles was not a scholar like James but he was a more refined man than his father. The behaviour at James's court had been undignified and disgusting. Women and men lay sick and drunk on the floor; food was thrown at meals; silly practical jokes, such as putting frogs in beds, were popular. During a visit to Madrid in 1623 Charles had admired the strict rules, exact timetables and elaborate ceremony of the Spanish court. The solemn, rather humourless young king decided to copy such customs.

The court was typical of the man. Charles made few friends and surrounded himself with a web of etiquette (good manners) which kept courtiers as well as crowds at a distance. On the other hand, the Caroline court (from Carolus, the Latin for Charles) became a meeting place for artists, poets, painters and musicians. Charles founded the Royal Art Collection, buying nearly 1,000 pictures during his reign. He also invited famous artists like Rubens and Van Dyck to work in England. Skilled architects were employed to build palaces and houses, writers were encouraged to produce plays for his court and he even hired a private orchestra.

The Caroline court had one big disadvantage – it cut the king off from his people. Unlike his father, Charles had a sheltered and pleasant upbringing. He had never been beaten, insulted or threatened. Charles rarely travelled and was unaware of many changes taking place in England. For most of his reign he lived in a dream world – a fairy prince in a fairy palace.

Charles I, painted by Anthony Van Dyck, a favourite court painter

The Petition of Right

James is supposed to have told his son, 'You will live to have your bellyfull of Parliaments.' If so, these were wise, prophetic words. From the start Charles acted and talked as though he was unaware of the growing power of Parliament. In 1626 he told the assembled Lords and Commons:

> I think it is more honour for a king to be invaded and almost destroyed by a foreign enemy, than to be destroyed by his own subjects. Remember that Parliaments are altogether in my power for their calling, sitting and dissolution; therefore as I find the fruits of them Good or Evil, they are to continue or not to be.

It is not surprising that his reign began badly. There were several reasons for this. One of his father's last acts had been to arrange for him to marry Henrietta Maria, daughter of Henry IV of France. Henrietta certainly brought elegance and beauty to the English court. Unfortunately, this Catholic girl also brought a host of French priests and advisers who encouraged her not to attend Charles's Protestant coronation.

An unpopular queen was only one of Charles's problems. His close friendship with the Duke of Buckingham disappointed those who had hoped to be rid of James's hated favourite. Parliament, in particular, showed its attitude to Buckingham quite early in the reign. When Charles suggested an expedition against Cadiz as part of the war with Spain, the members lost interest when Buckingham was appointed to command it. When the attack failed the Commons blamed him for the disaster, even though he had actually taken no part in it. In Charles's second Parliament a leading member, Sir John Eliot, declared: 'Our honour is ruined, our ships are sunk, our men perished, not by an enemy . . . but by those we trust.' This was a clear reference to Buckingham. Charles was furious. Eliot was arrested, only to be released because MPs refused to carry on their work without him. In the Lords there were suggestions that Buckingham should be charged with treason.

It seemed that Buckingham might suffer the fate of several of Henry VIII's ministers so the king hurriedly dissolved Parliament to save his friend. Later he raised money for an expedition to help the Huguenots (Protestants) of La Rochelle, France, in their battle with the French Catholic government (1627–8). This money was raised without Parliament's assistance and again the commander was Buckingham. Although the Duke did in fact fight bravely at La Rochelle, the attack was a failure.

When Buckingham came home he told Charles that he could persuade the Commons to finance yet another expedition to save the French Protestants. So Charles called a third Parliament. This assembly's first action was to refuse any money until their complaints were heard. To show the Commons meant business, Eliot and another parliamentary leader, Sir Thomas Wentworth, produced the Petition of Right (1628).

This important document contained demands that taxes collected without Parliament's permission and imprisonment without trial should be illegal. Other clauses condemned the custom of lodging troops in private houses and forcing civilians to obey military law. These grievances had arisen because of the bad behaviour of soldiers in England during the Cadiz and La Rochelle campaigns. Charles accepted the petition, probably for

A humble petition and protest from clergymen to the king in 1642. The names refer to their bishoprics, i.e. 'Godfr. Glouc.' is the bishop of Gloucester. Archbishops and bishops still sign letters in this way

To the Kings moft Excellent Majefty, and the Lords and Peeres now affembled in Parliament.

The humble Petition and Proteftation of all the Bifhops and Prelates now called by his Majefties Writts to attend the Parliament, and prefent about London and Weftminifter, for that Service.

That whereas the Petitioners are called up by feverall and refpective Writs, and under great penalties, to attend in Parliament, and have a cleer and undubitate Right to Vote in Bills, and other matters whatfoever, debateable in Parliament, by the ancient Cuftomes, Laws, and Statutes of this Realm, and ought to be protected by your Majefty, quietly to attend and profecute that great Service.

They humbly remonftrate and proteft before God, your Majefty, and the Noble Lords and Peers now affembled in Parliament, That as they have an indubitate Right to fit and Vote in the Houfe of the Lords, fo are they (if they may be protected from force and violence) moft ready and willing to perform their Duties accordingly. And that they do abhominate all Actions or Opinions, tending to Popery, and the maintenance thereof; as alfo, all propenfion and inclination to any malignant party, or any other fide or party whatfoever, to the which their own Reafons and Confciences fhall not move them to adhere.

But whereas they have been at feverall times violently Menaced, Affronted, and Affaulted, by multitudes of people, in their coming to perform their Services in that Honorable Houfe; and lately chafed away, and put in danger of their lives, and can finde no redreffe or protection, upon fundry complaints made to both Houfes in thefe particulars.

They likewife humbly proteft before your Majefty, and the Noble Houfe of Peers, That faving unto themfelves all their Rights and Interefts of Sitting and Voting in that Houfe at other times, they dare not Sit or Vote in the Houfe of Peers, untill your Majefty fhall further fecure them from all Affronts, Indignities and dangers in the premiffes.

Laftly, Whereas their fears are not built upon Phantafies and Conceipts, but upon fuch Grounds and Objects, as may well terrifie men of good Refolutions, and much Conftancy. They do in all duty and humility proteft before your Majefty, and the Peers of that moft Honorable Houfe of Parliament, againft all Laws, Orders, Votes, Refolutions, and determinations, as in themfelves Null, and of none effect; which in their abfence, fince the 27 of this inftant Month of *December*, 1641. have already paffed; as likewife againft all fuch as fhall hereafter paffe in that moft Honorable Houfe, during the time of this their forced and violent abfence from the faid moft Honorable Houfe; not denying, but if their abfenting of themfelves were wilfull and voluntary, that moft Honorable Houfe might proceed in all thefe premiffes, their abfence, or this their Proteftation notwithftanding.

And humbly befeeching your moft Excellent Majefty to command the Clerk of that Houfe of Peers, to enter this their Petition and Proteftation amongft his Records.

They will ever pray to God to bleffe and preferve, &c.

Jo. Eborac.	Geo. Hereford.
Thomas, Durefme.	Rob. Oxon.
Robt. Co. Lich.	Ma. Ely.
Jof. Norwich.	Godfr. Glouc.
Jo. Afaphen.	Jo. Peterburg.
Guil. Ba. & Wells.	Mor. Llandaff.

Vera Copia. Jo Browne *Cleric. Parliament.*

London, Printed for *Jofeph Hunfcutt.* 1642.

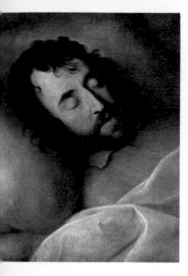

The murdered Buckingham. Van Dyck is said to have painted it

Buckingham's sake. It made little difference. Wentworth was satisfied but Eliot continued to attack the king's favourite.

The problem of Buckingham was solved in a tragic way. In August, 1628, John Felton, an army officer, stabbed and killed the Duke as he was coming out of his lodgings in Portsmouth. Charles was horrified at the death of his only friend. Even Felton felt sorry for what he had done. But the Lords and Commons were delighted and Londoners blessed Felton as he went to execution. As the gulf between monarch and people widened, the lonely king turned to his French wife for comfort and advice.

Laud and the puritans

A defiant Commons now started to criticise the king's Church policy. Charles was the first English king to be brought up in the Church of England. Whereas previous monarchs had upheld this Church for political reasons, Charles loved it as the one true way to salvation. Consequently he could never understand or tolerate anybody who wanted it changed. In his opinion, all complaints about the Prayer Book, all moves towards Presbyterian organis-ation, had to be crushed. Like Mary Tudor, it was his misfortune to rule many deeply religious men and women who disagreed with him.

After Buckingham's death, Eliot's chief complaint concerned the activities of William Laud, an important priest who later became Archbishop of Canterbury. Laud loved Church of England ceremonies as much as his master. He called puritanism 'the root of all rebellion . . . and sauciness in the country'. Laud believed bishops were chosen by God, and that even minor clergy were a superior breed of person. This enraged well-born puritans who despised Laud because he was a tradesman's son. They reacted by accusing Laud and the king of being secret Catholics who planned a return to 'popery'.

Charles told the Commons that religion was none of its busi-ness. As a sincere believer in Divine Right, he saw himself as the 'father' of his people and guardian of their Church. Eliot and his colleagues were not prepared to give way. They refused to grant the king any custom duties until he considered their criticisms. Charles decided to dismiss such a troublesome Parliament. He sent a messenger to the Commons' debating chamber with the news. There were shouts of 'No! No!' from the members and when the Speaker tried to leave the room he was held in his chair by force. One MP even locked the door and put the key in his pocket.

During the tense debate which followed, illegal taxation, imprisonment without trial and Church policy were again attacked. Anybody who disagreed with Parliament was condemned as 'a betrayer of the liberties of England'. Only after such open defiance, did the members unlock the door and go home. Eliot was put in prison by the king, and when he died there in 1632, he was regarded as a martyr. No Parliament met in England for the next eleven years.

Eleven years' tyranny

The years 1629 to 1640 were generally prosperous and peaceful. Charles had promised every man 'great peace and quietness' and to a certain extent he kept his word. His enemies, however, later called this period the Eleven Years' Tyranny.

There were many reasons for their dissatisfaction. Charles ruled without consulting his wealthy subjects. His government interfered with trading, starting new companies, disbanding old ones, seizing investors' savings, ordering merchants to do this and that. Besides raising most of the unpopular taxes used by his father, Charles solved his financial problems by extending Ship Money (a tax paid by ports for the upkeep of the navy) to inland towns (1635). This led to a famous court case when John Hampden of Buckinghamshire refused to pay. Although Hampden eventually lost the case, it aroused so much interest that the king's enemies were able to use it as propaganda against him.

Meanwhile, Laud continued his reorganisation of the Church. Much of his work was necessary and good. Dirty, neglected churches without windows and doors were common in those days. So were clergymen who avoided their duties, cut up clerical robes for towels and allowed parishioners to carry off gravestones to make walls. Laud stopped such behaviour when he could, insisting on hard-working priests, reverent services and well-ordered churches. At the same time, however, he punished puritans who wore the wrong robes, preached without permission or altered the wording of the Prayer Book.

Those who criticised Laud's policies were severely punished. In 1637 three puritans, William Prynne, Henry Burton and John Bastwick were sentenced to life imprisonment, a heavy fine and loss of their ears. Such punishments were frequent for common people but these were 'gentlemen'; this was unusual and shocked people of all classes. When the time came for them to suffer the penalty, Londoners laid sweet herbs in their path and gave them cups of wine. It was an impressive demonstration of how unpopular Laud's Church had become.

Revolt in Scotland

On 28 July 1637 English-style Prayer Books were issued to worshippers in St Giles Cathedral, Edinburgh, as part of Charles's scheme to enforce his religion north of the border. The Presbyterian congregation was well-prepared as the plan was no secret. They staged a riot. Bibles and folding stools were thrown at the bishop and his clergy. Crowds outside pelted the windows with stones and rubbish. The Prayer Book revolt had begun.

The St Giles riot was the signal to rouse Calvinist Scotland. There was similar uproar in many Scottish towns and villages. All over the south of Scotland men rushed to sign a National Covenant, promising to defend their Presbyterian Church 'against contrary errors and corruption'. Quite soon they numbered a large

The Prayer Book riot in St Giles

army, commanded by Alexander Leslie, a veteran of foreign wars. Happy preachers called this revolt 'the great marriage day of this nation with God'. A military expert told the king he would need 40,000 men to force the Prayer Book on a Presbyterian people.

When the king decided to fight he found that English puritans were unwilling to crush puritanism in Scotland. He formed a badly disciplined, poorly paid army which was forced back across the border by the Covenanters. Then came another surprise for him. When he called Parliament in April 1640, he expected they would raise money to fight the Scots. It showed he did not understand the bitterness roused by his 'personal rule' of eleven years. Parliament listened to John Pym, a lawyer, who spent two hours attacking the king's government. They refused to grant a war tax until Charles listened to their grievances.

The king was faced by puritan enemies in London, and a Presbyterian army of Scots poised to invade England. He dismissed his 'Short Parliament' but the Scots' army crossed the border, occupied the northern English counties, and demanded that Charles should pay their costs of £850 a day. The king had no choice but to summon another Parliament. The so-called 'Long Parliament' met in November 1640. It sat for thirteen years and destroyed his life's work.

Sources and questions

1. The historic events in St Giles's cathedral, Edinburgh on 23 July 1637 were described many years later in these two accounts.

   (a) On the Sunday morning appointed for the work, the chancellor of Scotland, and others . . . being present in the cathedral church, the dean began to read the liturgy [*prayers from Prayer Book*], which no sooner started, but a noise and clamour was raised throughout the church, that no words could be heard distinctly, and then a shower of stones, and sticks and cudgels were thrown at the dean's head. The bishop went into the pulpit, and reminded them of the sacredness of the place, of their duty to God and King; but he found no reverence, nor was the clamour and disorder less than before.

   Source: Clarendon, History of the Rebellion, *Oxford University Press, 1888*

   (b) No sooner was the [Prayer] Book opened by the dean of Edinburgh, than a number of the meaner sort, with clapping of their hands and outcries, made a great uproar; and one of them, called Jane or Janet Gaddis . . . flung a little folding stool, whereon she sat, at the Dean's head, saying, 'Out thou false thief! dost thou say the mass at my lug [ear]?' which was followed with a great noise.

   Sources: Phillips, Baker's Chronicle, *London, 1670. Quoted by T. Carlyle*, Oliver Cromwell

   (a) Both writers disapprove of the protest but which account do you think is the more hostile? Give reasons for your answer.
   (b) What evidence is there in (a) and (b) that the riot was carefully planned?
   (c) What did Janet Gaddis mean by calling the new liturgy a 'mass'?
   (d) Why were so many Scots against the Church of England forms of worship? What form of worship did they prefer?

2. This account of Prynne, Bastwick and Burton being punished comes from a *Book of Days* by R. Chambers. It was not published until 1863.

   In the palace-yard [*Westminster, London*] two pillories were erected, and there the sentence of the Star Chamber against Burton, Bastwick and Prynne was executed. They stood for two hours in the pillory. The place was full of people, who cried and howled terribly, especially when Burton was cropped. Dr. Bastwick was very merry; his wife got on a stool and kissed him. His ears being cut off, she asked for them, put them in a clean handkerchief, and carried them away with her . . . .

Source: Chamber, Book of Days. *Quoted by Millward,* Sixteenth Century Documents, *Hutchinson Educational, 1961*

(a) From the evidence of this source, which man was most popular?

(b) In what way does this source suggest that the writer was sympathetic to the three men?

(c) Was the crowd angry because they thought it cruel to cut people's ears off, or because they supported Burton, Bastwick and Prynne in their quarrel with Laud and the Star Chamber?

(d) What did the authorities hope to achieve by this public punishment of their critics? Do you think they were successful? Give reasons for your answer.

3. This puritan propaganda drawing shows 'Soundhead',

'Roundhead' and 'Rattlehead'. 'Rattlehead' has two faces, one meant to be Archbishop Laud (left) and the other the queen's Catholic chaplain (right).

(a) Which character is meant to be the puritan and which the Catholic? Give reasons for your answer.

(b) The priest is shown as 'Roundhead' because of his shaven head (tonsure). What person usually had this nickname? Do you think the artist meant this as a joke?

(c) What object in this drawing was particularly disliked by puritans? Explain why.

(d) What object on the front of the church (right) indicates that it is a Catholic church?

(e) How did the artist indicate that he regarded Laud as a friend of Catholics?

4. Imagine you are Archbishop William Laud. Write a letter to a parish priest, reporting that you have heard of his puritan ways, and ordering him to obey your instructions regarding services and so forth.

RISING AND REMONSTRANCE

The Long Parliament showed no interest in the Scottish threat. Indeed, many of its members, including Pym, were on friendly terms with the Presbyterian leaders in Scotland. Instead, it turned upon Charles's two chief ministers, William Laud and Thomas Wentworth, now Earl of Strafford. Both were sent to the Tower on charges of treason.

Strafford was the more feared of the two men. He had started as a Parliament man who had helped to frame the Petition of Right. Later he became one of the king's Ministers. For this reason, many MPs regarded him as a traitor. But 'Black Tom Tyrant', as they called him, had great ability. As governor, or Lord Deputy, of Ireland, he had ruled with efficiency and an iron hand. Seventeenth-century Ireland never knew such peace as Strafford gave it.

There now began a deadly game. Strafford hoped to force Pym to put him on trial so that he could defend royal policies and win a resounding victory. Pym, for his part, was afraid Strafford might reveal his own secret negotiations with the Scots. What if the Lord Deputy charged him with treason? What if he brought Irish troops to help Charles? There could be no mercy in such a struggle, for both men's lives were at stake.

Pym had to prove that Strafford was guilty of treason. Evidence was not easy to find. The best he could do was to quote a remark said to have been made by Strafford to the king – that he had an Irish army 'here to reduce [*conquer*] this Kingdom'. Such a phrase could have two meanings, to conquer Scotland or England. When Strafford's trial opened in March 1641, the Lord Deputy naturally claimed that 'this Kingdom' meant Scotland. His enemies said it referred to England. After three weeks' trial there was still no verdict. It was obvious there was not enough evidence to find Strafford guilty.

Parliamentary victory

Strafford's enemies were now desperate. They therefore decided to switch to a Bill of Attainder which needed no proof but simply declared a person guilty of treason. This was passed by 204 to 59 votes; figures which indicate that only half the MPs were present. Charles promised Strafford he would save his life. For a time he seems to have considered some sort of military action to save his minister. These rumours caused the London mob to riot; Pym's enemies suspected that he was behind the mob violence. There was such a scare that when a floorboard creaked in the House of Commons someone shouted 'gunpowder' and all the MPs rushed out!

In this mood Charles's opponents began to hint at charges against the queen herself. Strafford was now sick and weary. He advised the king to let him die. Charles decided to sacrifice his minister. 'If my own person only were in danger,' he explained, 'I would gladly venture it to save Lord Strafford's life; but seeing my wife, children and all my kingdom are concerned in it I am forced to give way.' In May 1641 Strafford went bravely to his death, blessed by the imprisoned Laud as he went by.

The stage was now set for Parliament to reduce the power of the king. Ship Money and other 'illegal' taxes were abolished. So were Royal Courts such as Star Chamber and the Church courts. Most important was the Triennial Act which started regular meetings of Parliament. Charles commented bitterly on this decisive change:

The execution of Thomas, Earl of Strafford, Tower Hill, London, 1641

. . . you have taken the government almost to pieces, and, I

A Doctor Vſher, Lord Prim
   te of Ireland,
B the Sherifes of London,
C the Earle of Strafford,
D his kindred and friends.

may say, it is almost off the hinges. A skilful watchmaker to clean his watch takes it asunder, and, when it is put together it will go better: but just remember if you leave out one pin the watch may be worse not better.

Until this time almost all MPs were against Charles's style of government. Now some members began to have doubts, as the vote for Strafford's attainder had shown. Were Pym and his men really going to take the 'government almost to pieces'?

The Irish Rebellion

Few people mourned 'Black Tom Tyrant'. Spectators at Strafford's execution rode home, waving their hats and shouting, 'His head is off! His head is off!' In Ireland far worse happened. No sooner was the Lord Deputy dead than the Irish broke into savage and disorganised rebellion.

Both James and Charles had continued the policy of 'grant and plant' (see Chapter 20). More and more English and Scottish settlers had been encouraged to 'colonise' Ireland. Such families took the best land and treated the inhabitants very badly, occasionally even hunting and killing them like wild animals. Strafford had tried to protect the Irish people. Now he was gone the Irish saw themselves at the mercy of a puritan Parliament. There was nothing to stop a national rising against the English.

Beacons soon spread the news of rebellion to wild clansmen who promptly attacked Protestant settlements. Farms were burned and their owners murdered or driven out. Hundreds, perhaps thousands, died. The grim story was exaggerated by the time it reached England. Puritan writers claimed it was a plot by the queen and the Irish to destroy Parliament's new power. Their pamphlets contained tales of raped women and children roasted by Catholic priests!

It was now that Charles's lack of contact with his people proved his downfall. The king was in Scotland trying to come to terms with the Covenanters when he heard the news. Instead of confronting his enemies as soon as possible, he travelled south in a leisurely fashion. By the time the king asked Parliament for an army to crush the rebellion, Pym was ready. No one knew better than the Parliamentary leader that his success, possibly his life, depended on the king having no armed forces. To allow Charles to raise an army would be madness from his point of view, for it would be used to crush Parliament, not reconquer Ireland.

Grand Remonstrance

Pym decided that his best plan was to remind the people what an untrustworthy king they had. A document called the Grand Remonstrance was prepared to be presented to Charles. It described every royal act of which Parliament disapproved and also proposed puritan changes in the Church of England.

The 'Short' Parliament in session, April 1640

This alarmed moderate-minded MPs. To object to illegal taxes and imprisonment without trial was one thing. To destroy both Church and royal authority was another. The danger of a too-powerful king seemed to them to have been replaced by that of a too-powerful Parliament. In the furious debate on the Remonstrance swords were rattled and members tore each other's clothes. At last Charles had a substantial number of Parliamentary supporters.

Those against the Remonstrance complained that no good could come from dragging up the past. They realised that the Bill, although addressed to the king, was in fact a direct appeal to the English people to support Parliament against Charles. Pym's defence was that Parliament was threatened by certain hotheads friendly with the king and queen. Liberty and religion were in danger and strong measures were needed. In the early hours of 22 November 1641 the votes were counted. It was a close victory for Pym – 159 members for and 148 against.

The result of this famous debate was obviously encouraging to Charles. Were his enemies falling out? He indignantly rejected a proposal by Oliver Cromwell, MP for Huntingdon, that any force assembled for the reconquest of Ireland should be commanded by the Earl of Essex, one of Pym's supporters. Consequently, no army was recruited and the Irish revolt continued. For the second time in two years the king had been refused the means to crush a rebellion.

The five members

London was in a violent and angry mood that Christmas. Armed bands roamed the streets, often with drawn swords. Mobs ran wild and rumours spread like forest fire. For the first time two abusive nicknames were heard. Royalists called their opponents 'roundheads' because so many of the mob were short-haired apprentices. Parliamentary supporters shouted 'cavalier [*horseman*]', comparing their opponents to the brutal Spanish 'caballeros' who had slaughtered the Protestant Dutch in the days of Alva.

Charles felt the time was ripe to hit back. On recent journeys he had seen plenty of evidence of loyalty and affection for himself. The Grand Remonstrance vote had shown he could count on many members of Parliament. He had to act quickly because rumours were reaching him of a possible trial of his queen. In January 1642 he gave orders for the arrest of five Parliamentary leaders: Pym, Hampden, Holles, Strode and Haselrig. When the Commons refused to surrender them he took the advice of Henrietta Maria, who suggested he should use force to capture them.

It was essential for Charles that the plan should succeed. If the five men were locked up opposition to him might well collapse. If they escaped, he would have struck what might well turn out to be the first blow of a civil war. Had Pym been less clever the king might have succeeded. But Pym knew from his spies exactly what Charles intended, and to make sure that the king and his soldiers did break into the Commons chamber he stayed there until the very last moment. Then he and his friends fled down river to the City (4 January 1642).

Charles entered the Commons chamber, leaving his soldiers at the door. There was a deathly silence as he asked for the five members by name. The Speaker refused to tell him whether they were present. Charles looked around. Significant empty seats told him all he needed to know. He knew the master stroke had failed and said:

> Well, I see all the birds are flown, I do expect from you that you shall send them unto me as soon as they return hither. If not, I will seek them myself, for their treason is foul . . . . But I assure you, on the word of a King, I never did intend any force, but shall proceed against them in a fair and legal way.

Approximate
division of
England at
the outbreak
of the civil
war in 1642

or Parliament

It was an important moment in English history. Since that day no British monarch has been allowed in the Commons whilst it is in session. This is more than a quaint custom. It reminds people that Parliament is the supreme power in the land, and that it must never be threatened with armed force.

The war begins

Londoners went wild on the night the five members escaped. Charles's action seemed to prove that Pym was right. The king *did* intend to destroy Parliamentary liberties. Barricades were set up, cannons dragged into firing positions and water boiled ready for throwing on the heads of royal soldiers. The houses of Catholics were attacked and several Catholic priests murdered. As one man remembered years afterwards, 'the war began in our streets before the King and Parliament had any armies'. It was no longer safe for Charles and his family to live in London. They left in January so that Charles could seek support for his cause. Enough men were ready to fight for him. On 22 August 1642 Charles raised his standard in a field near Nottingham as a signal for war.

It was a miserable scene for so important an event. Pouring rain reduced the number of spectators. The heavy flagpole needed twenty men to heave it upright. A gloomy Charles seemed more worried about the exact wording of his proclamation than anything else. There was a roll of drums and the sound of trumpets as the royal standard fluttered in the wind. Men cheered and hurried to shelter from the rain. Later that week a gale blew the flagpole down.

Charles I raises his standard at Nottingham. A drawing of the time

Nottingham

Sources and questions

1. Sir Philip Warwick was an MP who took part in the debates about the 'Grand Remonstrance' against King Charles. This description is from his *Memoirs of the Reign of Charles I*, published in 1701.

> Upon the King's return from Scotland, the City of London councillors entertained him splendidly and speeches flew in all directions saying how satisfied they were with what he had done in Scotland. Charles's opponents, however, prepared a Remonstrance to give the King as his first 'entertainment' amongst them . . . a worse libel could not be framed against either his person or government; and it was passed . . . two or three nights before the King came to town [*London*] . . . . At three o'clock in the morning, when the Commons voted for it, I thought we were all in the shadow of death; for we . . . grabbed at each other's hair, and would have put our swords in each other . . . had not . . Mr. Hampden . . . persuaded us by a short speech to adjourn our angry debate until the next morning. . . .

Source: Adapted from Millward, Sixteenth Century Documents, *Hutchinson Educational, 1961, pages 88–9*

(a) Do you think Warwick was for or against the Remonstrance? Give reasons for your answer.
(b) Who, according to Warwick, seemed well satisfied with the King?
(c) What evidence is there is this source that the country was near to war?
(d) Rewrite this account from the opposite point of view to Warwick. What part does not need to be changed?

2. Although the title of the source opposite reads '1641', this speech was printed after 5 January 1642 – in those days the dating of a year changed on 25 March, not 1 January.
(a) Why are there so few details of who printed this speech?
(b) Why did Pym and his supporters think it important to publish this speech?
(c) Would it have helped Charles if he had published *his* side of the story?
(d) What does the printing of this speech suggest to you about the way Charles's opponents were organised?
(e) Why do you think Pym's picture was put on the front?

3. Make up a play about the attempted arrest of the Five Members. Possible scenes would be:
(a) Five Members are warned and leave the Chamber.
(b) King and soldiers arrive.
(c) Dialogue between Charles and Speaker.

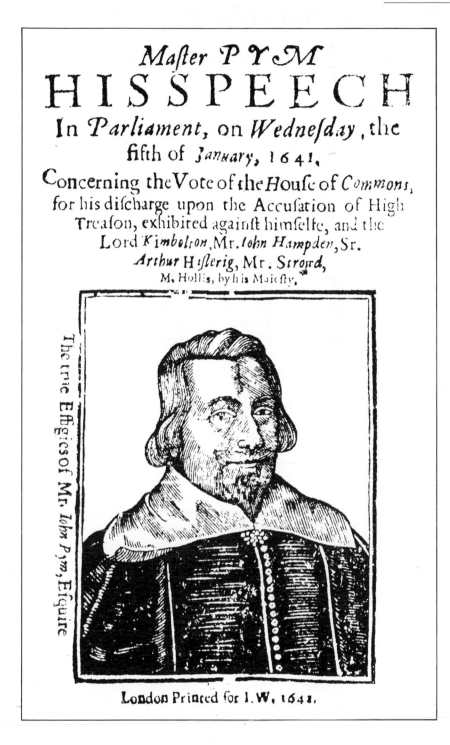

Master PYM
HIS SPEECH
In *Parliament*, on *Wednesday*, the fifth of January, 1641. Concerning the Vote of the House of *Commons*, for his discharge upon the Accusation of High Treason, exhibited against himselfe, and the Lord *Kimbolton*, Mr. *Iohn Hampden*, Sr. *Arthur Haslerig*, Mr. *Strodd*, M. Hollis, by his Maiesty.

The true Effigies of Mr. Iohn Pym, Esquire

London Printed for I. W, 1641.

(**d**) Afterwards Charles decides to leave London and seek support for his cause in the country.

4. Imagine you are living in Nottingham in August 1642. Describe the raising of the King's standard, and explain why you decided to fight for or against the King.

THE ENGLISH CIVIL WAR 1642–43

Guard your pan.

A civil war musketeer

The king's declaration alerted a country which had seen no serious fighting since the Wars of the Roses. An island state like England did not need large armies. Charles had only 300 infantry when he declared war. His nephew, Prince Rupert, son of Frederick of Bohemia, commanded 800 cavalry. The men of the Parliamentary militia which assembled at Coventry and Northampton were badly equipped and untrained. Few officers on either side were experienced soldiers, although there was a sprinkling of men who had served in European wars.

At that time the foot soldiers of an army were divided into pikemen and musketeers. Pikes were about 5 metres long and made of wood with a metal point. Muskets, of course, were for long-range fighting. They were slow to fire and reload. Musketeers carried a slow-burning fuse, the match, which fired the weapon. Later in the war firelocks, in which the bullet was fired by a flash pan of powder ignited by a flint, became more common.

Horsemen carried pistols as well as swords. Strangely enough, the tactic of 'charging home' into the army ranks had only just been introduced by Swedish cavalry in the German wars. This was done by all branches of the cavalry except the dragoons. These regiments got their name from the pistol called a 'dragon' which they carried. They were really mobile infantry who rode to a battle and fought on foot. An important cavalry task was to be the 'eyes' of the army – spying on the enemy, attacking supply waggons, seizing bridges and other strong points, even capturing enemy soldiers to obtain information.

Artillery had a less important role. Most English guns were old and out of date. They were cumbersome and difficult to move. The larger ones needed eight horses to pull them and a crew of three to load and fire. Consequently, their chief use was at sieges where they could be set in semi-permanent positions and used to batter down walls. The large number of barrels of gunpowder around an artillery battery often led to devastating explosions.

A big army problem in those days was food supplies. The relatively few villages and towns could not feed thousands of men for long. Only biscuits and cheese were ever issued as rations. Troops were expected to find any other food or drink for themselves. This led to much stealing and made the soldiers on both sides unpopular with the people. Fodder for horses was also a difficult problem. Good grass was available in spring and summer but there was little at other times. This fact, added to the bad state of the roads in the winter, meant that all major campaigns were fought in the summer.

The country divides

The king needed to win quickly if he was to win at all. London was the basis of Parliament's power and wealth and it also controlled the richest parts of the country, southern England and East Anglia. Another Parliamentary advantage was the support of the navy. This made it difficult for the Royalists to get help from abroad, besides giving the Roundheads customs' duties from the ports. The areas loyal to the king were Wales, the West Country and the North. These regions supplied good soldiers but little money. There were rich men who fought for the king, notably the Duke of Newcastle. But Parliament could call on the wealth of men like John Hampden who equipped a complete regiment out of his own pocket. If wealth had been all that mattered, the king would have stood no chance.

Each side claimed it was fighting for the king. At first, it was Parliament's aim to destroy Charles's army, and, once the king had agreed to their terms, to leave him on the throne. For Royalists the matter was simple. They fought for Charles the king even if they did not like Charles the man. Both Roundheads and Cavaliers thought God was on their side. The majority of ordinary people were not interested in the dispute. For them it was a quarrel between their masters; its causes were understood only by educated men. They fought for their local lord and master. If he changed sides they did the same! If they were taken prisoner they often enlisted in the ranks of the army which had captured them.

Prince Rupert of the Rhine

Edgehill

In the autumn of 1642 the king's army began to march towards London. Its aim was to capture the seat of Parliamentary power and so end the war at a stroke. Charles's cavalry was commanded by his twenty-two year old nephew, Prince Rupert. This young man had already fought on the continent where he had been taken prisoner by his Catholic enemies. In the first charge of the war, his men so terrified the enemy that they ran for nine miles. At that moment the 'legend' of Rupert was born. Tales of his deeds were exaggerated until he was supposed to be able to move faster than the wind, to be unhurt by bullets and to be a friend of the Devil. Even his little white dog, Boy, which ran beside his horse, was said to be a devil!

Parliament had appointed the Earl of Essex as Roundhead commander. He decided to get behind the Cavalier army and so

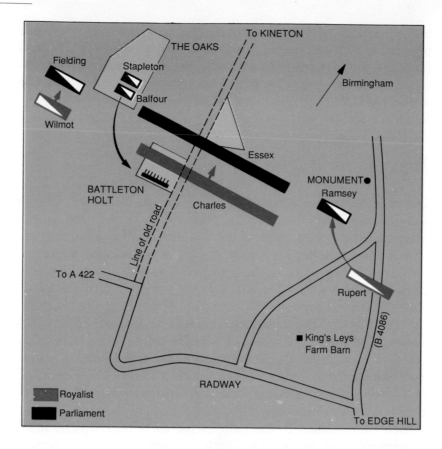

The first battle of the Civil War: Edgehill, October 1642

cut off its retreat. The king halted and offered battle at Edgehill, near Birmingham. About 14,000 men faced each other on 23 October 1642 in the first major battle of the war. Before the fighting started Charles rode along his lines and told his men, 'come life or death, your King wil bear you company'. Sir Jacob Astley, one of his generals, prayed, 'Lord, Thou knowest how busy I must be this day; if I forget Thee, do not forget Thou me'.

Rupert began the battle with an assault which broke Essex's left wing. He then led his men in a joyful and disorganised pursuit. Whilst he was away, the Roundhead cavalry smashed the squadrons facing them, leaving the Royalist infantry to fight both footsoldiers and horsemen. It was a desperate encounter in which Sir Edmund Verney, the king's standard-bearer, was cut down with sixty men of the royal bodyguard. Verney's severed hand was found still fixed to the captured staff. Eventually enough of Rupert's cavalry arrived back on the field to prevent a Parliamentary victory.

Next day Essex marched his men off towards London. The king's men were too weary to attempt to stop him; in any case Charles was horrified by the slaughter. A few weeks later Rupert moved towards the capital again but he found 24,000 apprentices barring his way at Brentford. He retreated to the Royalist base at Oxford for the winter. No royal army ever got as near London again.

Newbury

In 1643 Charles decided to attack London with three armies, one from Oxford, one from the west and one from the north. This plan failed because the western and northern forces could not fight their way through in time. So Charles moved west to help his men take Gloucester. This town was being defended heroically by the puritan citizens. When Essex realised London was no longer in danger he led his army of city apprentices to the relief of Gloucester. It was a dangerous march, across country swarming with enemy cavalry. But on 5 September the sight of his watchfires burning on the hills behind them forced the Royalists to give up the siege.

The Royalists now decided to move on London. Essex turned back, only to find the king's army barring his way at Newbury. If the Roundheads could be beaten, London would be in real danger. The Parliamentarians were tired, hungry and wet from frequent rain. The king, meanwhile, had been joined by fresh cavalry from Oxford. There followed a confused fight amongst narrow lanes and tall hedges. Men fought in desperate ambushes, hand to hand without formation or planning. Rupert's cavalry drove the Londoners back but suffered heavy losses from well-aimed musket fire. Essex's men were able to continue towards London where they were given a great welcome.

The year's fighting showed it was not going to be a short war. Both king and Parliament spent the winter looking for allies.

Oliver Cromwell

The obvious ally for Parliament was the Scots, who had done little to help their Puritan friends since 1641. This was because Scottish clergymen, besides hating the Church of England, also disliked those Puritans who wanted freedom of religious belief. Only when the Commons agreed to establish an English Presbyterian Church after the war did the Scots send aid. In November 1643 a Scottish army of 20,000 arrived to fight the king. Charles did not do so well in his negotiations. He signed a truce with the rebel Irish which meant that English troops could come home to fight for him. But when they arrived they were beaten by the Roundhead general Fairfax at Nantwich, Cheshire in January 1644.

Oliver Cromwell

The Scottish alliance was John Pym's last masterstroke before he died in December 1643. Royalists claimed he had been 'eaten by worms'; his supporters said he had died of overwork. Whatever the cause of his death, his achievement had been impressive. In three years he had destroyed much of the royal power established by the Tudors, making Parliament stronger than ever before. As he passed from the scene, a greater Roundhead leader arrived. Oliver Cromwell was distantly related to Henry VIII's minister, Thomas. During his short time at Cambridge University he lived the usual carefree life of a gentleman. But he also laid the foundation of a puritan belief which grew deeper and stricter with every year that passed.

Besides farming his lands in Huntingdonshire, Cromwell served as a Justice of the Peace and a member of Charles's third Parliament. In that assembly he became known as a rather uncouth critic of the king who stood up to speak in a 'plain cloth suit, which seemed to have been made by an ill country tailor'. He supported his cousin John Hampden in the Ship Money Case, was against a royal plan to drain the Fenlands near his home, and frequently demanded freedom of worship. He took this line where religion was concerned because he was an Independent, that is, one who disliked both Church of England and Presbyterian discipline.

In 1642 Cromwell joined the Parliamentary army as a captain of cavalry. From the start he showed natural ability as a soldier. He disciplined his men firmly, teaching them to advance to the attack in close formation and at a 'pretty round trot'. Such a charge was slower than Rupert's but easier to control. Above all, Cromwell recruited 'godly men' whose belief that God was on their side made them fight as well as any Cavalier. At Grantham in 1643 he won his first skirmish. Afterwards he reported, 'our men charging fiercely upon them, by God's providence they were immediately routed, and ran all away'. It was a story to be repeated many times in the years that followed.

When Pym died, Cromwell was a lieutenant-general in Lord Manchester's Army of the Eastern Association. Essex and Fairfax were then the most famous Roundhead generals. Yet one man who had seen Cromwell's cavalry in action told the king that Oliver was 'the most dangerous enemy his Majesty had . . . .'

Sources and questions

1. Here a soldier of Essex's army writes home. Wooden rails had been set up in front of communion tables by order of Archbishop Laud. Puritans disliked this because it reminded them of Catholic arrangements for the mass.

   Aylesbury, August, 1642

   On Monday August 8th we marched to Acton . . . we were late, and so many of our soldiers had to lodge in beds whose feathers were above a yard long. . . . Tuesday, early in the morning, several of our soldiers . . . went to the house of one Penruddock, a papist, and being insulted by him and his dog . . . entered his house and wrecked and robbed it . . . . This day also the soldiers got into the church, defaced the ancient and sacred glazed pictures, and burned the holy rails. . . . Saturday morning . . . we came to Wendover, where we refreshed ourselves, burnt the rails and accidentally one of Captain Francis's men, forgetting his pistol was loaded, shot a maid through the head, and she immediately died. . . . Sabbath day, August 13th. In this town a pulpit was built in the market-place, where we hear two worthy sermons.

   Sergent Nehemiah Wharton

Source: Quoted in The Oxford Book of Military Anecdotes, *ed. Max Hastings, Oxford University Press, 1986*

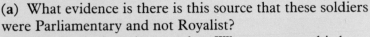

(**a**) What evidence is there is this source that these soldiers were Parliamentary and not Royalist?
(**b**) The war had not begun when Wharton wrote this letter. What does this letter suggest about the training and discipline of Essex's army?
(**c**) From this source, can you see why most civilians detested soldiers? Give reasons for your answer.
(**d**) What would we call 'ancient and sacred glazed pictures' today? Why did puritans destroy them?

2. Look at this comic drawing of a soldier. It was made during the Civil War. It shows how many civilians viewed soldiers as ruffians who plundered houses and stole food.
(**a**) Make a list of the food and drink the soldier has stolen. Why do you think soldiers stole food and drink?
(**b**) What old-fashioned methods of (i) Roasting a chicken, (ii) Cooking a stew, are illustrated in this source?
(**c**) What weapons should the soldier really be holding in his right and left hand? What might he be wearing on his head?
(**d**) Imagine you are a cottager. From this source, tell the story of what happened when soldiers came to your farm.

3. Imagine you are a Royalist pikeman at the battle of Edgehill. Write a letter home, describing what happened to you and your comrades, and mentioning any famous incident you may have seen.

THE ENGLISH CIVIL WAR 1644–46

The Scottish invasion of England made the Cavaliers' position in the north desperate. The Duke of Newcastle, their commander, put his army behind the defences of York and promised to surrender if not relieved by 4 July 1644. The king kept the Parliamentarians busy around Oxford and sent Rupert to the rescue. The young prince was at his best on such a mission. He stormed Stockport, Bolton and Liverpool, crossed the Pennine Hills, and entered York with three days to spare. Then, possibly because he misunderstood a letter from the king, he challenged the Roundheads to battle, although outnumbered three to two.

All through a hot summer day (2 July) the two armies gradually assembled on Marston Moor. The Royalists were on the moor and the Parliamentarians on higher but rougher ground. A ditch separated them although in certain places the cavalry of either side were very close. Cromwell commanded the Eastern Association cavalry on the left; Fairfax had his horsemen on the right and his infantrymen in the centre. Leslie, the Scottish commander, had chosen to fight beside Cromwell's men.

As evening came Rupert wished to attack but was persuaded by Newcastle to wait until next day. Both Newcastle and Rupert went to their coaches for the night. The men broke ranks and began to prepare for supper. Suddenly, at 7.30 pm, Cromwell's men crossed the ditch and attacked. An officer who rode with him described the charge like this:

> Our army in its several parts moving down the hill, was like unto so many thick clouds, having divided themselves into Brigades . . .the enemy (as some prisoners report) was amazed and daunted at our approach, not expecting any assault until next morning . . . .

This surprise action brought on a full-scale battle. Galloping horses and shouting men destroyed the peace of a summer evening. Musket fire lit the countryside with flame and sent clouds of smoke drifting across the moor. The Royalist centre quickly gave way. Only on the left, where the Royalist Lord Goring drove Fairfax's regiments from the field, did the king's men do well. As night fell, Rupert tried to rally his scattered horsemen but it was

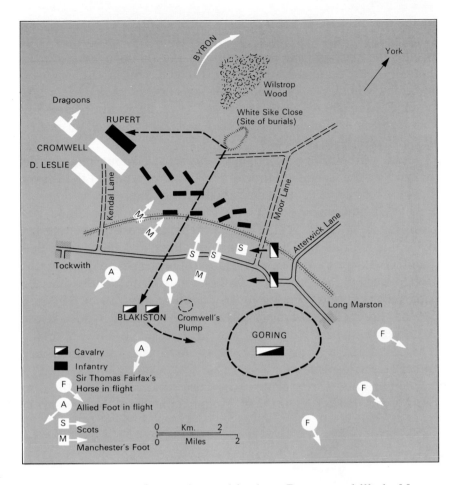

The turning point of the war: Marston Moor, 1644

no use. During a fierce charge his dog, Boy, was killed. Meanwhile, Cromwell was temporarily blinded by a powder flash during hand-to-hand fighting and had to retire from the field.

He returned to lead his cavalry in one devastating charge after another. Goring and his brave horsemen were driven from the field. In the end Cromwell's brigades had turned a full circle behind the enemy's original front. Thousands of Royalists were dead or wounded. The Prince himself had fled, leaving his battle flag. Alone in the moonlight one regiment remained firm. Newcastle's Whitecoats had sworn to stain their tunics red with Roundhead blood. They refused Fairfax's offer of surrender and fought on for hours in a wood. By midnight only thirty were left alive to lay down their arms.

Marston Moor shattered the legend of Rupert's superiority and gave Parliament control of the North. It was the turning point of the war.

Self-Denying Ordinance

Back in the South, Cromwell and other Independent generals were disgusted to find that Essex and Manchester had been beaten during the summer. They therefore suggested that no member of the Lords or Commons should be an army officer. This Bill, the Self-Denying Ordinance (Order), seemed a fair way to weed out inefficient officers. It was, after all, most difficult to make a man obey military rules if he enjoyed Parliamentary privileges. But behind the proposal lay an attempt by the Independents to gain control of the army because any MP could stay in the army by resigning whereas a lord could not give up his peerage in those days! Consequently, when it became law, the Roundhead army lost Essex and Manchester, the two generals Cromwell suspected of not fighting hard enough.

There were similar sweeping changes in religious matters. In January 1645 a Calvinist Directory of Worship replaced the Prayer Book, whose services were described by the Commons as 'unprofitable and burdensome'. On the same day Archbishop Laud was condemned to death at a trial in which the prosecution was led by William Prynne. The fact that the king had demanded that Laud should be pardoned was ignored. On the scaffold the Archbishop denied that he was a Catholic and claimed also that the king was 'as sound a Protestant . . . as any man in the Kingdom'. Such a dignified end did not satisfy one clergyman, who said the Archbishop should have been put in a sack and thrown in the Thames. Laud was the fifth and last Archbishop of Canterbury to suffer a violent death.

Even as Laud was executed a new armed force was recruited to destroy his master. The New Model Army was the first truly

Equipment of a new model trooper

professional army in English history. At first it consisted of 22,000 men, well-supplied with guns and other equipment. Infantry regiments were dressed in scarlet tunics; the cavalry wore brown leather coats. The new army was well-paid. Colonels received £1 a day, troopers 2s 6d (12½p) and privates 10d (4p). It was also well-disciplined. There was a death penalty for threatening an officer or hitting a civilian. Men who swore were whipped and had a hole bored in their tongues. An entire army was influenced by Independent religious ideas and taught it was fighting God's battles.

Naseby

Royalists sneered at this new force and called it 'The New Noddle'. Yet Charles's badly equipped troops stood little chance against it when the two sides met at Naseby near Market Harborough in Leicestershire on 14 June 1645. Rupert charged first, determined not to be surprised as he was at Marston Moor. His men did well until the Royalist infantry were overcome by superior numbers. Wave after wave of Cromwell's cavalry completed

The last major battle of the war: Naseby, July 1645. A drawing of the time

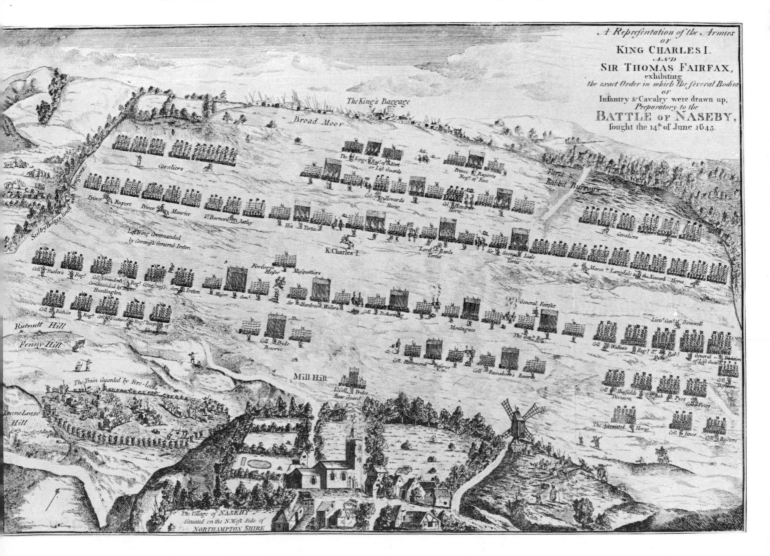

A Representation of the Armies of KING CHARLES I. AND SIR THOMAS FAIRFAX, exhibiting the exact Order in which the several Bodies of Infantry & Cavalry were drawn up, Preparatory to the BATTLE OF NASEBY, fought the 14th of June 1645.

the rout. Charles decided to gallop into the fray when he saw his enemies closing in. A Cavalier officer seized his bridle and persuaded him to turn back. By early afternoon there was 'not a horse or man of the King's army to be seen except the prisoners'.

The battle of Naseby was the final disaster for the Royalist cause. That evening Cromwell wrote to the Speaker of the Commons:

> Sir, Being commanded by you this service, I think myself bound to acquaint you with the good hand of God towards you and us . . . . We, after three hours fight very doubtful, at last routed his army; killed and took about 5,000 – very many officers, but of what quality we yet know not . . . . Sir, this is none other than the hand of God; and to Him alone belongs the glory . . . . *Honest men served you faithfully in this action. Sir, they are trusty; I beseech you, in the name of God, not to discourage them . . . . He that ventures his life for the liberty of his country, I wish he trust God for the liberty of his conscience, and you for the liberty he fights for . . . .*

The words in italic were a clear warning that the New Model Army had not fought for a Presbyterian church but for 'liberty of conscience'. These sentences were not published by the Parliamentary government in London.

There was fighting until March 1646 when Sir Jacob Astley was defeated at Stow-on-the-Wold. Two months later the king gave himself up to the Scots. They offered to help him if he would promise to establish a Presbyterian church in England. When he refused to do this the Scots handed him over to Parliament. The war was over.

Sources and questions

1. The particular tragedy of a civil war is shown in this letter from Sir William Waller, a Roundhead general, to his old friend, Sir Ralph Hopton, who commanded the king's army in the west of England. Hopton had suggested a meeting, perhaps hoping Waller would change sides. A few weeks later Hopton defeated Waller in a fierce battle at Lansdown near Bath.

   To my Noble friend Sir Ralph Hopton at Wells,

   Sir,
   The experience I have had of your worth, and the happiness I have enjoyed in your friendship make me sad when I look upon the present distance between us. Certainly my affections to you are so unchangeable, that war itself cannot violate our friendship . . . but I must be true to the cause wherein I serve. . . . That great God . . . knows with what a sad heart I go upon this service, and with what a perfect hatred I detest this war without an enemy . . . but . . . we are both set upon a stage and must

act those parts given us in this tragedy: Let us do it with
honour, and without personal dislike . . . .

> Your most affectionate friend
> and faithful servant,
>
> Wm. Waller

Bath, 16 June 1643

Source: Quoted in The Oxford Book of Military Anecdotes,
ed. Max Hastings, Oxford University Press, 1986

(**a**) What did Waller mean by 'a war without an enemy'?
What would he have regarded as a war *with* an enemy?

(**b**) Would Hopton have admired Waller if he had changed
sides?

(**c**) What evidence is there in this source that Waller felt
God was on the side of Parliament?

(**d**) What evidence is there in this source that the Civil War
was partly the result of a quarrel between the ruling classes?

2.

The moſt Illuſtrious and High borne PRINCE RUPERT,
PRINCE ELECTOR, Second Son to FREDERICK
KING of BOHEMIA, GENERALL of the HORSE
of H's MAJESTIES ARMY, KNIGHT of the Noble
Order of the GARTER.

This cartoon of Prince Rupert was published by the
Parliamentarians. It shows how he was portrayed by his
enemies.

(**a**) What do you think Rupert was accused of doing at

'Brimidgham' (Birmingham)?

(b) Why might Englishmen have disliked Rupert?

(c) What is the point of printing all Rupert's titles, commands, etc., under the drawing?

(d) Do you think the artist had ever seen Rupert or his dog? Give reasons for your answer.

(e) Do you think this source suggests that Rupert was feared or despised by his enemies?

3. On 5 July 1644, after the decisive victory at Marston Moor, Cromwell wrote this to a close relative, Colonel Valentine Walton.

> Truly England and the Church of God hath had a great victory given us by the Lord . . . . Sir, God hath taken away your eldest son by a cannon-shot. It broke his leg. We had to cut it off, whereof he died. Sir, you know my own trials this way [*Cromwell had also lost a son in the war*] but the Lord supported me . . . . Now is your precious child full of glory, never to know sin or sorrow any more. He was a gallant young man, exceedingly gracious. . . . Before his death he was so full of comfort . . . it was greater than his pain. This he said to us that one thing lay upon his spirit. . . . He told me it was, that God had not allowed him to be any more the executioner of His enemies. . . . You have cause to bless the Lord . . . Your son is a Glorious Saint in Heaven; wherein you ought exceedingly to rejoice.

> *Source: T. Carlyle*, Letters and Speeches of Oliver Cromwell, *Hutchinson, 1905*

(a) Cromwell was often accused by his enemies of being a hypocrite when he spoke about God. Why would you think he was writing sincerely in this letter in particular?

(b) What sort of man do you think Colonel Valentine Walton was, if this source is a guide?

(c) From this source, explain,
  i) How Cromwell and other puritans felt about the Civil War.
  ii) How they felt about their enemies.
  iii) How they felt about death.

(d) What evidence is there in this source of the primitive state of medicine and surgery at that time?

DOCUMENTS: THE VERNEYS, A FAMILY IN THE CIVIL WAR

The Verneys belonged to the top five per cent of the population in terms of money and influence. They owned property at Claydon in Buckinghamshire, where they lived in a fine house. Both Sir Edmund Verney (1590–1642) and his son Sir Ralph Verney (1611–96) were members of the Long Parliament. Both favoured Parliament, but Sir Edmund sided with the king when war came.

Claydon House, the Verneys' country home. It was altered in the eighteenth century

Document 1

Sir Edmund served with the king's army in which he carried the royal standard (flag). He was at York with the royalist troops when he wrote this to his steward at Claydon (July, 1642).

> I pray have the carbines [*muskets*] at home ready for the defence of the house if need be; and get powder and bullets ready; for I fear a time may come when rogues come thieving in such houses; therefore be not unprepared . . . . Have my waggon ready, if I should at any time send for it; get in all the money which is owing with all speed, for we shall certainly have a great war. Have a care of the harvest, and God be thanked for a good one. Your loving Master . . . .

Source: Memoirs of the Verney Family, *ed. Frances Parthenope Verney and Margaret M. Verney, Vol. I, Longmans, Green & Co, 1904*

Questions

1. How was the steward expected to defend the house 'if rogues came'? What does this tell us about the state of the country at this time?
2. What evidence is there in this source that Sir Edmund was a wealthy landowner?
3. Why did Sir Edmund think it important to get the harvest in as soon as possible?
4. What did Sir Edmund mean by 'such houses'?

Document 2

Sir Edmund made these remarks to a friend just before he was killed at the Battle of Edgehill, October, 1642.

> You have the satisfaction in your conscience of believing you are in the right; that the King ought not to grant what is required of him. . . . But for my part I do not like the quarrel, and do heartily wish that the King would consent to what they desire . . . my only concern now is to follow my master. I have served him for thirty years, and will not do so base a thing as to desert him; and I choose rather to lose my life (which I am sure I shall do) than defend things which are against my conscience. . . . For I will speak frankly with you, I have no liking for the Bishops, for whom this quarrel is being fought . . .

Source: Clarendon, A Life of Himself. *Quoted in* Memoirs

Questions

1. What does Sir Edmund mean when he says the Civil War was about bishops? Give reasons for your answer.
2. Which parts of this source show that Sir Edmund had been an opponent of the king's policies?
3. Why might Sir Edmund's job as king's standard bearer be particularly dangerous in a battle? What evidence is there that he knew this?
4. What particular reasons might a man of Sir Edmund's status have had to feel grateful and loyal to his king?

Sir Edmund Verney

Document 3

Even as Sir Edmund journeyed to Edgehill he wrote a letter to a family friend, Lady Sussex. She, in turn, wrote to his son Sir Ralph who had just taken the oath of loyalty to Parliament (September, 1642).

> Your father's letter was a sad one, and he said this of you, 'Madam, he has ever been near to my heart and truly is there still'. . . he is much troubled that you declared yourself for Parliament. . . . Let me beg you not to write angrily to your father . . . he is a good man who is very unhappy at the moment for many other things besides the differences between you two. For God's sake give nothing to Parliament, directly or indirectly: I hope in the Lord there will be peace and that Parliament will show their strength and so cause the King to yield to most of their demands . . . .

Source: Clarendon, op. cit.

Questions

1. Do you think Lady Sussex knew of the opinions expressed in Document 2? Give reasons for your answer.
2. Why did Lady Sussex think it dangerous to help Parliament at this time?
3. Do you think Lady Sussex was for or against Parliament? Give reasons for your answer.
4. Bearing in mind they had taken opposite sides, what particular troubles might have befallen the Verney family if Sir Edmund had lived?

Document 4

Ralph left England for reasons of conscience during the Civil War. By the time he returned he was a widower. Here he writes to his friend, Dr Denton, asking for help in settling once more at Claydon.

> If I must keep house . . . I will employ but one woman, who must wash my small linen (bed and board linen shall be put out) and she must clean the house and its contents. . . . I should like her to cook as well . . . . for men servants, I intend to keep a page and a footman. . . . Tell me what napkins, table clothes, sheets, pillow-cases and coverlets [*outside cover for bed*] are in the house . . . what store of beds for masters and servants . . . also what silver spoons . . . dishes, pie-plates, candle-sticks, basins, wooden trenchers [*plates*], beer and wine glasses . . . spits and such like matters . . . . tell me if the locks and glass-windows are in order. . . . Repair the chicken-house, next to the slaughter-house . . . that I may not be troubled with workmen on my return. . . . If Mrs Alcock [*his mother's old housekeeper*] cannot brew ale, a brewer must be found . . . we need 6 barrels a week for my table and the servants' Hall . . . . tis cheaper than wine and will please the servants better. . . .

Source: Clarendon, op. cit.

Questions

1. In Documents 1 and 4, Sir Edmund and Sir Ralph write letters about their estates. Do you think these letters show any changes in the social life of the time as a result of the war and execution of the king? Give reasons for your answer.
2. Using this Document as a guide, write a short character sketch of Sir Ralph Verney.
3. What parts of this source would concern a modern house-owner, and what parts indicate that it was written a long time ago?
4. From this Document, explain the sort of relations which existed at that time between:
   (a) father and son
   (b) master and servant
   (c) men and women.

Document 5

In 1643 Parliament decided that its supporters should agree to the Solemn League and Covenant, which aimed to establish a Presbyterian church system in England. Rather than do this, Sir Ralph chose to go abroad, where he remained until 1653. One of the many problems he faced in connection with running his estates from abroad, was the question of marriages for his five sisters. In 1647 his wife, Mary, returned to England to help. Here is what she wrote about one sister, also called Mary but known as 'Mall'.

(a) Will Roades tells me he has always paid 18 pounds a year for Mall's food, and truly 12 pounds a year, as you suggest, is very little for her clothes considering how everybody dresses here; I see by one of your letters that you reckon she shall cost you only 30 pound a year in all . . . . Miss Ise says that there was an allowance paid for Mall's washing besides her food and she had the help of a maid as well . . . all this will cost more than 18 pounds a year . . . .

(b) Your friend Mr Brown was with me yesterday, so I told him plainly that if he wished to marry I would help him get a wife; I told him of the condition [*social status*] of the woman [*it was Mall*] and how she had been brought up in the country which pleased him. . . . I told him that her dowry★ was to be a thousand pounds . . . he seemed to like this very well, but said his own fortune was too small to deserve her, for he had but fifteen hundred pounds a year. . . . I did not name the woman nor told what relation she was to us; I confess I like the man but his fortune is poor and whether Mall will accept him I know not . . . .

★ a sum paid by bride's family to the bridegroom

Source: Clarendon, op. cit.

Questions

1. From this source, what were the main considerations when planning a marriage?
2. Why do you think Ralph was anxious to get Mall married?
3. Why do you think Mr Brown was pleased that Mall had been brought up in the country and not in a town?
4. Explain Mall's feelings as an unmarried woman. Do you think she would have preferred to be married? Give reasons for your answer.

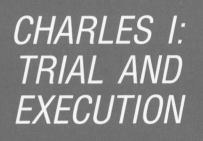

CHARLES I: TRIAL AND EXECUTION

Parliament seemed to have won a great victory. But two problems remained. What if the Independents in the army refused to allow the Presbyterian system which Parliament had promised the Scots (see Chapter 25)? What if the king still refused to give way to Parliament's demands? If either of these things happened Parliament would have lost the war as surely as the king.

The army was the more urgent problem. By 1646 there were soldiers in its ranks with unusual religious and political beliefs. A few were 'wild men' who thought Christ was about to return to earth. They called themselves 'Saints' and dreamed of building a 'New Jerusalem' in England. Others demanded far more political freedom than the mere 'parliamentary liberties' for which the war had been started. 'Honest' John Lilburne, for example, was afraid that his comrades had beaten one set of tyrants only to be crushed by another. He belonged to a group called the Levellers who demanded a vote for most men over twenty-one.

Cromwell did not see eye to eye with these men. His religious ideas were revolutionary by seventeenth-century standards. His political views were not. Cromwell was a landowner, the grandson of a baronet. 'I was by birth a gentleman', he once said and this was true. Like most of his class, Cromwell thought only those who owned valuable property should have a say in running the country.

John Lilburne

Seizure of Charles

Old Sir Jacob Astley had told his enemies after the last Roundhead victory, 'You have done your work and may go and play, unless you fall out among yourselves.' Within a year Parliament and the army did 'fall out'. In 1647 Parliament ordered some of the New Model Army to disband and the remainder to crush the rebellion in Ireland. Its terms were harsh; no pensions for the wounded or for widows, no backpay, although cavalrymen were owed forty-three weeks' pay and infantrymen eighteen.

The New Model saw all it had fought for at risk. It refused to obey and elected 'agitators' (agents) to take its grievances to London. At first Cromwell stayed out of the quarrel. Then, when it became

The Rump roasted salt it well it stinks exceedingly.

The Rump and dreggs of the house of Com: remaining after the good members were purged out.

Oliver declars himself and the Rebells to be the Gadly Party

Royalist playing cards. The roasting of the 'stinking' rump. The Rump Parliament shown as dregs left in a wine barrel. Cromwell declares his supporters to be the godly party

clear it would be a serious clash, he took the side of his men. This set the pattern for the rest of his career. However much he disliked its political ideas, Cromwell needed the army. Without it, the religious freedom which he believed God had granted England on the battlefield would be lost. The army, for its part, might have lost without Cromwell's firm leadership and great reputation.

It was clear that possession of the king would be a trump card in the 'game' about to be played. Since his surrender Parliamentary officials had guarded him at Holdenby House in Northamptonshire. After a secret meeting of officers at Cromwell's house in Drury Lane, London, a force of 500 troopers seized Charles and carried him off to Newmarket (June 1647). The Commons was furious and tried to arrest Cromwell as a traitor but he escaped. Soon afterwards the army occupied London and expelled eleven important Presbyterian members of Parliament.

Crisis at Putney

The New Model generals now offered the king their terms. In a document called the Heads of Proposals they suggested religious freedom for all except Catholics, Parliamentary elections every two years and a return to both bishops and Prayer Book. They also proposed that a Council of State appointed by the army, and ministers appointed by Parliament should rule the country for the next few years. Charles's friends advised him to accept. 'A crown so near lost was never recovered so easily as this would be', one man told him.

Charles rejected the offer for several reasons. First, he disliked Cromwell as a religious extremist whose soldiers had damaged cathedrals. Second, he knew that Parliament and the army had quarrelled and he hoped to play off one against the other. This turned out to be a fatal mistake on his part. The army represented the only effective power in the land. No agreement that the king might reach with Parliament or the Scots could succeed unless the New Model was beaten, and this was unlikely.

Meanwhile, many troopers were dissatisfied by the behaviour of the 'grandees', as they called Cromwell and his generals. The Heads of Proposals, in their opinion, let the king off too lightly. They met to debate an alternative solution to the crisis, at Putney, near London. They called their suggestions the Agreement of the People and it was suggested by the Levellers. The Agreement wanted complete religious toleration, no bishops, elections every two years and absolute power for Parliament. Even more revolutionary was the proposal that all 'freeborn Englishmen', that is, heads of families, should be allowed to vote.

Such ideas led to serious disagreements in the army. At Ware in Hertfordshire, two cavalry regiments drove off their officers and paraded with copies of the Agreement of the People in their hatbands (November 1647). Cromwell is said to have drawn his sword and ordered them to throw down these papers. The sight of their Lieutenant-General so angry made the troopers obey. Afterwards, one of the ringleaders was court-martialled and shot.

'A more prodigious treason'

At this critical moment the king made the wrong move. He escaped to the Isle of Wight, where he was well-treated by the Governor of Carisbrooke Castle. Within weeks of his arrival there he was able to meet Scots representatives. In return for military aid from a Scots' army, he promised to set up Presbyterianism in England for three years. At the same time he promised the Scots that he would put down 'the opinions and practices of the Independents'. A copy of this 'Engagement' was wrapped in lead and buried in the garden of the castle.

Charles's action united the army. They forgot their differences and appealed once more to God. The 'Second Civil War' was over in a matter of weeks. Cromwell destroyed the main Scots' army in a three-day battle near Preston (August 1648). Royalist risings timed to coincide with the Scots' invasion were suppressed in Kent, Essex and Wales. Now the generals prepared to settle with both Parliament and king once and for all. Charles Stuart, that 'man of blood', as they called him, was to be put on trial. Parliament, which had signed the agreement with the king, was invaded by soldiers led by Colonel Pride. He arrested forty-one moderate members and expelled ninety-six. Only a hard-line 'rump' of the Long Parliament now remained.

Cromwell was campaigning in the north when 'Pride's Purge' took place. He returned to London determined that the king must die. He was particularly angry about the invasion of a Scottish, 'foreign' army, possibly forgetting that one such army had been on his side at Marston Moor! He wrote indignantly,

This is a more prodigious treason than any that hath been perfected before; because the former quarrel was that Englishmen might rule over one another; this is to vassalise [*make slaves of*] us to a foreign nation.

Royal trial

On 20 January 1649 a court consisting of 135 commissioners assembled in the Painted Chamber of Westminster Palace to try King Charles. Its President, John Bradshaw, wore a special hat lined with metal in case anybody tried to murder him.

In this grim situation a mysterious change came over the king. The shy, hesitant man became bold and determined; even his stutter left him. Perhaps it was because his task was simple; all he had to do was die bravely. For a courageous person like Charles this was not too difficult. It was his enemies who had now made a mistake. This trial was an illegal act by men who claimed to have been fighting to defend the law. It would replace a king who was

Metal hat worn by John Bradshaw, president of the court which tried Charles in Westminster Hall. He was afraid he might be killed by a royalist.

A nineteenth century drawing of the trial of Charles I. Cromwell is standing right

a prisoner with one who was abroad and free – the future King Charles II. Finally, it would horrify all moderate men and women and create sympathy for the victim.

Charles was charged with a 'wicked design' to be a dictator and 'overthrow the rights and liberties of the people'. He was also blamed for the wars and the deaths of innocent men, women and children. He reacted contemptuously, refused to remove his hat and laughed when Bradshaw called him a 'tyrant, traitor and murderer'. Then he asked what right the court had to try him:

> 'I would know by what power I am called hither . . . I would know by what authority, I mean lawful? . . . Remember I am your King, your lawful King, and what sins you bring upon your heads and the judgement of God on this land.
> 'By the authority of the Commons of England, assembled in Parliament', came the answer.
> 'The King cannot be tried', retorted Charles.

This was the weak point of the proceedings. As one lawyer told Cromwell, 'The King can be tried by no court'. Then he added that 'this particular court' was not fit to try anybody. He was referring to the fact that the army, not Parliament, was behind the trial since the 'rump' was merely a puppet of the New Model Army.

So the king was able to pose as a defender of the people's rights. 'If Power without law can make law . . . I know not what subject in England can be sure of his life or anything he calls his own . . .', he remarked. The court sentenced him to death as a 'Tyrant, Traitor, Murderer and a public enemy . . . .'

Royal execution

On Tuesday, 30 January 1649, Charles I was brought to his own Banqueting Hall in Whitehall, London. It was a gloomy, cold day, white with frost and snow. A procession of soldiers beating drums escorted him. They surrounded the black-draped scaffold whilst the king went to a room in the Palace.

At about two in the afternoon a Colonel Hacker tapped quietly on Charles's door. The king finished praying and walked to the place of execution. Dense crowds surged forward, stretching their necks to see him and calling out prayers and blessings. The scaffold itself was crowded with army officers and clergymen. Charles's executioners wore disguises, masks and false beards, to save them from Royalist revenge later. Charles decided to speak even though he knew the spectators were too far away to hear him. Briefly he summed up the principles for which he believed he was dying. They were noted down by Bishop William Juxon who was his chaplain that day.

> For the people truly I desire their liberty and freedom as much as anybody whatsoever; but I must tell you that their liberty and freedom consists in having government, those laws by which their lives and goods may be most their own. It is not

The execution of the king, 1649

their having a share in the government . . . a subject and sovereign are clean different things.

Of his faith he remarked, 'I die a Christian according to the profession of the Church of England'.

Charles then stripped off his jewels, the badge of the Order of the Garter, and his outer clothing. The block was only ten inches high so he was forced to lie flat to put his head on it. After a few seconds he gave a signal to the executioner. The axe swung down, cutting off his head at one blow. A great groan went up from the crowd as the head was held up by the axeman. Cavalry quickly herded them away. Only a few managed to dip their handkerchiefs in the blood that dripped from the scaffold.

As a king, Charles Stuart nearly ruined the English monarchy. His brave death saved it. Few English kings since 1066 have been saintly. Only one is a 'martyr'.

Sources and questions

1. Here are three comments upon Charles I's character and actions. (a) is by Lord Clarendon, Charles's friend and minister, writing many years after the events he describes. (b) is by a Catholic, Cardinal Rinuccini who went as papal nuncio (ambassador) to Ireland in October 1645. (c) is the report of a sermon preached by William Goffe to the New Model Army at the start of the Second Civil War in 1648.

(a) . . . he [*Charles*] was the worthiest gentleman, the best master, the best friend, the best husband, the best father and the best Christian, that the age in which he lived produced. And if he were not the best king . . . no other prince . . . possessed half his virtue.

Source: Clarendon, History of the Rebellion, OUP, 1885

(b) I am alarmed by the general opinion of His Majesty's unreliability . . . which suggests that whatever promises he may make, he will never carry them out unless it pleases him. . . . He has not appointed a Catholic governor [*in Ireland*] so I am afraid he might be persuaded by his Protestant ministers to avenge himself on the Catholic noblemen of Ireland and renew heresy [*he means Protestantism*] in this island.

Source: The embassy in Ireland of Monsignor G. B. Rinuccini, *Translated by Annie Hutton, 1873. Quoted by Godfrey Davies*, The Early Stuarts, *OUP, 1959*

(c) . . . and presently we were led and helped by God to a clear agreement amongst ourselves . . . that it was our duty . . . with the forces we had, to go out and fight against those powerful enemies which that year in all places had appeared against us . . . and that it was our duty, if ever the Lord brought us back again in peace, to call Charles Stuart, that man of blood, to account for all the blood he had shed, and mischief he had done . . . against the Lord's cause and the people of our poor nation.

Source: Somers Tracts (1811). *Quoted by Davies*, op. cit.

(a) Of the writers of these sources only Clarendon knew the king well. Does this make his evidence more or less reliable? Give reasons for your answer.
(b) Why might (b) contain a prejudiced view of Charles?
(c) Goffe was preaching to an army about to go to war. How might this affect what he had to say?
(d) Note the date when (b) was written. Would Charles have been more or less likely to break promises at that time?
(e) In your opinion, which source is openly hostile to Charles's behaviour as king? Which seems to have doubts as to his ability as a king?

2. The New Model Army's discontent at the way it was treated by Parliament after the Civil War is illustrated by this 1647 drawing.
   (a) What has happened to the woman?
   (b) What is the figure on the right doing? Why would this make his supporters angry?
   (c) Why would the figure on the left have particular reason to feel annoyed at his treatment?
   (d) What does this drawing suggest to you about the way the New Model Army was organised and supported?

3. Look at the Royalist playing cards on page 214. Why was it a good idea to print propaganda on playing cards?

DOCUMENTS: THE DEATH OF CHARLES I

Document 1

The picture on page 218 was drawn by a Dutch artist. It shows scenes at the execution of Charles I on 30 January 1649 outside the Banqueting Hall in Whitehall, London.

Questions

1. Why do you think Charles was executed in a public street before a large crowd?
2. Why do you think there are numerous drawings of the king's execution?
3. In this drawing the king is shown standing up *and* beheaded. Why do you think the artist did this?
4. What other section of this drawing is imaginary? Why do you think the artist put it in?

Document 2

John Rushworth was probably present at the execution. He wrote a long account of it which was eventually published in his *Historical Collections of private passages of state . . . in five Parliaments, 1659–1701*. Here is part of that account. Dr Juxon was a doctor of divinity, not medicine.

> From thence he [*the king*] was accompanied by Dr Juxon, Colonel Tomlinson, Colonel Hacker and the guards before mentioned through the Banqueting House, near to which the scaffold was erected. . . . The scaffold was covered in black cloth and an axe and block laid in the middle. . . . There were companies of foot and horse on every side . . . and the crowds of people . . . were very great. The King look'd very earnestly at the block and asked Colonel Hacker if there was not one higher. . . . The King made some speeches until Dr Juxon said to him, 'There is but one stage more. This stage is turbulent and troublesome . . . But soon you will travel from earth to heaven, and there you shall find, to your great joy, the prize. You haste to a crown of glory. . . .' Then the King took off his cloak and his George [*the Order of the Garter*] giving it to Dr Juxon. . . . After a while the King, stooping down, laid his neck upon the block; and after a little pause, the king stretched forth his hands, and the executioner at one blow severed his head from his body.

Questions

1. What points about the death of the king does Rushworth seem anxious to stress?
2. Do you think the artist of Document 1 had read this account? In what ways does this account confirm or contradict it?
3. What words spoken by Dr Juxon remind us of part of Document 1?
4. Which do you think is the most reliable and useful, Document 1 or 2? Give reasons for your answer.

Document 3

The news of the king's death spread rapidly. Here is a Mr Cockram, an English merchant living in Rouen, France, writing to his friend, Sir Ralph Verney, who had fled to France to escape the Roundheads. The letter is dated 20 February 1649 but as France used the Gregorian Calendar at that time and England the Julian, this date was about ten days ahead of the dating used in England.

> I doubt not but ere this you have heard the doleful news of our King's death, who was beheaded last Tuesday, at two of the clock, before Whitehall, which is the most barbarous act and lamentable sight that ever any Christians beheld. The numerous guard of horse and foot-soldiers . . . did bind the hands and stop the mouths of many thousand spectators, but could not keep their eyes from weeping . . . His Majesty behaved upon the scaffold with admirable courage . . . he did make a worthy speech showing he was innocent of what he was accused and condemned for, yet with great charity did freely forgive his enemies. . . . And to satisfy the people concerning his religion he declared that he died a true Christian according to the Church of England . . . and so . . . he submitted to his woeful end . . . which is the beginning of England's misery. . . .
>
> *Source*: Memoirs of the Verney Family, *ed. Frances Parthenope Verney and Margaret M. Verney, Vol. I, Longmans, Green & Co, 1904, pages 444–5*

Questions

1. Rushworth wrote many years after the event; Cockram within a few days. Why do you think his account has more details than Cockram's?
2. What does the fact that Cockram wrote such a letter tell us about means of communication at that time?
3. Cockram wrote to tell his friend of the king's death. What else was he anxious his friend should know?
4. Why might Charles need to satisfy his people that he died a true member of the Church of England?

Document 4

After Charles II's restoration some of the men who had condemned his father were themselves executed. Here, two of them, John Cook, who conducted the prosecution against Charles at this trial, and Major-General Thomas Harrison, one of Cromwell's most famous generals, give their reasons for executing the king.

> (a) We are not traitors, nor murderers, nor fanatics, but true Christians and good Commonwealth men, fixed and constant to the principles of . . . truth, justice and mercy, which the Parliament and Army went to war for. . . . [W]e fought for the public good and would have given the people more control of the government as well as securing the welfare of the whole nation . . . had not the people preferred slavery to freedom . . . .
>
> *Source: John Cook, writing to his wife in 1661. Quoted by Wedgwood, The Trial of Charles I, Collins, 1964*

Questions

1. What two reasons does Harrison suggest for putting the king on trial, rather than murdering him secretly?
2. What sort of God did Harrison believe in?
3. In what ways had the people chosen slavery rather than freedom in Cook's opinion?
4. From these sources, explain the two reasons for killing the king given by Cook and Harrison. In what way were they different?
5. Cook claims that the men who killed the King were *not* fanatics. After reading these sources, would you agree with him? Give reasons for your answer.

(b) I do not come here to deny anything but rather to bring it forth into the light . . . . The King's execution was not a thing done in a corner. I believe it has influenced most nations . . . the terror of the presence of God that was with us in those days meant that I did not follow my own judgement; I did what I did . . . out of fear of the Lord . . . . Maybe I might have been a little mistaken, but I did it all according to the best of my understanding, desiring to obey the will of God in his Holy Scriptures . . . .

Source: Thomas Harrison, at his trial in 1661. Quoted by Wedgwood, op. cit.

Document 5

On the day Charles was buried in St George's chapel, Windsor, a book called *Eikon Basilike* (Royal Image) was published. It consisted of thoughts and prayers supposed to have been written by the king during his imprisonment. This is unlikely, but it certainly contained plenty of the king's opinions. Here is the frontispiece of that book.

Questions

1. Do you think *Eikon Basilike* was intended for an educated readership? Give reasons for your answer.
2. What object in this source reminds you of Juxon's words in Document 2?
3. Why does the artist show Charles holding a crown of thorns? How would Roundheads have felt about this?
4. This frontispiece makes a clear statement about the death of the king. What is it? What other sources in this study contradict such a statement? Give reasons for your answer.
5. From these sources, and other information you have gathered, *either* explain how royalists felt about the death of Charles I *or* explain why Cromwell and his followers put the king to death.

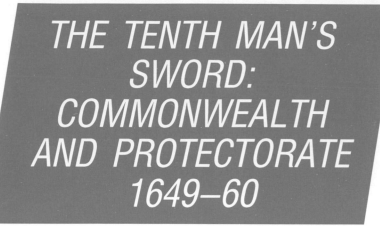

THE TENTH MAN'S SWORD: COMMONWEALTH AND PROTECTORATE 1649–60

Now that there was no king a Council of State was set up to rule the new 'Commonwealth'. It faced grave difficulties at home and abroad. The Scots regarded Charles's eldest son as King Charles II; the Stuarts were a Scots royal family anyway. The Irish continued to live in defiance and disorder. Foreign countries looked upon England as an outcast because it had killed its king. The Tsar of Russia ordered the Commonwealth representative from his court. The Dutch did nothing about finding the killers when the Commonwealth ambassador at their court was murdered. At sea, French privateers and a Royalist fleet commanded by Prince Rupert attacked English merchant ships.

The New Model Army was disturbed by more mutinies. These men were different from the soldiers of earlier times. Cromwell's soldiers had experienced more in seven years than their grand-parents in a lifetime. They had met and talked freely with people they would never have known, and seen parts of the country they would never have laid eyes on in ordinary circumstances. Most of the men, particularly the foot-soldiers, wished for little more than food and pay. But in the ranks of the cavalry enough 'extreme' ideas were discussed at this time to make the ruling classes afraid of the people for centuries to come.

A typical set of extremists were the Diggers. They were led by Gerard Winstanley, an Independent who claimed he received orders directly from God. In his opinion men without land were entitled to 'all the commons and waste ground in England'. In April 1649, at St George's Hill near Cobham in Surrey, he and a few friends dug up some rough ground and planted parsnips, carrots and beans. The idea was to share the work and the crops. The local inhabitants had other ideas. They complained to General Fairfax who sent soldiers to disperse the community. Their commander decided Winstanley and his friends were harmless lunatics. He reported to Fairfax that the Diggers had promised to use only common or park land, not private property.

Fairfax decided to leave them alone. This did not satisfy the people of Cobham. Local farm-workers pulled up the Diggers'

crops. A Justice of the Peace arrested the Diggers and confiscated their equipment. A novel experiment was crushed almost before it started.

Ireland and Scotland

The Commonwealth government tackled its problems quickly. In 1649 Cromwell was asked to go to Ireland to crush the rebellion. He captured a town called Drogheda and allowed his men to slaughter both soldiers and civilians. At Wexford the same thing happened without his permission. Cromwell was cruel because he was determined to avenge the deaths of Protestants in 1641 (see Chapter 23). He was also in a hurry to get back to fight the Scots. But this whirlwind campaign remains a blot on his reputation.

At sea the government appointed an ex-soldier, Robert Blake, to take charge of the fleet. Blake proved to be a brilliant admiral. During 1650 he drove Rupert's ships all the way from Ireland to the Mediterranean. Finally the Prince's fleet was smashed up on the rocks off Carthagena in Spain, 'not a mast standing', as Blake reported. Meanwhile Cromwell took over the New Model Army when Fairfax retired. He marched it north but found southern Scotland deliberately stripped of crops and food. His opponent was Alexander Leslie who had fought on the Parliamentary side at Marston Moor.

Cromwell would have preferred to avoid bloodshed. All he wanted the Scots to do was expel Charles II from their country and allow religious freedom. He wrote a letter to the Scottish General Assembly in which he begged the elders of the Church to 'think it possible you may be mistaken'. He was wasting his time. Presbyterians, like the Independents, were sure God was on their side. At first it did seem that God favoured the Scots. Cromwell could not capture Edinburgh; it was well-defended and he had no heavy siege guns. The New Model was soon a 'poor, shattered, hungry, discouraged' army, according to Cromwell. It fell back to Dunbar, where the English hoped to get fresh supplies by sea. The Scots left their trenches near Edinburgh and occupied the pass leading south through the Lammermuir Hills. Cromwell was now trapped between the sea and the mountains. It was the most dangerous moment of his military career.

Dunbar and Worcester

So far all had gone well for Leslie. He knew that it would be safer to starve the English into surrender than to fight them. The Scottish clergymen, however, disliked this waiting game. They demanded that he leave his defences and give battle. Leslie was forced to give way. As the Scots formed ragged battle-lines, with too many men on the right and not enough on the left, Cromwell could hardly believe his luck. 'God is delivering them into our hands, they are coming down to us', he exclaimed.

At dawn on 3 September 1650 Cromwell led his men to the attack. A man who rode with him wrote afterwards, 'He did laugh so excessively as if he had been drunk, and his eyes sparkled with spirits . . . .' While one wing shattered the weak Scottish left, guns

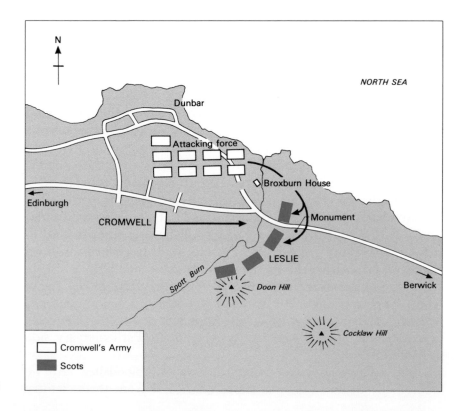

Cromwell's victory at Dunbar, 3 September 1650

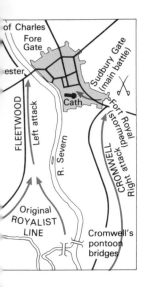

Battle of Worcester, 3 September 1651

pounded the men crowded on the right. The Scots were soon utterly defeated and running from the battlefield. Afterwards, happy New Model troopers grouped themselves around Cromwell and joined him in singing Psalm 117 – 'O give praise unto the Lord, all nations that be'.

Dunbar was a shattering blow to the Scottish Presbyterians. They had never believed God would 'desert' them in this awful way. They arranged public debates to discuss 'the dreadful appearance of God against us at Dunbar'. The men who had once humbled Charles I were now themselves humbled. Never again would they be so confident of God's favour or so certain they could turn England Presbyterian. They took no part in Charles II's invasion of England the following year. His mixed army of Scots and Royalists was trapped by Cromwell at Worcester. On the first anniversary of Dunbar, 3 September 1651, Charles was beaten in a fierce five-hour fight through the streets of the town.

Charles escaped abroad after many exciting adventures. Cromwell never fought again. Worcester, as he wrote, afterwards, was 'a crowning mercy'.

The Dutch war

England had virtually ceased to be a naval power after the death of Elizabeth. There was no money to build and maintain expensive warships. The country which took most advantage of England's weakness was Holland. In America the Dutch founded the colony of New Holland in the heart of English territory. In the East they drove English traders out of the Spice Islands. By the 1650s the Dutch East India Company was the wealthiest corporation in the world. At the same time its ships carried so much cargo for foreign countries that the Dutch were nicknamed 'the waggoners of the seas'.

The Commonwealth government levied heavy taxes so it had the money to contest the Dutch supremacy at sea. First, it ordered the building of forty new ships of war. Then, in 1651, Parliament passed a Navigation Act. This stated that no goods could enter English ports except in English ships or the ships of the country which produced the goods. This meant war with Holland, for their riches depended on remaining 'waggoners of the seas' for other nations. The fierce sea-battles which followed were fought for what one English MP called 'the fairest mistress in the world – trade'.

In spite of their aggressive behaviour the Dutch were at a disadvantage. All their trade had to pass through the English Channel. Consequently they were forced to protect every merchant ship. In any battle the English only had to fight whilst the Dutch had to fight and protect these 'lame ducks'. Even so it was a close contest. In December 1652, the Dutch admiral Maarten Tromp appeared off Margate with 400 ships and beat Blake. Later, in the Battle of Portland, Blake all but destroyed Tromp's fleet in a three-day battle near Calais. An English newspaper reported of the many captured Dutch ships, 'all their men-

A battle of the first Dutch war, 1652–4

of-war who are taken are much dyed with blood, their masts and tacks moiled with brains, hair, pieces of skull'.

It had been a clash of naval giants but there was no doubt who had won. Thousands of Dutch merchant ships had been taken and destroyed. Holland was forced to make peace because its trade was facing ruin.

Rump and Barebones

By 1653 the army leaders had grown tired of the Rump Parliament – all that was left of the Parliament which had fought the Civil War. One of the New Model's finest generals, John Lambert, wanted a Parliament based on the Heads of Proposals (see Chapter 26). General Thomas Harrison, a religious fanatic, preferred an assembly of 'godly' men to run the country until Christ returned. Cromwell was not so extreme. He knew the army was unpopular but he hoped that people would gradually grow to like the rule which God intended for them.

In April 1653 Cromwell took the plunge. Here is a description by an eyewitness of how he ended legal government in England:

Wednesday, 20th April. The Parliament sitting as usual, . . .
the Lord General Cromwell came into the House, clad in plain

clothes, with grey worsted stockings, and sat down as he used to in an ordinary place. After a while he rose up, put off his hat, and spake; at the first . . . he spake to the commendation of Parliament, for their pains and care of the public good; but afterwards he . . . told them of their injustice, delays of justice, self-interest and other faults. . . . After this he said to Colonel Harrison . . . 'Call them in'. Then Harrison . . . presently brought in five or six files of musketeers . . . with their muskets . . . .

The sight of musketeers with loaded weapons helped clear the Chamber; only John Bradshaw dared to protest. That night somebody wrote on the locked door of the empty room, 'This House to let, now unfurnished'. From that moment Cromwell was a reluctant dictator, ruling by military force alone. Once when he was told that one of his schemes would annoy nine out of ten people, he replied, 'But what if I should disarm the nine, and put a sword in the tenth man's hand? Would that not do the business?'

Cromwell's Parliaments were probably disliked by nine out of ten of the people. They, in turn, quarrelled with Cromwell. 'Barebones' Parliament', named after an MP called Praisegod Barbon,

Cromwell dissolves the 'Long' Parliament, April 1653. On the wall is written 'This House is to Let'

consisted of 140 'persons fearing God, and of approved fidelity and honesty' who were appointed, not elected. When that assembly was dispersed by the army, Cromwell took the advice of Lambert and became Lord Protector. He was advised by a Council of State and one House of Parliament. This Parliament later quarrelled with Cromwell and was dissolved. The Protector then divided the country into eleven districts each ruled by a Major-General.

The Major-Generals' rule was the most unpopular of all Cromwell's experiments. These officers closed theatres and inns, and applied the old laws against swearing and drunkenness so thoroughly that in 1657 Cromwell abolished their rule and tried his final experiment. A new constitution allowed for two Houses of Parliament, one elected, the other appointed by Cromwell. At this time Cromwell himself was offered the crown. Perhaps 'King Oliver' might have been the answer to the country's problems, especially since Charles II was hardly known in England. But the army would not allow Cromwell to become king.

The sword falls

The hardships of warfare had ruined Cromwell's health. He died on 3 September 1658, the anniversary of Dunbar and Worcester. Without his strong hand, military government collapsed. For a time his ineffective son, Richard, nicknamed 'Tumbledown Dick' ruled as Protector. He was forced out by the New Model generals, but they spent their time quarrelling among themselves. Finally, George Monck, commander of the army in Scotland, crossed the border at Coldstream and marched on London. Here he persuaded the army leaders to begin the process of bringing back legal government. The old Long Parliament was recalled and then persuaded to dissolve itself so that there could be free elections. These elections, of course, led to the formation of a Royalist Parliament which eventually brought about the return of King Charles II.

An undefeated army disbanded itself at the same time. Only three New Model regiments remained in the royal army which Charles formed in 1660. They are now the Life Guards, the Royal Horse Guards and the Coldstream Guards. The sword had fallen from the 'Tenth Man's Hand'.

Cromwell's skull, put on a spike after he was dug up and hanged. It is now buried at Sidney Sussex College, Cambridge where he studied as a young man

Sources and questions

1. Edward Hyde, Earl of Clarendon, was a member of the Long Parliament who joined the king's side at the time of the debate about the Grand Remonstrance. He served both Charles and his son, Charles II. When forced by his enemies into exile in 1667 he carried on writing his *History of the Great Rebellion*, a work he had begun in 1648. He died in 1674. The book was first published in the reign of Queen

Anne (1702–14). Clarendon's summing-up of Cromwell is famous.

> To reduce three nations [*England, Scotland and Ireland*], which perfectly hated him, to complete obedience . . . to govern these nations with an army which detested him, and wished his ruin, was a mighty achievement. But his greatness at home was but a shadow of the glory he had abroad. It was hard to discover which feared him most, France, Spain or the Low Countries [*Holland*]. . . . As they did sacrifice their honour and their interests to his pleasure, so there is nothing he could have demanded, that any of them would have denied him. . . . In a word, as he had all the wickedness . . . for which hell-fire is prepared, so he had some of the virtues . . . and he will be looked upon by posterity [*future generations*] as a brave bad man.

Source: Clarendon, History of the Rebellion, *Oxford University Press, 1888*

(a) What 'virtues' did Clarendon think Cromwell possessed?

(b) From what you know of Cromwell's career, do you think any parts of this source are exaggerated?

(c) Is this source more or less reliable because it was written by one of Cromwell's enemies?

(d) From this source, what do you think Clarendon's attitude was to foreign countries?

2. An artist/supporter of Cromwell sums up his hero's achievements on page 231. Cromwell is shown crushing under his feet a woman who represents the Catholic Church.

(a) What does the left-hand column represent? (There is a clue near the bottom.)

(b) Which three countries are illustrated in the right-hand column? How does this reference agree with parts of Source 1?

(c) Two drawings at the top indicate that the artist thought Cromwell had led England through storms to calm and peace. What famous story has the artist used to illustrate this?

(d) What does the bird above Cromwell's head symbolise?

(e) What languages and what book would a person need to know about to appreciate and understand this drawing?

3. Do you think Cromwell should have become king? Do you think British history would have been changed if he had done so?

THE RESTORATION WORLD: LIFE IN CHARLES II's ENGLAND

On 29 May 1660 John Evelyn, lawyer and author, wrote in his diary: 'This day, His Majesty Charles the Second came to London after a sad and long exile . . . . This was also his birthday'. Evelyn went on to describe how the king was greeted by the Lord Mayor in full regalia, lords dressed in velvet and cloth of gold and 20,000 soldiers who shouted and waved their swords. It was a day to

Charles II enters London in 1660

remember, with church bells ringing, streets decorated with flowers, houses hung with tapestries and fountains running wine. Less than a week before, the warship *Naseby*, which brought Charles to England, had been hastily renamed *Royal Charles*. The rule of the Saints was over.

The thirty-year-old king stood 'above two yards high'. He was a far different man from his father. Charles II loved wine, women, gambling, yachting and horse-racing. He was talkative and witty, with a love of pleasure which earned him the nickname the 'Merry Monarch'. On a more serious level he was interested enough in science to become the first patron of the new Royal Society formed in 1660. This was a club of scholars and scientists who met for discussions and lectures. Charles was religious in an easy-going way with a secret leaning towards the Catholic Church. But the martyr's son did not care much about old beliefs and superstitions. Once when an astrologer offered to foretell the future he invited him to come to Newmarket races and spot winners!

Beneath the charm and laughter lay an experienced man of the world. As a teenager he had lived through the defeat and death of his father and had courageously tried to regain his crown at Worcester. He had known what it was to be a hunted fugitive and an almost penniless exile. He came to the throne with no high and mighty ideas about 'divine right', knowing that if he ruled like his father he would, as he put it, 'go on his travels again'. Deep down he seems to have believed that his family's right to the throne must be safeguarded. Otherwise he had few principles which he would not alter to suit the occasion.

Second-class citizens

The easy-going king was prepared to forget the past, well knowing that ex-Roundheads as well as Cavaliers had put him back on the throne. 'Mercy and indulgence is the best way to bring men to a true repentance', he told his first House of Lords. His chief minister, Edward Hyde, Earl of Clarendon, agreed with him and begged the Commons to 'restore the whole nation to . . . its old good manners, its old good humour, and its old good nature'.

The so-called 'Cavalier' Parliament which sat until 1678 felt differently about the more dangerous or extreme of its old enemies. Soon after the 'Restoration' (Charles's return) the bodies of Cromwell and his son-in-law Ireton were dug up and hanged. Cromwell's head was fixed on London Bridge and is now buried in Sidney Sussex College, Cambridge. Nine survivors of the fifty-nine who had signed Charles I's death warrant were executed. Four men closely involved in Charles's execution were also hanged, drawn and quartered. General Harrison died in this way but Lambert was imprisoned for life. Otherwise, those who had fought against the king in the wars were pardoned.

As far as religion was concerned the few Presbyterians who had supported Charles's return were soon disappointed. The Cavalier Parliament felt it was essential to preserve the Church for which

Charles II

Charles I died. Various Acts of Parliament, the so-called Clarendon Code, gradually prevented all persons who were not members of the Church of England (called nonconformists) from sharing in the government, administration or education system of their country. A Corporation Act (1661) dismissed all town councillors who were not Church of England; nonconformists were also excluded from the universities. The Act of Uniformity (1662) authorised a new edition of the Prayer Book. Nearly 1,000 puritan clergymen and university teachers who would not use this form of prayer were sacked. Another 700 left of their own accord. Further, the so-called Test Acts in 1673 and 1678 stopped nonconformists being MPs or holding government posts.

Two other laws wiped out the religious toleration of Cromwell's day. The Conventicle Act made it a crime to worship anywhere but in a Church of England church. The Five Mile Act forbade nonconformist ministers to live within five miles of a town, or their old parishes. The idea was to stop them preaching. The Clarendon Code made Charles II's reign a time of great unhappiness for many sincere Christians. It created a large class of second-class citizens, the nonconformists, whose distinctive way of life continued long after the Code itself was forgotten.

Samuel Pepys

In 1665 England again went to war with Holland. There was fighting in North America, where the Dutch colony of New Amsterdam was captured and renamed New York in honour of the king's brother. Most battles, however, took place in the waters off southern England and were fought by hundreds of warships

Samuel Pepys by John Hayls, 1666. He is holding the manuscript of one of his songs

at murderously close range. Of the Battle of Lowestoft (June 1666), a certain Samuel Pepys recorded in his diary:

> The Earl of Falmouth, Muskerry, and Mr Richard Boyle killed on board the Duke's ship, the *Royal Charles*, with one shot. Their blood and brains flying in the Duke's face and the head of Mr Boyle striking down the Duke, as some say . . . .

The Duke of York was Charles's brother, James, who commanded the fleet in this battle. James returned, according to Pepys, 'all fat and lusty, and ruddy by being in the sun', but a wounded sailor who brought news of the battle had 'a face black as the chimney and covered with dirt, pitch and tar and powder, and muffled with dirty clouts [*rags*] and his right eye stopped with oakum'.

Pepys began his diary in 1660, writing in a special shorthand so that it would be difficult to read. After his death in 1703 it was given to the library of Magdalene College, Cambridge, where it remained unread until decoded in 1822. The effect was almost miraculous – out of the dusty sheets emerged a vivid picture of life at the time.

The Great Plague

As Pepys rode through London in June 1665 his coachman complained of feeling ill. He was one of many being taken sick at this time, for the capital was in the grip of bubonic plague. Plague had been rife in Britain since the Black Death (1348–51). There had been bad outbreaks in Elizabeth's reign and in 1625 and 1647 thousands had died in London alone.

By August many rich people, including the king and his courtiers, had fled from the narrow, infected streets of London. Pepys stayed, although he sent his wife to Woolwich, a town a few miles down river from the capital. On 7 June he had noted:

> This day . . . I did in Drury Lane see two or three houses marked with a red cross upon the doors and 'Lord have mercy upon us' writ there which was a sad a sight to me, being the first of that kind that I ever saw.

This referred to a City Council rule which ordered that once there was plague in a house it was to be shut with the family inside for forty days and a red cross painted on the door.

As the plague took a grip on the city, Samuel Pepys wrote, 'Every day looks with the face of a Sabbath day. Now shops are shut in, people rare and very few that walk about, in so much that the grass begins to spring in some places.' At night carts moved through the streets, pulled by men shouting 'Bring out your dead'. With people dying at such a rate there was no time for proper burial. Large pits were dug to take the corpses. Bills of Mortality (death) were published weekly; this one records the deaths during the height of the plague in August 1665.

Doctors were helpless. Some suspected that 'small worms' carried by rats or cats ate into human bodies. None knew the real

Bills of mortality were published weekly, showing the number of deaths and their causes. This one records a week in August 1665, when the plague was at its height

The Dise[ase]

Abortive ———
Aged ———
Apoplexie ———
Bedridden ———
Cancer ———
Childbed ———
Chrisomes ———
Collick ———
Consumption ———
Convulsion ———
Dropsie ———
Drowned two, one at St. [ ]
  Tower, and one at Lamb[ ]
Feaver ———
Fistula ———
Flox and Small-pox ———
Flux ———
Found dead in the Stre[et]
  St. Bartholomew the L[ ]
Frighted ———
Gangrene ———
Gowt ———
Grief ———
Griping in the Guts ———
Jaundies ———
Imposthume ———
Infants ———
Killed by a fall down sta[ ]
  St. Thomas Apostle ———
Christned { Males ———
           { Females ———
           { In all ———
Increased in the [ ]
Parishes clear of the [ ]

The Assize of Bread set fo[ ]
A penny Wheaten [ ]
  half-p[ ]

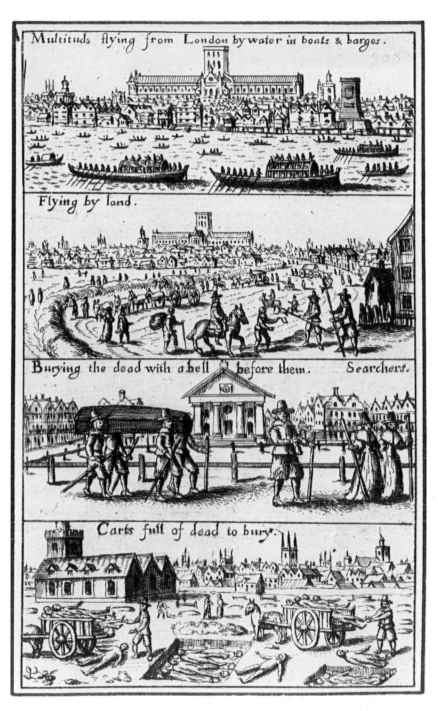

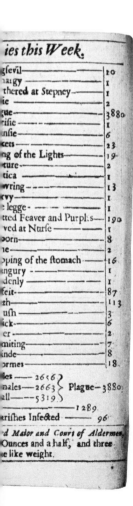

Plague scenes

cause, that the disease was carried by the fleas of the black rat. Even if it had been known there would have been little hope of preventing the disease while people washed so rarely and lived in filthy, crowded conditions. When the plague died down, 100,000 people had lost their lives – nearly a quarter of London's population. That winter, so Pepys reported, many still refused to buy wigs in case they had been made from the hair of plague victims.

London's burning

Early next year Charles II returned to Whitehall and his people hoped for better things. Unfortunately 1666 proved nearly as bad. In January the French joined the Dutch in fighting England. Despite another naval victory in June, rumours of an invasion by 30,000 Frenchmen caused thousands of Englishmen to join the militia. Londoners were therefore in a dangerously excited mood when early on Sunday, 2 September, a fire broke out in the house of Thomas Farrinor, a baker in Pudding Lane.

At first it seemed a small incident. Farrinor and his family escaped through an upstairs window. Only his maidservant, who refused to jump to the cobbles below, was burned to death. Then a steady east wind caused the fire to spread swiftly through the narrow alleys and overhanging houses. Worse still, the flames destroyed the lead pipes and the water-wheels at London Bridge. Thus there was little water with which to fight the blaze. All day the fire raged out of control. Smoke clouds, reckoned to be 90 kilometres long, hung over the inferno and at Oxford, over 80 kilometres away, the citizens looked towards London and saw 'a dim reddish sunset' as night fell.

London's Lord Mayor at first underestimated the danger. When he did try to fight the fire the task overwhelmed him. Pepys met him and was told, 'Lord! What can I do? I am spent; people will not obey me. I have been pulling down houses, but the fire overtakes us faster than we can do it'. Eventually, the king and his brother James took command of the fire-fighting. Sailors were brought ashore to blow up houses; this created spaces which the fire could not cross. A circle of fire-posts, manned by soldiers and civilians, was set up around the disaster area.

After three days the wind veered south, driving the flames back on the fire damage. This slowed the fire down, although it did not stop the destruction. Old St Pauls Cathedral burned from the roof downwards, its stones exploding with the heat, its 2.5 hectares of

FAC SIMILE OF AN EXTRACT FROM THE SHORT-HAND M.S. DIARY
(Vide Page 1. 3rd sentence)

The condition of the State was thus - viz. The Rump after being disturbed by my Lord Lambert, was lately returned to sit again. The Officers of the Army, all forced to yield — Lawson lies still in the River. & Monke is with his Army in Scotland.

An example of Pepys's shorthand with translation. This is from his diary

Fire of London, 1666, by a Dutch artist

lead roof melting like 'snow before the sun'. The city's widest street, Cheapside, was crossed by the fiery sparks which fed on piles of timber left in the middle. London Bridge was saved but only just. When the fire died away the centre of the city was like 'some dismal desert'.

Wren's London

Only a few days after the Great Fire, Sir Christopher Wren placed before the Royal Society a plan for a 'new city' to replace the old. Wren was a mathematician, astronomer and scientist as well as an architect. His ambitious scheme would have made London one of the wonders of the world. But those who had lost their houses wanted them built exactly where they had been before, so Wren's wide streets and squares remained a dream. Despite this setback Wren built at least sixty new churches and a tall column to commemorate the Fire. It is called the Monument and stands about 40 metres from the site of Farrinor's baker's shop.

Wren's most famous task began in 1673, when the king ordered him to prepare plans for a new St Pauls. The work lasted the rest of Wren's long life. It was 1711 before the huge dome was in place and

Wren's most famous achievement: St Paul's Cathedral, London

another five years before the Cathedral was open for services. Year after year Wren supervised the work, travelling to the top in a basket, arguing with authorities who grumbled at the cost, trying to solve the problems of placing such a weight on wet sand and gravel. His salary worked out at £4 a week. He died in 1723 and was buried in St Pauls. The words on his tomb are most appropriate. They are in Latin and read, 'Si Monumentum Requiris Circumspice' – if you seek his monument, look around you.

Sources and questions

1. One of the most famous stories about Charles II tells of his adventures after the Battle of Worcester in 1651, when he fled from the Roundheads and was forced at one point to hide in an oak tree at Boscobel House in Shropshire. He first told this tale to Samuel Pepys as they sailed back to England in 1660. Twenty years later he dictated a full account to Pepys when the two were staying at Newmarket.

> Upon the Quarter-deck he [*Charles*] fell to talking of his escape after Worcester. . . . [*how*] he travelled four days and three nights on foot, every step up to the knees in dirt, with nothing but a green coat and a pair of country breeches on and a pair of country shoes, that made him so sore all over his feet that he could scarce stir. Yet he was forced to run away from a miller . . . that took them for rogues. He told of sitting at table in one place, where the master of the house, that had not seen him for eight years, did know him but kept it private. . . . In another place, at his inn [*The George at Brighton*] the master of the house, as the King was standing by the Fireside, knelt down and kissed his hand, saying that he would not ask who he was, but bid God bless him wherever he was going.

Source: Pepys's diary, 23 May 1660. *Full account in Pepys's shorthand, in PL 2141, later published by Sir David Dalrymple as* An Account of the preservation of Charles II, 1766. Pepys diary, *G. Bell & Sons, 1970*

(a) Charles first told this story to a stranger. Can you think why he was fond of telling it?

(b) Charles had not told this story until he met Pepys on his way back to be King of England. Can you think of a reason why?

(c) Why should 'country shoes' have made Charles so sore?

(d) Why would Charles be pleased to have reached Brighton during his escape?

(e) What particular skill did Pepys possess that made Charles confident he would write an accurate account of what he said?

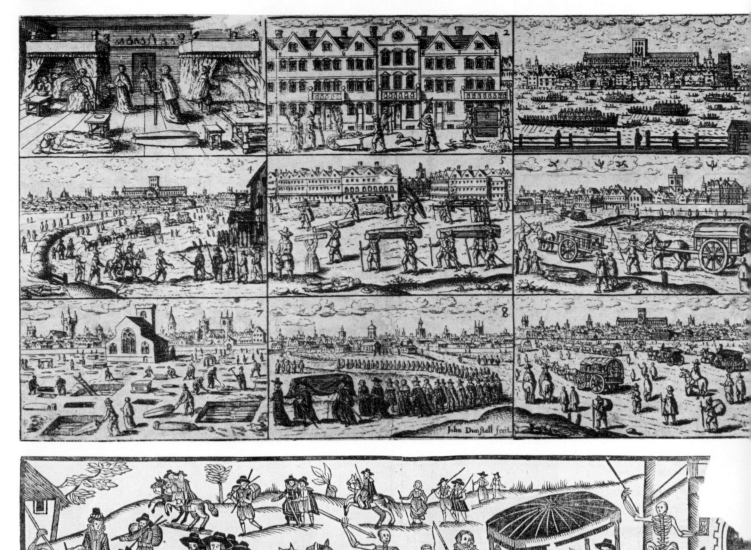

2. **(a)** Why are the people in the lower drawing leaving town for the country?
   (b) How does the artist show us the reason for their leaving?
   (c) How does the artist show that rich as well as poor could catch the plague?
   (d) What information does this source convey regarding transport in those days?

3. Look at the nine scenes at the top of the page. Using them as a guide, write a letter to a friend describing life in London during the plague.

DOCUMENTS: THE GREAT FIRE OF LONDON, 1666

Here are four eyewitness accounts of the Great Fire of London.

Document 1

Lady Hobart wrote this letter to a friend as the fire still raged.

> O dear Sir Ralph, I am sorry to be the messenger of so dismal news, for poor London is almost burnt down. It began on Saturday night and has burnt ever since and is at this time more fierce than ever. It did begin in Pudding Lane at a baker's where a Dutch rogue was staying and it burnt to the Bridge and all Fish Street. . . . It is caused by the Dutch. . . one Dutchman was captured in Westminster setting his outhouse on fire and other Dutchmen have attempted to set light to many places. . . . A number of Dutchmen have been arrested with grenades and gunpowder. . . . I am almost out of my wits. We have packed up all our goods to leave, but cannot get a cart for money. . . people are paying 5 and 10 pounds for carts.
>
> *Source: Clapp, Fisher and Juraci*, Documents, *George Bell, 1977*

Questions

1. Why would Lady Hobart particularly dislike Dutchmen at this time?
2. How do you think Lady Hobart got her information about the Dutch 'fire-makers'?
3. Why do you think carts were so expensive?
4. Lady Hobart wrote that she was almost 'out of her wits'. What parts of this source seem to confirm this?
5. In what way would a letter written at the time be a better/worse source than one written weeks or even months later?

Document 2

Edward Hyde, Earl of Clarendon, was a friend and minister to both Charles I and II. He was Charles II's Chancellor at the time of the Fire. Some years later, Clarendon wrote this.

> Monday morning produced first a suspicion and then a universal conviction that this fire was not an accident . . . rather that it was the result of a conspiracy. . . the wicked men who were thought to have done it were the Dutch and French who lived in London, though they had lived in the city for nearly twenty years . . . . Shortly after, all the Roman Catholics were blamed as well. When this rumour spread . . . every hour brought reports of some bloody attacks on foreigners . . . the king ordered many [*members*] of the privy council to go into the city to prevent these cruelties . . . . The trouble was that people could not work out how a house that was distant a mile . . . from the fire could suddenly be in flame . . . . Soon there were witnesses who said they had seen this villainy committed. . . .
>
> *Source: Clarendon's* History of the Rebellion *and* The Life of Himself. *Selections edited by Huehns, Oxford University Press, 1978*

Questions

1. Pick out the parts of this document which suggest that Clarendon did not believe the tales of Frenchmen and Catholics starting the fire.
2. What reasons does Clarendon give for people believing that the fires were started deliberately? What do you think was the actual reason for what had happened?
3. Why would Clarendon have been interested in reports of fires being started deliberately?
4. What parts of this document suggest that Clarendon held an important position in the government?

Document 3

These extracts about the Great Fire come from Pepys's diary. They were written later from rough notes scribbled at the time.

2 [*September*]   Lord's day. . . . Jane [*their servant*] called us up, about 3 in the morning, to tell us of a great fire they saw in the city. . . . I rose . . . and went to her window, and thought it to be on the back side of Mark Lane . . . but . . . I thought it far enough off and went to bed again. . . . about 7 . . . Jane tells me that she hears that . . . 300 houses have been burned down . . . and it was now burning down all Fish Street by London Bridge. . . . So down. . . to [*see*] the Lieutenant of the Tower [*of London*], who tells me that it began this morning in the King's bakers in Pudding Lane. . . . So I went down to the water-side . . . and there saw a lamentable fire. . . . Everybody endeavouring to remove their goods, and flinging them into the river. . . .

7 [*September*]   Up at 5 o'clock and, blessed be to God, find all well, and by water to St Paul's wharf. Walked thence and saw all the town burned, and a miserable sight of St Paul's church [*cathedral*], wish all the roofs fallen. . . . [I]t is a proper time for discontentment. . . . [A]ll men's minds are full of care to protect themselves and their goods. . . . Our fleets [*the Dutch and British*] have been in sight of one another, and were parted, to our great loss . . . the Dutch being come out [*of port*] only . . . to please their people; but in very bad condition as to stores, victuals [*food and drink*] and men. . . .

Source: The Diary of Samuel Pepys, *ed. Robert Latham and William Matthews, Vol. VII, Bell and Hyman, 1972, pages 267–79*

Questions

1. Can you think of any reason why Pepys was not surprised to hear that a fire had broken out?
2. What parts of this source suggest that Pepys was an important and well-off person?
3. Why did Pepys know so much about the movements of the British and Dutch fleets?
4. What reason does Pepys give for suggesting that the British might have beaten the Dutch had there been a battle?
5. Compare the accuracy of Documents 1 and 3. Explain why you think one source is more accurate than the other.

Document 4

William Taswell was a schoolboy of 15 when the Great Fire occurred. Many years later he wrote this account of what he heard and saw.

On Sunday [*2 September*] between 10 and 11 forenoon . . . a report reached my ears that London was on fire. . . . I saw four boats crowded with homeless people. They had escaped from the fire with hardly any other covering than a blanket. . . . Meanwhile, the ignorant . . . mob . . . hurried away with a kind of frenzy, vented their rage against the Roman Catholics and Frenchmen. . . . A blacksmith in my presence meeting an innocent Frenchman . . . knocked him down . . . with an iron bar. . . .

On Thursday . . . I tried to reach St Pauls. The ground was so hot as almost to scorch my shoes. . . . [W]hen I got there I saw

Questions

1. Why were Frenchmen and Catholics regarded as enemies?
2. Compare Documents 1 and 4. What did Taswell know that Lady Hobart did not? Why was this?
3. What part of this source contradicts one of the known facts about the fire?
4. What methods of escape from the fire are mentioned in Documents 1, 3, and 4? What clues are there that these methods were ineffective or inefficient?

the metal belonging to the [*cathedral*] bells melting, the walls in ruins, and heaps of stones tumbling down with a great noise. . . . I should also mention that near the east walls . . . I saw a human body. . . . This was an old . . . woman who [*had*] fled here for safety. . . . Her clothes were burnt and every limb reduced to coal. . . .

But what made the loss of our house greater was this. Certain persons, pretending to be porters, but in reality nothing else but downright robbers, offered to help us remove our goods. We accepted their offer: but all they did was to steal goods from us to the value of forty pounds. . . .

Source: Clapp, Fisher and Furacci, op. cit.

Document 5

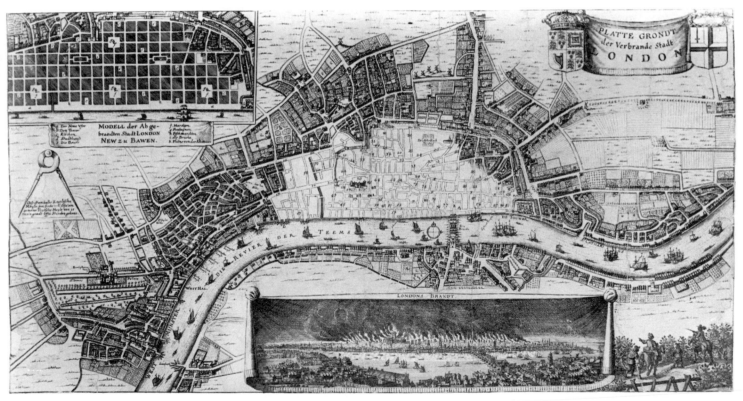

Map showing the extent of the fire. The light coloured areas were those devastated

Questions

1. Using this map as a guide, what made escape especially difficult for the inhabitants in those days?
2. What were places like Temple Stairs, Milford Stairs, etc., used for? Why would they not be needed today?
3. What important parts of London were *not* affected by the fire? How did the survival of one in particular help the king?
4. What famous landmarks, streets, etc., are mentioned in the other sources? Apart from personal losses, what particular destruction seems to have horrified people most?

The Monument. In the Pepys Library at Magdalene College, Cambridge there is this drawing of the Monument erected to commemorate the Great Fire. One improvement as a result of the fire was included in this drawing. What was it? *An insurance badge.* One good result of the Great Fire was the founding of fire insurance schemes. Each insurance company had its own fire brigade. Houses insured by a company displayed this badge. Can you think why?

CHARLES II: FROM POPISH TO RYE HOUSE PLOT

In August 1678 Charles II heard rumours of a plot to kill him. When he asked for proof, a Dr Israel Tonge was brought before his Council. Tonge said that there was indeed a conspiracy by the pope, the French king and the Jesuits to murder Charles and place his Catholic brother James on the throne. He also admitted that a certain Titus Oates had told him this. The tale, like the names, was strange. Oates was a shady character whose evidence consisted of obviously forged documents. He changed his story frequently and when examined by the Privy Council contradicted himself.

The king was sure Oates was a liar, yet he did nothing about it. There were several reasons for his silence. In the first place Charles was fond of the Catholic faith which he had once described as 'the only religion fit for a gentleman'. His enemies would have liked to accuse him of being a 'Papist', a charge used against his father. Secondly, in 1670 he had signed the Treaty of Dover with the French king, Louis XIV. Officially this treaty was a military alliance of France and England against Holland. But it also contained a secret clause in which Charles promised to declare himself a Catholic in return for a pension from the French king. Whether Charles ever intended to do this is doubtful; he was more interested in money which would make him independent of Parliament.

The nearest Charles ever got to keeping his promise to Louis was in 1672 when he cancelled the Clarendon Code laws by a Declaration of Indulgence. This would have made it easier for nonconformists, including Catholics, to worship freely and get good jobs. Parliament's reaction was a warning to the king. They were furious and compelled him to give up even this small step in the direction of religious toleration. In such circumstances Charles dare not appear friendly towards Catholics. If men 'discovered' Popish plots it was best not to speak, for some already suspected his religious beliefs and if the secret Treaty of Dover became public he might well lose his throne.

After the Privy Council had finished with Oates, Charles went off to enjoy some horse-racing at Newmarket.

The Earl of Shaftesbury, Whig leader during Charles II's reign

An unsolved murder

Protestants who discovered 'popish' plots were fairly common in seventeenth-century England. Generally they were exposed as liars and forgotten. This time two dramatic events appeared to confirm the story. Edward Coleman, secretary to James's wife, was found to have written to foreign Catholics discussing ways of changing England's religion. Then, in October 1678, the country was alarmed by an unsolved murder.

Sir Edmund Berry Godfrey, the magistrate to whom Oates had made his first statement, disappeared. Later his body was found in a ditch on Primrose Hill near London. Nobody knows exactly how Godfrey died. Doctors certified that he had been strangled, although a sword was fixed through his body. In recent times it has been suggested that Godfrey might have committed suicide and that friends made it look like murder so that he could have a Christian burial. Whatever really happened, his death convinced every loyal Protestant that Catholics had killed him to destroy evidence of their wicked schemes.

For the next two years there was panic in England as Charles's political opponents, led by Lord Shaftesbury, used the plot as a way of attacking the king's government. Wild rumours alarmed the country. Tales of French armies landing in Kent, of Catholic troops advancing underground, and of 'cellars full of swords', became commonplace. James, the Catholic heir to the throne, felt it safer to retire abroad for a time. His friend, honest Samuel Pepys, was put in the Tower as a suspected Papist because he knew a Catholic musician! The Commons even set up a special committee to examine the royal fireworks-maker because he had a French name.

Altogether thirty-five men, including Coleman, a lord and an archbishop, were executed, and Oates and his friends made a comfortable living 'discovering' plotters.

Whigs and Tories

The Popish Plot panic gradually became a battle over the succession to the throne. Charles II had several children, but none by his wife, the Portuguese Catherine of Braganza whom he had married in 1661. As a result his Catholic brother James was due to succeed him. It was a fact which numerous Protestants were not ready to accept. One group wanted Charles to follow Henry VIII's example and divorce *his* Queen Catherine; a new marriage might produce a son to succeed him. This idea did not appeal to Charles who seemed to dislike divorce more than adultery. Another suggestion was that James's Protestant daughter by his first marriage should rule after Charles's death. This was Mary, wife of the Dutch King William of Orange.

A third, more dangerous scheme was to allow Charles's illegitimate son, James, Duke of Monmouth to become king instead of James. His mother, Lucy Walter, had been one of Charles's mistresses. Some people wanted James proclaimed legitimate.

Less honest men remembered that Charles had known Lucy before his marriage. They whispered of a mysterious 'black box' which contained the marriage certificate of Charles and Lucy. Had this been true it would have made Monmouth heir to the throne. Charles always denied that such a marriage had taken place, and in 1679 signed this declaration in the presence of some of his Councillors:

> For the voiding of any dispute which may happen in time to come concerning the succession to the Crown, I do here declare in the presence of Almighty God, that I never gave nor made any contract of marriage, nor was married to any woman whatsoever, but to my present wife, Queen Catherine, now living . . . .
> Charles R.

During the fierce war of words which followed, Shaftesbury's followers placed a Bill before Parliament proposing that James should not be allowed to become king. This was called the Exclusion Bill. The battle which followed saw the birth of the first political parties in English history. Those who wanted to get rid of James were called Exclusionists. Those against interfering with the succession to the throne were referred to as Abhorrers because they abhorred (detested) the suggestion.

Such clumsy names were soon replaced by simpler ones as each side called the other names. Abhorrers called their opponents 'Whiggamores' or Whigs after the Presbyterian rebels still fighting against the Royalist government in Scotland. Exclusionists called their enemies Tories, the name given to Irish Catholics battling to be free of English rule.

One should not think of these rivals as political parties in the modern sense. Nobody joined them by filling in a form and paying a subscription. The present idea of an opposition party which has a useful job to do and is really an alternative government never entered the minds of seventeenth-century people. Opposition to royal policies, however peaceful, was still seen as near to treason. Nevertheless, the two groups did have different points of view. Whigs stood for many of the ideals of those men who had gone to war against Charles I. Shaftesbury, for example, had fought for Parliament and served in Cromwell's government. Such men believed that royal power should be limited and Parliament powerful. Tories stood more firmly for the Church of England and many still believed in the divine right of kings. These people were ready to accept James because he was the rightful heir to the throne, even though they disliked his Catholic faith.

The Rye House Plot

When it became clear that Charles had organised enough parliamentary support to defeat the Exclusion Bill his Whig opponents acted very differently from a modern political party. During 1682, Shaftesbury plotted an armed rebellion. His supporters included

Charles II attends a horse race near Windsor. The Rye House plotters planned to kill him on his way back from another of his favourite courses, Newmarket

old Commonwealth republicans as well as Exclusionists. This plot was discovered, so he fled abroad where he died in December.

Some of Shaftesbury's more extreme followers decided on a 'Guy Fawkes' style solution to the 'problem'. They planned to shoot both Charles and James as they rode along a narrow lane near Rye House at Hoddesdon in Hertfordshire, on their way home from the Newmarket races. Monmouth was involved in this conspiracy. He claimed later that he never wished to kill his father. 'I wish I may die this moment I am writing if ever it entered into my head', he said of such a thought. But he had sided with Shaftesbury during the Exclusion quarrel, had been barred from court and certainly knew of the plot.

The plot misfired because the royal pair travelled to London earlier than expected due to a fire which devastated parts of Newmarket. One of the plotters then betrayed his companions. The investigations which followed led to the execution of several Whig lords and the flight of Monmouth abroad. It also marked the end of the Popish Plot panic. People began to see how foolish they had been. James himself became more popular. Soon afterwards Oates was flogged and imprisoned for daring to call James a traitor.

In 1685 Charles suffered a stroke. Anxious doctors gathered at the palace, bleeding him repeatedly and putting hot coals on various parts of his body. When their efforts failed Charles sent for a Catholic priest. It was a difficult, dangerous moment. His room was filled with Church of England priests who would have been horrified if they had known. A Father John Huddleston was found. By a strange coincidence, he had helped to hide Charles when he fled from Cromwell's troops after the Battle of Worcester. James cleared the bedroom and when Charles saw the priest he exclaimed, 'You that saved my body are now come to save my soul.' Huddleston gave the dying king the last rites of the Catholic Church. Just before midday on 6 February 1685 Charles II died.

Years before, a witty courtier had suggested Charles's epitaph:

> Here lies our sovereign lord the King
> Whose word no man relies on
> He never said a foolish thing
> And never did a wise one.

It was clever but not true. Charles had done many wise things. He had kept England at peace after a long period of upheaval. He had fought off a challenge to the throne. He had made sure that the rightful heir to the throne became king. Personally he did not think James would last very long, but he had done his best for his brother.

Sources and questions

1. Here, Lady Fox writes to her daughter to tell her about the excitement in London at the news of the Popish Plot.

> You cannot think how busy a place this is and how full everybody is of this damned plot. I pray God they get to the bottom of it, which will be hard to do, for sure it was hatched deep and in the dark. Every day brings more to light. This day were two letters read in the House of Commons, which were found in a Jesuit's room and had been written by him to another member of the order. These tell of a great design [*plot*] and of a great meeting; and this does agree with Oates's evidence . . . .
>
> Here is great strictness in Whitehall [*palace*]; all the locks changed on the private lodgings and all the gates of the courtyards kept shut and none allowed in unless they are known. The French cook . . . is discharged already by the King's command and there is no other Papist [*left*] below stairs . . . . I am heartily sorry for our good friends who must suffer with the rest if this [*matter*] be pursued.
>
> 29 October and 2 November 1678

Source: Audley End Archives, Essex Record Office (D/DBy C14). Quoted by Millward, Seventeenth Century Documents, *Hutchinson Educational, 1961, pages 121–2*

(a) What evidence is there in this source that Lady Fox was a woman of position and influence?

(b) Do you think Lady Fox believed there was a plot? Give reasons for your answer.

(c) Why were English people particularly suspicious of French people and Jesuits?

(d) What evidence is there in this source that Lady Fox knew some Catholics?

(e) What suggests that security had been rather lax at Whitehall *before* the Popish Plot scare?

2. The drawing opposite was published at the height of the Popish Plot scare.

(a) Who are the men standing round the table at the bottom of the picture? Look at their hats and robes for a clue.

(b) A shaft of light containing the words, 'Heaven shall turn thy weapons against thee' is pointing at the man in centre. Look at the crown he is wearing and work out who he is meant to be. In what way was this man thought to be connected with the Popish Plot?

(c) The angel on the right is holding a crown, the one on the left is holding a church. In what way did people of the time think that 'angels' had helped save the English Church and Crown?

(d) Charles and his brother James are seated at the top, right. The figures on the left represent two men who 'saved' them from the plot. Can you guess the name of one of them?

3. Here Bishop Gilbert Burnet gives his opinion of Charles II. This comes from Burnet's *History of His Own Times*, published in 1724. Burnet had known Charles. He was a friend of William of Orange.

> He had a very good understanding. He knew well the state of affairs both at home and abroad. . . . He seemed to have no sense of religion. . . . He once said to myself . . . he could not think God would make a man miserable . . . for taking a little pleasure. . . . He disguised his Popery to the last. . . . He was friendly and easygoing. . . . His understanding was sharp, and his memory good. He was an everlasting talker. . . . He had a very poor opinion of both men and women; and did not think there was either sincerity or chastity in the world. . . . He thought that nobody served him out of love: and so loved others as little as he thought they loved him. He hated business . . . but when it was necessary . . . he would stay as long as his ministers had work for him.

Source: Quoted by Millward, op. cit., pages 47–8

(a) Do you think Burnet liked Charles? Give reasons for your answer.

(b) Why might a king of those times decide that nobody served him 'out of love'?

(c) Why might a Protestant like Burnet think that Charles had no sense of religion?

(d) What evidence is there in this source that Burnet thought Charles was an intelligent man?

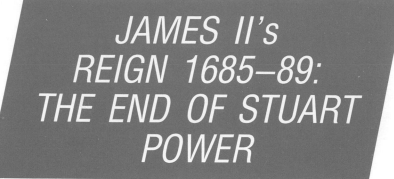

JAMES II's REIGN 1685–89: THE END OF STUART POWER

James II, the new king, had proved himself brave in war and a capable organiser in peace. In his early years he had been a Protestant; both daughters of his first marriage were of that faith. After the Restoration his beliefs had changed, especially after his second marriage to a Catholic, Mary of Modena. In 1670 he openly announced his conversion to the Catholic Church – a courageous act which Charles never dared make.

Charles had worked hard in his last years to fill the House of Commons with Royalists. Consequently, the Parliament that James summoned turned out to be the most loyal Parliament of the century. The majority of Tory MPs felt that the new king had served his country well in the Dutch wars. They thought he should be given a chance to prove himself as king. Of course, Tories particularly disliked his religion but they stressed he had a right to the throne by birth. All he had to do was respect the rights, and maintain the privileges, of the Church of England. His faith could then be a private matter which was none of their business.

Rebellion in the West

The first two rebellions against James's authority were easily crushed. Monmouth had sailed to Holland after the Rye House Plot in which he had treacherously given evidence against his fellow conspirators. Here he was joined by the Presbyterian leader in Scotland, the Earl of Argyle, who was discontented with the persecution of Presbyterians by Charles's government. When James became king the two plotted his overthrow. In May 1685 Argyle went to Scotland and raised a rebellion. It failed and he was executed.

Next month Monmouth landed at Lyme Regis in Dorset to a disappointing welcome. Local Whig leaders were not interested in such a weak, unreliable leader. Those who did rally to Monmouth's army were mainly discontented nonconformist peasants. After he had been proclaimed king at Taunton, Monmouth published a 'Declaration'. In it he accused his uncle James of starting the Great Fire of London, conspiring in the Popish Plot and even poisoning

James II

The battle of Sedgemoor, July 1685

his brother! He then advanced to meet the royal army which was at Sedgemoor, 5 kilometres from Bridgwater in Somerset.

By this time Monmouth was in a gloomy state of mind. He realised that his position was hopeless. He had only a small army and many of his soldiers were untrained and badly equipped; some had only scythe blades fixed on poles. Once, when Monmouth stood watching the enemy troops from the tower of Bridgwater Church, he saw the flags of a regiment he had once commanded. 'I know those men. They will fight', he remarked.

Monmouth decided that his only hope was a surprise attack on the royal camp after dark. Unfortunately for him, flooded streams slowed down the advance so much that it was nearly daylight when the royal camp was reached. The battle of Sedgemoor (July 1685) which followed, although remembered as the last fought on

Primitive scythe weapons used by Monmouth's men

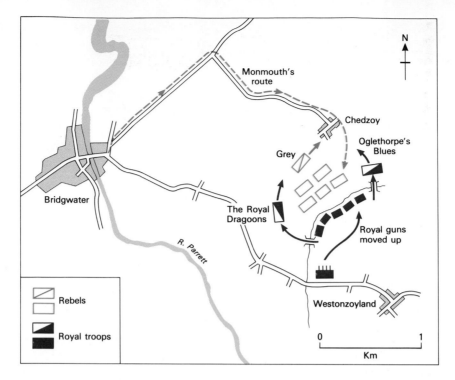

A plan of Sedgemoor. The dotted line shows Monmouth's advance during the night

English soil, was really a massacre. The royal commanders acted quickly to avoid panic. Drummers ran barefoot through the camp, awakening the infantry to the danger. Guns were dragged across the soft ground and put in firing positions. Cavalry engaged the rebels first, then the infantry ran forward to cut Monmouth's army to pieces.

Monmouth galloped towards the Hampshire coast, only to be captured near Ringwood. He was taken to London where he begged James to spare him. But he had gone too far this time and was beheaded.

The Bloody Assize

Monmouth was clumsily executed. It took three blows and a final cut with a knife to get his head off. His followers suffered even worse punishments. They were tried by Lord Chief Justice Jeffreys, a friend and adviser to James. Jeffreys had made his name trying the Rye House Plotters. He was a brilliant lawyer and a keen Tory who supported king and Church. During what Whig writers later called the Bloody Assize, he and his fellow judges toured the West Country on a special commission sent to deal with the rebels.

The driving force behind the commission was James himself. Instead of executing a few ringleaders, the king ordered large numbers of Monmouth's followers to be severely punished. Altogether about 1,300 men and women were condemned, of whom about 200 suffered hanging, drawing and quartering. Another 800 were given to the queen and her courtiers to be sold as slaves in the West Indies.

Most accounts of Jeffreys's bullying behaviour at these trials were written by Whigs after his death in 1689. They presented him as a devil in human shape who joked as he passed sentence. He was even described as being ugly, when all portraits show him to have been handsome. Actually his behaviour was no worse than that of many judges of the time. James, rather than Jeffreys, was responsible for the Bloody Assize (see Documents, page 260).

Royal indulgences

The Monmouth rebellion showed that James was unlikely to be deposed if he supported the Church of England. But he went too far and decided to grant toleration to Catholics and nonconformists.

During 1686–7 James made his intentions clear. Tory ministers were replaced by Catholics. Parliament was first adjourned and then dismissed. The rules of certain corporations (chartered towns) were altered to allow Catholics to be town councillors. The Test Acts were bypassed so that Catholics could become army officers. Cambridge University's vice-chancellor was sacked for refusing to grant a degree to a Catholic priest. At Oxford, Magdalen College was forced to accept a Catholic president.

Such actions frightened both rich and poor. Ordinary folk were afraid of a return to army rule, this time by Catholics instead of 'Saints'. Churchmen were horrified at the thought of their university training grounds coming under Catholic influence. After all, most of them had been trained at Oxford or Cambridge where lecturers had to be members of the Church of England. Political leaders saw their power being taken away by representatives of a religious minority. Even other nonconformists were not happy; James's moves would only make them more unpopular. They also knew that his real interest was in Catholic freedom, not their own.

In April 1687, James issued a Declaration of Indulgence which virtually cancelled the Clarendon Code. In it he admitted that he wished 'all his subjects were members of the Catholic Church'. Soon afterwards it became known that the queen was pregnant. This was bad news for all Protestants. As matters stood, the fifty-four-year-old James would be succeeded by his Protestant daughters, Mary and Anne. If a boy was born to his second wife, England would be faced with a line of Catholic monarchs. Suspicious Protestants wondered whether the queen was really pregnant or whether the country was about to be tricked.

Events moved to a crisis in 1688. In April, James published a second Declaration of Indulgence. Sancroft, the Archbishop of Canterbury, and six bishops asked permission not to read it in the churches under their control. Of the Declaration they wrote:

> That Declaration is founded upon such a dispensing power as hath often been declared illegal in Parliament . . . . Your petitioners therefore most humbly . . . beseech Your Majesty that you will . . . not . . . insist upon the distributing and reading of Your Majesty's said declaration.

James lost his temper when he read this petition. 'This is a great surprise to me', he exclaimed, 'I did not expect this from you. This is a standard of rebellion.' He immediately charged them with seditious libel.

The 'Warming Pan Baby'

Sancroft and his six colleagues were tried in Westminster Hall in June 1688. By this time public opinion had been roused against James; this was, after all, the country which had believed the Popish Plot scare a few years before. Although the judges were friends of James, they and the jurymen had seen the mob which filled the streets. They were aware how unpopular they would be if they condemned bishops. When at last they returned a verdict of 'Not guilty' there were cheers in court which were taken up by the crowds outside. In the next few days the whole country celebrated with bonfires.

It was the first time an English monarch had lost an important law case and a shattering blow to a king who believed in divine right. That night the 'impossible' happened. Leading Tories and Whigs met together and wrote an invitation to William of Orange, James's son-in-law, to come to England, save the Protestant faith and restore the country's 'true liberties'. They were influenced by the fact that three weeks before (June 1688), the queen had given birth to a son. The people did not want a Catholic prince. They were prepared to believe any wild rumours. The baby had been born in a crowded room with the king present. Why then had the infant been carried instantly into the next room?

Protestant writers soon supplied an answer to this question. The real prince, they wrote, had died within a few seconds. A miller's son had been smuggled into St James's Palace in a warming pan from a Catholic convent nearby. In another version the prince died a few weeks later and was replaced by a brickmaker's son. These stories were false, of course, but they were believed for many years and James's son was known by his enemies as the 'Warming Pan Baby'.

Sources and questions

1. On 29 March 1687 James II wrote this to a Catholic friend. At that time James was due to be succeeded by his Protestant daughters, first Mary, then Anne.

   Not only could it never enter my head to think of changing the succession to the throne, but I know well that it is not in my power to do it, even if a Pope and a Parliament joined with me. For where the crown is hereditary [*passing from father to eldest child*] (as it is in these kingdoms, thanks be to God) His Almighty power alone can dispose of it because not only the hearts of kings but their Crowns being in his hands.

Source: James to Albeville, 29 March 1687. Archives des Affaires Etrangères, Paris, Correspondance Politique, Angleterre, 164, fol. 28. Quoted by John Miller, The Glorious Revolution, *Longman Seminar Studies, 1983*

(a) What parts of this source show that James believed in the Divine Right of Kings?
(b) What evidence is there in this source to suggest that James was a Catholic?
(c) What event soon afterwards made it possible for the succession to the throne to be changed?
(d) Why was James glad that the succession was hereditary even though it meant that he would be succeeded by Protestants?

2. Anne, later Queen of England, and step-sister of James's new-born child, was not present when the boy was born (1688). She had this to say about his birth to her elder sister Mary, wife of William of Orange.

My dear sister, you can't imagine the concern and vexation I have been in, that I should be so unfortunate to be out of town [*London*] when the Queen [*Mary of Modena*] was brought to bed, for I shall never now be satisfied whether the child be true or false. It may be it is our brother, but God only knows, for she never took care to satisfy the world [*of her pregnancy*], or give people any demonstration of it . . . tis possible it may be her child; but where one believes it, a thousand do not.

Source: Brown, Letters of Anne. *Quoted by Henri and Barbara van Zee,* William and Mary, *Macmillan, 1973*

(a) Why was Anne unhappy that she was not in London when the baby was born?
(b) Why would Anne wish to believe that the child was not her step-brother? Why would Mary have been anxious to know whether the child was really the son of James and Mary of Modena?
(c) Do you think there would have been any query about the child's birth if James had not been a Catholic? Give reasons for your answer.
(d) Do you think James was the sort of man to accept a child as his son if he suspected he was not the father? Bear in mind the opinions he expresses in Source 1.

3. Look at the epitaph to Charles II on page 251. Write your own four-line epitaph on James II.

DOCUMENTS: THE BLOODY ASSIZE

After the Monmouth rebellion in 1685, King James sent a team of lawyers led by the Lord Chief Justice, George Jeffreys, to the West Country. They were to apply the usual punishment for high treason – hanging, drawing and quartering. About 1,300 men and women were condemned to death. Of these, 200 were executed; the rest were transported as slave-convicts to the West Indies. The downfall of James three years later meant a pardon for these rebels – and a far different attitude towards those who marched with Monmouth.

Document 1

On 16 November 1685 Edward Hobbes, the Sheriff of Bath, sent the following orders to his constables and other local officials. Similar orders would have been sent by other sheriffs in the rebellious areas.

> These orders . . . require you immediately . . . to erect a gallows in the most public place of your said city to hang the said traitors on. . . . [Y]ou are to provide nooses to hang them with, a sufficient supply of logs to burn the bowels of the four traitors and a . . . cauldron to boil their heads and quarters, and salt to boil them with. . . . also tar to preserve them and a number of . . . poles to fix and place their heads and quarters on . . . .

Source: Collinson, Somerset, *1791. Quoted by J. G. Muddiman in* The Bloody Assize, *William Hodge & Co., 1929*

Questions

1. What, according to this source, happened to the bodies of executed traitors?
2. What effect do you think such executions might have on spectators?
3. Do you think the authorities did this to traitors because,
   (a) They enjoyed inflicting such punishments.
   (b) They wanted to discourage other people from being traitors.
   (c) This is how traitors had always been dealt with.
   Explain your choice(s).
4. This letter is from a sheriff. Why might this be considered a reliable source?

Document 2

This is an extract from Henry Pitman's book, *Relation of his great sufferings and strange adventures*. Pitman was surgeon to the Duke of Monmouth. He was captured after the battle of Sedgemoor, tried, condemned, and sent to the West Indies. He was pardoned in 1689 and returned to England. Here he describes what happened in Ilchester gaol.

> Certain persons . . . called us [*the prisoners*] out of our cells one after another, and told us, 'That the King was very gracious and merciful, and would not let any be executed but those who had been officers . . . and therefore we would . . . get . . . the King's Grace and Favour . . . if we gave an account of where we joined the Duke's army . . . otherwise we could expect no mercy'. In this way they drew us into a confession of our guilt,

Questions

1. Why do you think the officers of the rebel army were treated more harshly than the ordinary soldiers?
2. Why were the authorities anxious to know *where* each rebel had joined Monmouth's army?
3. Why, according to Pitman, did the rebels write confessions?
4. Who, according to this source, decided who should be executed?
5. Was there any point in any of Monmouth's soldiers claiming they were not rebels?

and . . . these confessions were written down and sent to the King before the Lord Chief Justice [*Jeffreys*] ever came to Dorset to try us. So Jeffreys knew beforehand our particular crimes and had received orders from the King (as 'tis supposed) who and what number to execute.

Source: Quoted by Muddiman, op. cit.

Document 3

John Tutchin took part in Monmouth's rebellion, was captured, and sentenced to be whipped, although this sentence does not seem to have been carried out. Here he gives his opinion of Jeffreys's behaviour, in a book called *The Western Martyrology* published in 1712.

> His [*Jeffreys's*] treatment of the rebels is not to be equalled in history . . . . People could not offend so much as to deserve the punishment he inflicted. A certain . . . Joy and Pleasure grinned from his brutal soul through his Bloody Eyes, whenever he was sentencing any of the poor souls to Death and Torment . . . . He showed neither humanity to the dead, nor civility to the living in his behaviour. . . . Nothing could be more like hell in those parts he visited, nothing so like the devil as he. Caldrons hissing, Carcasses boiling, pitch and tar sparkling and glowing, blood and limbs boiling and tearing and mangling . . . and he the Great Director of all. . . .

Source: Quoted by Muddiman, op. cit.

Questions

1. Tutchin writes of Jeffreys himself inflicting these punishments, and describes him as the 'Great Director of all'. What parts of other sources in these Documents suggest that this was not true?
2. Choose three phrases of this source which show what the writer thought of Jeffreys.
3. Choose three phrases which suggest that the writer was exaggerating.
4. Is it fair to blame Jeffreys for the way traitors were executed? Give reasons for your answer.

Document 4

Not everybody thought the Monmouth rebels were martyrs; some thought they had deserved their punishment. In a book called *A Caveat [warning] against the Whigs*, a Tory had this to say about the Whigs.

> But the Whigs have gone farther yet, and in imitation of the Catholics, have given us a new kind of martyr – those Holy Ones who died for rebellion and treasons. In this way they . . . make rebellion seem like religion, and by a dash of the pen change a crew of rebels and traitors into a Noble army of Saints and Martyrs. . . .
>
> I have indeed sometimes thought that Jeffreys was more fond of Justice than Mercy . . . but when I consider in what way several of those people who were pardoned spent the rest of their lives, as for example, the late scribbler Tutchin . . . . I cannot but think that it might have been better if he [*Jeffreys*] had hanged a few more of them on that occasion. . . .

Source: Quoted by Muddiman, op. cit.

Questions

1. What does the writer of this source accuse the Whigs of doing?
2. What does the writer think of (**a**) Judge Jeffreys, and (**b**) John Tutchin?
3. In what way had Catholics been 'martyrs' in England for many years?
4. In what way was the Monmouth rebellion a 'religious' rebellion?
5. What phrase sums up how the writer regarded Monmouth's army?
6. What other source in these Documents suggests why this writer would have liked Tutchin to have been hanged?

THE COMING OF WILLIAM 1688

A great deal now depended on affairs abroad. William was the sworn enemy of France. If he did come to England would Louis XIV, the French king, try to stop him? William himself found the decision easy. He cared little for England's parliamentary liberties or even its Protestant religion. What he did wish to prevent was a Catholic England in alliance with France against him.

On 1 November 1688 he sailed from Holland with an army of 15,000 Dutch and English troops. At first he was delayed by bad weather. Then the fleet benefited from what was later called a 'Protestant wind' which blew it swiftly down the Channel. The English navy, meanwhile, did nothing to stop it; it had already staged a near mutiny when a Catholic admiral was put in charge of it. Louis XIV was in two minds what to do. He offered to let James use the French fleet against William but in fact he was anxious not to do anything which would unite England and Holland against him.

William decided to land in England on 4 November because it was his birthday and wedding anniversary. But his English friends advised 5 November for obvious reasons. They got their way. In later years Whig writers made much of the fact that England had been twice saved from a Catholic plot on that date.

James's flight

William spent his first night in a fisherman's hut. Next day his troops started to advance along bad roads in pouring rain. At most places he was joined by important local gentlemen or blessed by poor folk who came to get a look at their 'Protestant saviour'. In London his 'orange' colours began to appear on men's coats and ladies' petticoats.

Since 1685 Protestants had been afraid of James's 'standing' (regular) army. Now that it was called upon to fight they found they had nothing to worry about. The royal troops were dispirited and mutinous. James had stationed them at Hounslow near London to frighten the city. In fact, the soldiers had been infected with the fanatical Protestant beliefs of some Londoners. They

William III

often disobeyed their Catholic officers and some had celebrated the acquittal of the seven bishops.

James joined them at Salisbury. At once his experienced soldier's eye told him that they were not to be trusted in battle. As he explained, 'It was in no ways advisable to venture myself at their head.' When his best general, John Churchill, deserted to William, taking with him details of the army's size and strength, James knew it was hopeless. He fled towards the coast where he was captured by some fishermen at Faversham in Kent.

An ill-treated and ragged James returned to London. He tried to behave as though he was still in charge, calling a Council meeting and attending Mass. But it was no use. Orders came from William that he was to leave the court and accept Dutch soldiers to guard him.

James was now afraid he would suffer the same fate as his father:

> If I do not retire I shall certainly be sent to the Tower and no King ever went out of that place but to his grave. It is a cruel thing for a subject to be driven out of his native country, much more for a King to be driven out of his three Kingdoms.

William was James's nephew as well as his son-in-law. He had no wish to kill him. Consequently, James was allowed to escape to France. For the second time in forty years the English had rid themselves of a Stuart king.

Settlement and toleration

With James gone, Parliament decided the question of who should succeed to the throne. At first it was agreed that William and Mary should be followed by their children. If they had no children the throne would pass to Mary's sister Anne and her family. Few expected Mary to become a mother and in fact she died childless in 1694. When the last of Anne's seventeen children died in 1701 the descendants of James I's daughter Elizabeth were named as her successors. Since Elizabeth had married a German prince it was George, Elector (ruler) of Hanover, who became king when Anne died in 1714. Thus the Catholic line founded by James II was excluded from the throne.

Side by side with this settlement went new freedoms. A Toleration Act of 1694 cancelled many of the laws against nonconformists. In future they could worship openly, although they were still disqualified from government jobs or university training. The following year Parliament showed that it no longer regarded the open discussion of religion and politics as a threat to law and order. The Licensing Act, which allowed the government to control all printed material, was conveniently dropped. By such deliberate 'forgetfulness' it became possible for authors and publishers to write and print what they liked, subject to the law of libel.

The events of 1688–9 were a turning point in British history. A new kind of monarchy had been established by men who regarded William as less of an evil than James. On the other hand, they were not prepared to give William some of the powers of previous kings. William still appointed his own cabinet, negotiated with foreign governments and saw to the day-to-day running of the country. The essential difference was that he had been *chosen* by Parliament, not born king by 'Divine Right'. In effect, William signed a contract with his wealthy subjects. A Bill of Rights (1689) gave to Parliament alone the right to raise taxes, pass laws and control the army. It laid down that elections should be held frequently and that MPs should have the right to speak freely during debates. Since 1689 many English monarchs have influenced their ministers; none has wielded 'God-given' power.

So rule passed to a Parliament controlled by a minority of rich people. It was to be the twentieth century before Parliament was controlled by all adult people through secret votes in free elections.

Sources and questions

1. Here two leading politicians, Lord Henry Sydney and Thomas Coningsby, explain to one of William's ministers how to manage Parliament.

> It is without question impossible for a King of England to do any considerable thing in a House of Commons, without . . . a number of men on whom the King may confidently rely, joined with the Speaker (who is now most certainly yours) meeting privately every night, there to work out how and by what methods they will oppose anything which might obstruct His Majesty's affairs, or propose anything that will further his interest the next day; amongst these ought to be . . . two or three men who have fair reputations in the House, such as [William] Sachaverell, Leveson Gower and Sir Thomas Clarges, who must by no means have any employments during the sessions but be rewarded afterwards. . . . [W]e look upon these three . . . to have the greatest influence over the three parties in the House that are not for King James: Sachaverell for the Whigs, Leveson Gower of the middle party and Sir Thomas Clarges of the High Church.

> *Source: S. Baxter*, William III, *Longman, 1966. Quoted by John Miller*, The Glorious Revolution, *Longman Seminar Studies, 1983*

   (a) Explain why a king needed to work with the House of Commons after 1689.
   (b) What evidence is there is this source that bribery was to be used to 'manage' the House?
   (c) Why was there no point in trying to influence the party which favoured King James? What was it called?
   (d) What evidence is there in this source to indicate the growth of political parties?
   (e) Why would William in particular need advice on how to manage the House of Commons?

2. On 2 February 1689 the House of Commons drew up a long list of its grievances. Some of these points were later put in the famous Bill of Rights, which guaranteed many freedoms which had been threatened in the long years of struggle between King and Parliament.

> The said Commons so elected, being now assembled in a full and free representation of this nation . . . unanimously declare . . .
>
> That the pretended power of . . . suspending laws . . . by regal authority, without consent of Parliament, is illegal . . .
>
> That levying [*raising*] money for . . . the use of the crown . . . without permission of Parliament . . . is

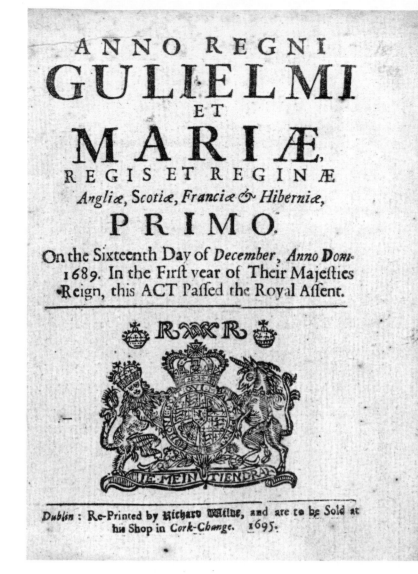

ANNO REGNI
GULIELMI
ET
MARIÆ,
REGIS ET REGINÆ
Angliæ, Scotiæ, Franciæ & Hiberniæ,
PRIMO.

On the Sixteenth Day of *December*, *Anno Dom*
1689. In the First year of Their Majesties
Reign, this ACT Passed the Royal Assent.

Dublin: Re-Printed by Richard Milne, and are to be Sold at
his Shop in *Cork-Change*. 1695.

Title page of the Bill of Rights. The two names mean 'William' and 'Mary'. Can you work out which words mean England, Scotland, France and Ireland?

illegal . . .

That the raising and keeping of a standing army . . .
during time of peace, unless it be with the consent of
Parliament, is against the law . . .

That election of Members of Parliament ought to be
free . . .

Parliaments ought to be held frequently. . . . None of
the royal family to marry a Papist. . . . Every King and
Queen of this realm . . . to take an oath for the
maintaining of the Protestant religion.

Source: Commons Journals, *Vol. X, pages 21–2. Quoted by
Miller, op. cit.*

(a) Which parts of this list applied directly to James II?
(b) Which parts would have annoyed James I and Charles I?
Give reasons for your answer.

(**c**) Why was William III in a weaker position than other monarchs where Parliament was concerned?

(**d**) Imagine you are a believer in the Divine Right of Kings. Make a speech commenting on this list.

3.

'*Lilliburlero*'. This song was sung by the enemies of James II, 1688–89. The words are meaningless – possibly a password used by Irish rebels in 1641. Because the song had been composed originally to make fun of James's representative in Ireland, the Earl of Tyrconnel, it became a protest song against the king as well.

Write your own protest song about James II using the tune of 'Lilliburlero', or another well-known tune.

INDEX